FLAMING MINISTER

FLAMING MINISTER

A STUDY OF
OTHELLO
As Tragedy of Love and Hate

G. R. ELLIOTT

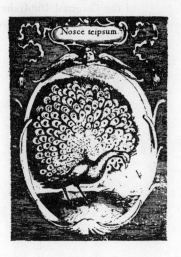

Nosce teipsum

AMS PRESS, INC.
NEW YORK
1965

AMS Press, Inc.
New York, N.Y. 10003
1965

Manufactured in the United States of America

To

my wife

WHO GREATLY HELPED THE COMPOSITION

AND THE SPIRIT

OF THIS BOOK

PREFACE

On the Restudy of Shakespearean Tragedy

Taken together this book on *Othello* and its predecessor, on *Hamlet*, constitute an essay towards a fresh view of Shakespearean tragedy. The main theme of that "essay" is given by a word common to the titles of my two Introductions, the word pride; and of course the titles of the two books, *Scourge and Minister* and *Flaming Minister*, point to a close relationship.[1]

My first intention was to write a book on Shakespeare's tragic work as a whole. Later, however, I came to believe that *Othello* and *Hamlet* provided the crux of the whole matter. Criticism had regarded those two plays as extraordinarily different from each other and from all the rest of their author's works. But the more I reread, with as open a mind as possible, the writings of Shakespeare (and incidentally of his contemporaries) the more I felt that the distinctive features of those two dramas had been grossly overstated. The result was that, from the prevailing standpoint, those two great tragedies did not really belong in "Shakespearean tragedy" and, indeed, that this categoric term had not much depth of meaning. Moreover, the characters of Othello and Hamlet, together with certain of their chief associates, were considerably divorced from that common humanity which Shakespeare designed them to have, like all his other leading personages. The truth is, surely, that those two central and companion plays, capping the climax of the first half of Shakespeare's career and initiating the second and greater half, must be read in the light of his work (and of Renaissance literature) as a whole and in vital relation to the series of his tragic and semitragic plays.

But false generalizations, especially those containing a good

[1] Much of the Preface and Introduction of the earlier book applies to this one, which, however, is designed to be read quite independently.

deal of truth,[2] cannot be effectually overthrown by further generalizations. My project demanded a close-up restudy of *Hamlet* and *Othello*, scene by scene.[3] And that method seems to be
in accord with the spirit of our time. This is an age of revisions
and, somewhat, of re-vision. Stock notions coming down to us
through the past two or three centuries, in all the main fields
of thought, are being overhauled in the light of a close scrutiny
of the relevant facts. This is occurring in the field of Shakespearean criticism and scholarship; my footnotes, especially
those for the Introduction, pay tribute, though very inadequately, to the work of other scholars.[4] Our present immense

[2] In the present book as in the preceding one I have tried to do justice to
the individualistic or nineteenth-century insights into Shakespeare: time was
when they dominated my mind, and I am sympathetic to them still.

[3] The scene-by-scene method brings into right prominence the *doings* of
the dramatis personae. In real life it is a truism that a person's utterances
must be judged in the light of his actual conduct. But Shakespeare's continual recourse to that obvious fact has been obscured for many readers,
including some teachers of English, by the modern novel, wherein the author
comes on the stage to expound the disconcerting difference between his pro-
tagonist's words and deeds. Shakespeare displays that difference through
dramatic action. Of course he often employs illuminating comments by other
personages upon the mental state of the person in question; but this is not
possible when the latter hides his feelings successfully from the others—sometimes also from himself. This situation is particularly true of Hamlet and
Othello; and here the dramatist, time and again, precedes or follows up a
speech of the hero by a stroke of conduct sharply at variance with it. But
the intended implication is apt to be missed by readers accustomed to having
everything told them in explicit words. A reviewer of my preceding book,
a learned and able scholar in the field of the novel, accused me of reading
into Hamlet motives which in fact are read into him, through the means
just described, by Shakespeare himself. See the item "implicit motives" in
the Index of my *Scourge and Minister*. Incidentally, many scholars now know
that the phenomenon of subconsciousness, though not the term, was familiar
to the leading Elizabethan dramatists. A striking example is Othello's famous
speech, badly sentimentalized by Romantic critics, at the beginning of the final
scene (see page 212 below). Here Othello, unlike Posthumus in *Cymbeline*
(V.i.1-11), will not confess the iniquity of his murder of his wife; but in
his "soul," i.e. subconsciously, he is deeply aware of it.

[4] Two new works which bear upon my main theme (but with standpoints
different from mine) are: Clifford Leech's *Shakespeare's Tragedies and Other
Studies in Seventeenth Century Drama*, stressing the idea of pride; and
E. M. W. Tillyard's *Studies in Milton*. My Introduction considers Shakespeare's relation to Milton; his relation to Spenser was touched upon in my
previous book. This matter is the subject of a new book by W. B. C. Watkins, *Shakespeare and Spenser*. Professor Alfred Harbage's brilliant *As They
Liked It, An Essay on Shakespeare and Morality*, has many challenging pas-

restudy of Shakespeare in detail can result eventually in a fresh and larger vision of his work—a not unimportant contribution to the new vision of humanity towards which our century is painfully striving. But first, certain truisms of the modern or humanitarian era (so to term it) must be shown to be untrue, and certain truisms belonging to *all* eras must be shown to be demonstrably truer than our forebears, from the Renaissance on, knew; including various truisms regarding "common humanity" (a favorite modern phrase, used by me above) and, in this connection, the import of pride. Here I must declare emphatically that I did not reapproach Shakespeare with the motif of pride[5] in mind: it was forced upon my attention by a restudy of *Hamlet* and *Othello* and Shakespearean tragedy.

In this book, perhaps even more than in its predecessor, I have tried constantly to visualize the action of the play on the stage. And I would point out that the interpretation here given of *Othello* can solve the dilemma of the modern leading actor who is painfully uncertain as to whether the hero or the villain provides the greater role—so heavily and so long has Iago been overstressed by modern criticism. Shakespeare's friend, the great Richard Burbage, who "created" the part of Othello (as well as Hamlet and Lear, and probably Henry V, Brutus, Angelo, Macbeth, Antony, etc.) was not thus embarrassed. He played the hero always; nor is it conceivable that he permitted his subordinate who acted the villain (John Lowin, ap-

---

sages upon the tragedies. Especially valuable is William Haller's "What Needs My Shakespeare?" in the *Shakespeare Quarterly* for January, 1952.

[5] This word appears, but very subordinately, in my essay on "Othello as a Love-Tragedy" in the *American Review* (now defunct) for January, 1937. The present book is developed from that essay but with several marked divergences. In particular I found that only through a scene-by-scene interpretation of this play could I hope to do any justice to its amazingly cumulative effect. Here as in no other drama every episode, one might say every word, prepares the way for what ensues; Shakespeare writes as though from the very first he has fully in mind *every detail*, almost, of the finale. Notice, for instance, the profound effect of the sudden appearance, near the close, of the word "wedding" (IV.ii.105), hitherto unused but prepared for subtly in many ways. Flash backs could be employed with telling effect in a moving-picture production of this drama.

parently) to make the slightest semblance of stealing the show.[6] A close restudy of this drama in the original texts and in the light of Elizabethan conditions makes very clear the fact that Othello was designed to overtop Iago just about as much as Hamlet overtopped Claudius (also played by Lowin) in theatrical effect. Shakespeare and also Burbage conceived the hero as far more humanly complex and vividly interesting than the villain. Othello, not Iago, is the main motive force of the tragedy—particularly by reason of his superb, subtle, baleful pride.

G. R. E.

Brunswick, Maine
October 2, 1952

[6] See T. W. Baldwin's *The Organization and Personnel of the Shakespearean Company* and Ronald Watkins's *On Producing Shakespeare*. The latter demonstrates convincingly that Shakespeare's dramas cannot be rightly and fully understood unless and until produced, today, in a fully (not just partially) reconstructed Elizabethan theater.

CONTENTS

(The design on the title page, like the one in *Scourge and Minister*, is from *Emblemata Politica*, 1617, in the Treasure Room of the Duke University Library.)

INTRODUCTION

On Pride, Renaissance Tragedy, and the Design of *Othello*

IN OLD TIMES, pagan and Christian times, pride—wrong pride as distinguished from right self-esteem—was regarded as the worst of all evils and the central source of tragedy in human life and art. The reasons are obvious enough. Pride fixes us where we are, preventing growth of spirit and initiating decay; it is deadly. Traditionally it is the one unforgivable sin, hopelessly affronting God or the gods or supernal law. In other words pride is the essence of all spiritual evil: the insulation of oneself from that which is supremely real in life; the self's refusal of a truer and larger vitality for the self. Pride is therefore not merely *a* sin: it may rightly be regarded as synonymous with sin itself; at any rate it is Sin capitalized. It makes all sins or faults capital by establishing them as unconfessed obstacles to growth. It nullifies our so-called divine dissatisfaction, the human humility essential to human development. Hence it is not merely immoral, in the ordinary or puritan sense of that term, a naughtiness denounced professionally by ancient saints and sages. It is the perennial deadly enemy of humanity, the adversary, the "Satan," opposed to right fulness of human life.

Such is the picture of pride limned in the world's greatest literature considered as a whole. Of course innumerable causes of human unhappiness and misery appear in that literature, but the central one is pride. It alone is regarded as supremely tragic and, at the same time, as supremely dramatic. For the poet in proportion to his greatness tries to see life whole and to discern, within that whole, those great contrasts that are the lifeblood of art. And chief of these is the contrast between that which is most vital, most healthful, in mankind and that which is most limiting and toxic. So extreme, moreover, is that conflict in the vision of the world's chief poets that they perceive it to be, while never unhuman, in some sense preterhuman. Whatever is best in man, his magnanimity, nobility, charity, is supernal; intimately allied, in pagan poetry, to the gods at *their* best. But pride derives from the gods at their worst—in Christian poetry, from the devil; it is satanic. Thus the main struggle that goes on in the human breast is at once thoroughly human and grandly cosmic. And from the standpoint of world literature, whether secular or religious, all supreme tragedy, particularly in the form of drama, must turn upon pride.

Very paradoxical therefore seems the fact that modern criticism, while certain that Shakespearean tragedy is supreme, has not regarded pride as its main motif. Generally speaking the critics and interpreters of Shakespeare during the past two hundred years have relegated pride, when they have dealt with it at all, to a subordinate position in his tragic dramas. Can it be that Shakespearean tragedy is *not* supreme? Certain hardened classicists have all along maintained that opinion and have believed that, in Dogberry's words, "it will go near to be thought so shortly"; that is, when future generations have discarded our primitive Shakespeare-worship. On the other hand the proud classicists and, more importantly, the world's chief authors, all except Shakespeare, may be wrong. Perhaps he inaugurated a new and truer view of tragedy in human life and art; though it is generally admitted, sometimes with regret by his admirers, that by disposition he was just the reverse of an inaugurator. More probably Shakespearean criticism, which, as many voices have of late been reminding us, is still young, is at fault in the matter under discussion. Inevitably modern criticism of Shakespeare has been much affected by modern thought in general; and this has shown a really extraordinary lack of interest in the tragedy of pride.

The least objectionable label that has so far been found for the modern movement is, I think, the term "humanitarianism." It is clumsy enough but suggestive and comprehensive: it can comprise or at least connote rationalism, individualism, romanticism, naturalism, and many other isms that have beset the modern soul. The great humanitarian movement, emerging from the Renaissance, rose in the seventeenth and eighteenth centuries, culminated in the nineteenth, and is visibly dissolving in the twentieth. It was a magnificent movement; never before in the whole course of history has the welfare of mankind been advanced so rapidly in so many ways. But the leaders of the movement assumed that the spiritual welfare of man was progressing equally, or at least comparably, with his material welfare; that the spirit of *humankindness,* not created but widely diffused by that movement, was able to remedy, with the aid of science, the basic ills of human society. The falsity of that assumption is generally seen today. Consequently the spiritual pride implicit in that assumption, though not yet so generally recognized, is being and is bound to be more and more perceived. Our present period of unprecedented warfare in the world, following hard upon an era of unprecedented belief in the efficacy of mundane kindness, is a great and inescapable humiliation for modern man. It is clear that the proverb "pride goeth before a fall" is not out of date and that in the modern era, as in every past era, pride has been fatally self-concealing. Man's worship of man's powers, a worship that flourished in many a century before the nineteenth and in many forms, hid from itself, always, its own ruinous weakness under its great achievements: it built magnificent cities and empires. But these decayed, and the pride became bare; as humanitarian pride is now in process of becoming.[1]

Accordingly a remarkable change, a slow revolution, is taking place in the realm of Shakespearean criticism. Some signs of it appeared a good many years ago; evidences of it are frequent in recent books and articles. The humanitarian interpretation, so to call it, of Shakespeare's tragedies and semitragic plays has been increasingly found unsatisfactory: it is seen to be

[1] A fuller treatment of this subject and of its general bearing upon literature is given by my essay "The Pride of Modernity," in the symposium *Humanism and America* (1930).

deficient in dramatic and tragical reality. On that negative
score the new Shakespeare studies are unanimous; their positive
outlook is still somewhat various, tentative, and obscure. But
their general trend, I think, is towards the recognition of the
tragedy of pride as central in the Shakespearean drama. This
trend is parallel to new developments appearing in the fields
of religious, psychological, and political thought. Our modern
catastrophe is bringing the subject of pride into a vital[2] prominence it has not had for well-nigh three hundred years. Of
special importance for my present purpose is the fresh attention
which scholars in all fields are now devoting to the great movement that shaped Shakespeare's mind and art, the Renaissance.

In the Renaissance the subject of human pride was outstanding. For on the one hand the age-old tradition of the deadliness
of pride was fully alive. Conspicuous in the pages of the pagan
classic authors, now being freshly studied, it had been immensely
reinforced by medieval Christianity: it was a main theme in the
Christian humanism that was predominant in art and literature
from the thirteenth to the seventeenth century. On the other
hand modern pride was rising. Men were inflated by the great
discoveries and creations, including the new natural science,
though this was still subordinate, that were being achieved by
European man.[3] Thus there was a deep-going conflict in the
Renaissance spirit. The extraordinary development of man was
engendering a pride that was bound finally to undermine, as
it has now patently done, that very development. But in the
chief creative minds of the time the classic and Judeo-Christian
tradition[4] was thoroughly alive: it was not a mere moral con-
vention (as it became in the eighteenth century), but a fresh
and vital experience. The greatest thinkers, artists, and poets

[2] Vital, in contrast with the more or less conventional treatment of that
subject in the eighteenth century. Pope in his *Essay on Man* was impelled
by tradition to attack human pride; but the attack is more notable for exquisite witty poetry than for experienced conviction.
[3] This subject has interested a number of scholars recently. See Abraham
C. Keller's very suggestive essay on "The Idea of Progress in Rabelais,"
PMLA for March, 1951.
[4] The part played by the great Jewish and other non-Christian thinkers
of the Middle Ages in maintaining the tradition should be emphasized.

of the Renaissance *knew* that humility before the Highest was the *sine qua non* of true human growth. And that vital experience of "high humility"[5] in conflict with the new and vivid rise of human pride is a central source of the poetry, and especially the drama, of the Renaissance.

That fact stands out in the last supreme poem of the period, *Paradise Lost*. Milton, it is clear nowadays, was in the main animated, not by Puritanism, but by the whole Renaissance outlook. And what he said of the work of his predecessor Spenser is true of his own epic, as of all great poetry: "more is meant than meets the ear."[6] In his Satan he consciously presents the perennial nature of spiritual pride but also, and unconsciously, he adumbrates the special qualities of *modern* pride. Hence the modern popularity of Satan and the unpopularity of Milton's attitude towards him—a revealing paradox. The fallen archangel goes in for a romantic naturalism, a pseudodemocratic spirit, and an autocratic, hellish communism that are remarkably prophetic. And the human vividness of Milton's Satan in contrast with Dante's—in lesser but still strong contrast with the various figurations of pride in *The Faerie Queene*—is indicative of the human appeal of pride, modern pride, in the last phase of the Renaissance. Very different, naturally, is Milton's method of representing Satan's opposite, the Son of God, symbolizing "high humility" (the contemporary phrase cited above) and all that belongs therewith. At some future time, one hopes, the poetic as well as the religious beauty and power of this great figure will be generally recognized. In the nineteenth-century view, which is still with us, Milton's divine Son is extremely pallid and uninteresting. The truth of the matter is, I think, that Milton in depicting the cosmic unworldliness, so to call it, that the Son must always have along with his hu-

[5] From Henry Vaughan's poem "They Are All Gone into the World of Light." It is given on page 801 of Hebel and Hudson's *Poetry of the English Renaissance* (1929), an excellent anthology, expressive of the growing American interest in that period.

[6] The allusion of the famous passage in "Il Penseroso" is of course not confined to Spenser, there unnamed. See the footnote on page 199 of the *Paradise Regained* volume (1937) of Merritt Y. Hughes's fine edition of Milton.

manity, also depicted, unawares, the special remoteness which "the sovran Presence"[7] of divine-human humility has from the standpoint of the modern pride of worldly achievement.[8]

Thus *Paradise Lost* is at once the upshot and the essence of the Renaissance. This epic, so very brief in comparison with its lengthy predecessors in that era, is an intense condensation of Renaissance tragedy—the tragedy that was actually occurring more and more in the soul of the Renaissance, and the tragedy that was written out in letters, above all in the drama. In his hero,[9] Adam, Milton laid bare, made naked—the pun is irresistible and meaningful—the dilemma of the typical hero of Renaissance tragic drama. To be fully human that hero had to have a proper self-esteem. This virtue, slurred by ascetic religion, was stressed by Christian humanism and is at the center of Adam.[10] But it was not a virtue in the narrow, moralistic sense of that term: it was the normal and vital posture of the human self. And it was as strenuous and difficult to maintain as human life when fully lived, in body and spirit, has to be. Right self-esteem demanded humility before the Highest while it excluded all groveling to the gods as well as to men. But proper human dignity could very easily pass over into wrong pride. Indeed the hero's liability to that evil was proportionate to his human greatness; and only divine grace, or the same thing under another term, could prevent his slipping from vital into baleful self-regard, or recover him after his fall—the Fall of Man.[11] In Milton's story Adam and Eve,

[7] *Paradise Lost* X.144.

[8] Partly the modern movement substituted humanitarian or democratic modesty for fundamental humility; partly it confused the two.

[9] Our literary grandfathers thought of *Paradise Lost* as an epic without a "hero," unless Satan could be regarded as such. But nowadays it is quite *au fait* to apply the term to Adam.

[10] See note 39 to Act V below (page 238). Significant of the modern movement was Emerson's choice of "self-reliance" instead of "self-esteem" as title for his famous essay, an essay great in spirit but confused in thought. "Trust thyself: every heart vibrates to that iron string." The vibration would be different but the epigram just as true if we should substitute "distrust" for "trust." But if we should read, "Esteem thyself truly . . . ," the epigram would be as firm as Renaissance epigrams, notably in Milton, generally are and as Emerson's epigrams often are not.

[11] *Secular* interest in that ancient myth was characteristic of the Renaissance. Later that interest disappeared; but it has recently been reviving.

ruined by the satanic spirit working within them, are recovered, though very far from fully, except in hope, by the spirit of the Son of God at work within.[12]   And that story, doubtless without Milton's full awareness of the fact, is the distilled essence of the story of the chief heroes and heroines of Renaissance tragic dramas.

Renaissance tragedy including Shakespearean tragedy is the tragedy of pride.   Indeed there is no such thing as *Shakespearean tragedy,* in any deep and inclusive sense, apart from the motif of pride.   Consider the extreme contrast between the first and last of the main tragedies: *Hamlet,* so humanely various and charming, and *Coriolanus,* so very univocal and harsh. They might well have been written by two different authors: actually modern criticism has conceived them as written by two very different Shakespeares, i.e. Shakespeare in two utterly diverse states of mind.   But in fact the two plays have a central theme in common: right self-esteem turning into wrong pride.[13] And that is the main theme, more or less, of Shakespeare's tragic and semitragic plays from the beginning to the end of his career. I say more or less because in the shallower personages, such as Richard III, the element of right self-esteem is at its minimum. But in richer characters, for example Richard's successor Macbeth with his native loyalty, openness, poetic sense, and magnanimity, the self-esteem is humanly valid.   These characters have both a right and a wrong pride; and their inward catastrophe is therefore humanly typical and great.   Of course Shakespeare's tragic protagonists are highly individualized; each has his own particular values and defects.   But the values center in self-esteem and the defects in wrong pride: the defects are rendered *essentially* tragic by, and only by, the pride.   The *motives* in Shakespearean tragedy are many, various, and fascinating: its *motif* is pride.   In *Coriolanus* that motif is exceptionally bare, though we can see it tending to become so in preceding works

---

[12] The inwardness of that working is represented or suggested with exquisite art in a series of passages alternating with episodes wherein the Son and Satan appear externally as dramatis personae.

[13] See the excellent chapter on *Coriolanus* in Willard Farnham's *Shakespeare's Tragic Frontier* (1950).

from *Lear* on. In his final great tragedy Shakespeare was impelled—no doubt quite subconsciously, for his main aim here as
ever was to make an excellent dramatic story—to display the
very skeleton of his tragic creation as a whole. Hence the hard
grandeur of *Coriolanus*. It is a bald peak at the end of a moun-
tain range: it is made of the igneous rock, pride, underlying the
various strata and variegated landscapes of the total range.

The underlying pride in *Julius Caesar, Hamlet,* and *Othello*
is not so readily discernible by the modern reader as it was by
the spectator in the Elizabethan theater. For that spectator was
prepared by long tradition to perceive it; and the modern reader
has been rendered obtuse to it by the humanitarian outlook, now
quite traditional. The modern theatergoer is more likely than
the reader to sense it, because the actors, in their efforts to wring
from the lines the fullest histrionic effect, cannot entirely miss
the pride of the dramatis personae. And doubtless that motif
will become increasingly apparent as time goes on: a deepening
and broadening discernment of the human meaning of the
tragedy of twentieth-century society will sharpen our feeling
for the tragedy in the life and art of earlier eras. Perhaps after
two or three hundred years the theater audience will be as well
aware as Shakespeare's audience must have been that pride is
the main cause of the inner and outer disasters of all the most
active personages in his tragic plays, including the three named
above.

That awareness, so humanly normal, was counted upon by
Shakespeare very particularly in the case of Brutus, Hamlet, and
Othello. In earlier and later protagonists, Richard II and Hot-
spur, Lear and Antony, the urge of pride is comparatively obvious. And so it is in the secondary characters in the three
dramas under discussion, for instance Caesar and Cassius, Polonius and Laertes, Brabantio and Iago. But be it noted that
these and others serve to set off by contrast the far more subtle
pride of the three principals. In Brutus, Hamlet, and Othello
the grounds for self-esteem are peculiarly valid and the emer-
gence of wrong pride is a psychologically subtle process. Apparently the dramatist was unconsciously impelled to show in

those three persons, created at the outset of his tragic period,
how devilishly insinuating and elusive pride can be before pro-
ceeding to display it more broadly in his later protagonists. The
character of Othello is at once the culmination of the first group
and the precursor of the second. In him appears a depth of
primitive passion absent in the case of Brutus but considerably
present in the case of Hamlet and very outstanding in the later
heroes; but also Othello exhibits the covert pride of his immediate predecessors.

Pride is no less powerful in Brutus, Hamlet, and Othello
because it is subtly so. It is not baldly obtruded in their speeches
nor in the utterances of others concerning them: it is deeply implicit in their conduct. Increasingly it informs their decisions
and deeds as these become more and more disastrous. And I
would urge that modern criticism in slurring that motive has
made Brutus more theoretic, Hamlet more unaccountable, and
Othello more naïve than their creator intended. It is not
mainly the fault of Shakespeare if today Brutus seems to people
in general much of a stick, Hamlet really a weakling, and
Othello, when all is said and done, a noble fool. But in truth
their pride, if only we will see it, makes them humanly repre-
sentative and vitally dramatic.

Those two aspects of pride are emphatically given in a well-
known passage in *Measure for Measure* (II. ii. 110 ff.), written
at the beginning of Shakespeare's tragic period:

> Could great men thunder
> As Jove himself does, Jove would never be quiet,
> For every pelting petty officer
> Would use his heaven for thunder;
> Nothing but thunder. Merciful heaven,
> Thou rather with thy sharp and sulphurous bolt
> Splitst the unwedgeable and gnarled oak
> Than the soft myrtle. But man, proud man,
> Drest in a little brief authority,
> Most ignorant of what he's most assured—
> His glassy essence—like an angry ape

> Plays such fantastic tricks before high heaven
> As make the angels weep; who, with our spleens,
> Would all themselves laugh mortal.

Those lines, less characteristic of the inexperienced Isabella who speaks them than of the great and now fully mature dramatist who wrote them, strike the keynote of Renaissance and Shakespearean tragedy. Here pride is not conceived as one sin, though the greatest, among others: it is an evil human *posture*.[14] Like its opposite, humility, it is a bent of the whole man—"man, proud man"—a power pervading the self and determining the quality of all that a man thinks, feels, and does. And pride is intensely dramatic: it elicits the most vivid and radical contrasts that there are in human life. Extremely wicked, it is also extremely abnormal and absurd. Ignorantly, "like an angry ape," it nullifies that which is most essential to man, mercy and charity, derived from "heaven";[15] without which he is merely a "glassy essence," a brittle, fragile thing playing "fantastic tricks before high heaven": the "angels weep"[16]—but if they had human "spleens," along with their heavenly insight, the spectacle would make them laugh themselves to death. In other words the more deeply we look into "proud man" the more tragic he appears and, incidentally, the more "fantastic"[17]—a creature supremely dramatic.

[14] But it is regarded merely as a particular moral fault by A. C. Bradley in his *Shakespearean Tragedy*; see Lecture I. For him the essence of tragedy is "waste": he fails to see that "waste" is supremely tragic only when it is due to pride. That, I think, is the fundamental defect in his conception; others, to be noted later, follow from that. His book, in its second edition, is referred to below as "Bradley." But here I must say that I dislike criticizing this distinguished work, to which so many of us owe so much. First issued in 1904, it embodies the nineteenth-century or humanitarian conception of Shakespeare at its reasonable best. But see Lily B. Campbell's penetrating critique of Bradley in the appendices of her interesting book on *Shakespeare's Tragic Heroes*, 1952.

[15] Isabella's earlier words on "mercy" (50 ff.) in the same scene, especially the passage "Alas, alas! / Why, all the souls that were . . . " (72-79), obviously prepare for her present climactic speech. Note that the "angry ape" is, by implication, at once "petty," "unmerciful," "ignorant," and "fantastic."

[16] Compare the "Angelic Guards . . . mute and sad / For Man" after his fall, *Paradise Lost* X.18-19.

[17] The fantastical and comic effect of pride, a common theme in the Renaissance and played up by the dramatists, e.g. Ben Jonson, is elaborately pictured in the central cantos of the first book of *The Faerie Queene*.

The pride of Angelo, whom Isabella is adjuring, is not greatly tragic nor highly fantastic: her words are too grand for the core of the matter; Shakespeare is really thinking of far greater tragic figures. With that in mind let us consider three significant incidents in the tragedies closely contemporary with *Measure for Measure:* Brutus's mastery of his sorrow for the death of Portia (*Julius Caesar* IV. iii. 145-195); Hamlet's refusal to kill the King in the Prayer scene (III. iii. 73 ff.); and Othello's crucial concealment of his jealousy from Desdemona in the Handkerchief episode when he has every reason to interrogate her frankly regarding her relations with Cassio (III. iii. 260-290). In those incidents the three heroes, so notable for their love of truth, are notably unveracious in spirit and speech: they become, for the nonce, liars. But most disconcerting from the standpoint of the modern reader is the fact that each of the three seems here quite inhuman: Brutus, a coldhearted pedant; Hamlet, a weak-willed emotionalist; and Othello, a dunce of the first water. In fact, however, the tragic hero is intended by the dramatist to be here, as ever, thoroughly human: we can see this if we attend to his pride. In these episodes the three protagonists cover up their inmost feelings by means of a pride that is at once tragic, especially in the case of Othello, and very preposterous.[18] Here "proud man," as continually in Renaissance literature, is playing his "fantastic tricks," though more covertly than usual.[19]

In such episodes we are especially aware of Shakespeare's great charity. It is one, or at one, with his great art. But we cannot see that fact fairly and fully unless we abandon the hu-

---

[18] But pride is not mentioned in the lengthy discussion of the Brutus episode in the *Furness Variorum* edition of *Julius Caesar*, pages 222-225; some of the comments exemplify strikingly the limitations of the humanitarian outlook. For Brutus the immediate sequel of this episode is, suggestively, his stubborn determination to proceed at once to Philippi and, thereupon, the apparition of his "evil spirit" in the form of the Ghost of Caesar. The case of Hamlet is dealt with in my *Scourge and Minister*, pages 108-111. For Othello see pages 124 ff. below.

[19] At the other end of the scale—but the same scale—are such obviously fantastic themes as Shylock and his pound of flesh and Richard II with his mirror. Unlike them, Malvolio in his cross-garters is comically conceived, not tragically proud; but he is the immediate predecessor of the tragicomic Polonius, whose fantastic conceit has in it a vein of catastrophic pride.

manitarian tendency to identify charity with sympathy. This tendency can blind the modern reader to the meaning of the divine Love building hell in Dante's allegoric imagination. It can make the gentle Spenser seem in certain passages of *The Faerie Queene* nonplusingly severe, Milton far more harsh than he really is, and Elizabethan tragedy fundamentally gloomy. It can read a basic bitterness into Shakespeare's satiric vein, notably in *Troilus and Cressida* and *Measure for Measure*.[20] But there are many signs at present of the rise of a truer concept of charity wherein the ancient view will be enriched, instead of undermined, by the modern development of sympathy.

Charity or high love, as normally conceived, is no more sympathetic, patient, merciful, and kind than righteous and just: unkind justice is unjust, but also unjust kindness is unkind. And the boundless sympathy found by many in Shakespeare and discounted sharply by others, including Tolstoy, is really anomalous. His pouring sympathy is bounded, is directed and *empowered*, by his extraordinary justness. His charity is powerful because it is at once just and kind—and intensely dramatic. Aesthetic persons are annoyed, understandably, by the osseous principles that religionists and moralists dissect out of the Shakespearean drama. On the other hand common sense is outraged by the claim that Shakespeare is purely aesthetic. The fact is that his poetry at its best is pure and supreme because therein the true charity and the finest dramatic art (both inspired by richest humor) are completely interfused—most remarkably in his treatment of pride.

That human posture is in Shakespearean drama, as it is in real life, tragicomic or comicotragic as the case may be. Pride is comical in proportion as it is a minor constituent of vanity,

[20] See the lengthy and revealing footnote in Bradley, page 275. Since his time criticism has increasingly tended to deny the "spirit of bitterness and contempt" that he felt in the two plays named above. Bradley missed the relation, now generally perceived, between *Measure for Measure* and Shakespeare's main tragedies. The new and truer view is contemporaneous with the decline of the humanitarian principle of "appeasement" of evil autocracy in international politics, a principle that carried sympathy to a bad extreme. But the wrong view still persists, notably in Donald A. Stauffer's otherwise charming book, *Shakespeare's World of Images* (1949).

conceit, arrogance, and the like; but wherever it is present in the slightest degree it is potentially disastrous. It is tragic in proportion as it concentrates and erects itself "before high heaven." But since it is always fantastic it is always potentially comic: the Shakespearean smile flickers ever, no matter how remotely, in the background. When pride is utterly catastrophic it could make heavenly (and dramatic) charity laugh if it did not make it "weep." That is the situation pre-eminently in *Othello*. This story, more than any other of Shakespeare's stories, made very extreme demands upon both his charity and his art. And he met those demands with triumphant success. The general conviction that this play is Shakespeare's greatest achievement in tragidramatic *form*, whatever its deficiencies in other respects, means really that it is his main drama of pride.

Incidentally it is in a broad sense his most Christian drama. Christian believers discern that Shakespeare was a Christian believer; unbelievers believe that he was not. The former are wrong when they find an explicit theology in his work; the latter, when they assert that no theology at all is implicit there. At the least it is certain that the Shakespearean drama is based on the Judeo-Christian conviction, held also by leading pagan thinkers and artists, that *reality* is not monistic but has three distinct (not separate) levels: deity, man, and nature. This conviction underlay Renaissance art and literature as a whole; it was essential to their great dramatic quality.[21] It provided those utmost contrasts which Shakespeare and his fellow playwrights, in England and elsewhere, sought when their art was most intense. The clash in man between the divinely magnanimous and the diabolically brutish was both ultimately real and intensely dramatic. The triform constitution of life and being is in Shakespeare not a dogma: it is, like charity, one with his art. And it is the source of that cogent cosmic atmosphere in his tragedies which modern criticism has tended to regard as

[21] The monistic tendency of nineteenth-century thought, while animating the nature lyric, sapped vitality from the drama, as noted in my *Cycle of Modern Poetry*. The monism of Bradley (see particularly the final section of Lecture I) is comparatively moderate and circumspect; yet it renders his view of Shakespeare essentially nondramatic.

merely imagistic, and to eliminate entirely in the case of *Othello*.
This play has been regarded as peculiarly domestic and mundane, giving us a sense of "confinement to a comparatively narrow world"²²—a view incompatible, really, with our belief that
Shakespeare's tragic art is in this play supreme. But in fact, as
I have tried to show in my text, the cosmic implications are no
less potent in *Othello* than elsewhere because less obtrusive.
Indeed God and nature are the more intensively at strife here
just because that strife is extraordinarily *domesticated*.

And it is significant that in *Othello* as in *All's Well That
Ends Well, Measure for Measure,* and *Hamlet,* four plays
composed at the start of Shakespeare's tragic period, Christian
imagery and reflections of Christian doctrine are especially
prominent. Christianity had greatly emphasized just and merciful charity, the human need of humility and conversion, the
insidious power of pride, and the mystery of grace, i. e. the
divine will at work through and with the human will. Not
one of those things was entirely foreign to the classic pagan
humanism upon which Occidental culture was founded and
which was very much alive in the Renaissance mind; but
Christianity had stressed them in a revolutionary manner: thus
they were strong strands in the very texture of the secular, as
well as the religious, imagination of the time. And it was
natural that Shakespeare should be particularly conscious of
them when he began to face the full tragedy of human life
and to seek the means of wringing the fullest possible dramatic
effect from the stories he had in hand. Certainly his interest,
as a secular poet, in the leading Christian ideas was far more
dramatic than religious. But to claim it was "merely dramatic"²³ is to miss an essential element of his work—"sheerly
dramatic" would be a truer though still inadequate term. The
pagan-Hebrew-Christian belief that "There's a divinity that
shapes our ends" (*Hamlet* V. ii. 10) was a main *shaping* factor

²² Bradley, page 181.
²³ Bradley, page 38. Note that the theme of "grace," in particular, is
scanted in this book as a whole. In this connection see A. S. P. Woodhouse's
timely essay on "Nature and Grace in *The Faerie Queene*" in *ELH*, XVI, p.
194 ff.

of the Renaissance: it informed the thought and art, especially the dramatic art, of that era.[24] It is implicit in the Shakespearean drama from first to last and, often enough, very patent; though the modern reader is apt to be misled by the Elizabethan dramatists' custom, followed by Shakespeare, of referring to the deity under various poetic synonyms, such as the "heaven" and "Jove" in the passage quoted above. All those terms, whether pagan or Christian, point to the one "divinity that shapes our ends." But the specific Christian conception of that shaping, the idea of divine grace, is significantly prominent in the four plays named above.[25] The reason, I think, is that Shakespeare was here especially conscious of the prime evil that only "grace" (or its equivalent) can overcome: the subtle insidiousness of pride.[26]

The chief cause of Othello's downfall is not his jealousy but the fact that he conceals it from all concerned—except his evil other self, Iago—by reason of his pride. That is the main point of this story; but also the whole pattern of the play turns upon pride. With the exception of Emilia all persons who take any decisive part, even the least, in the main action are in one way or another, and in varying degrees, actuated by pride. Most obvious is the case of Brabantio. In the beginning the old man's violent imperiousness (later to be developed fully in Lear) blasts open, so to speak, the drama's underlying vein of pride. At the opposite pole is the surreptitious arrogance of Iago, displayed to us at the start and at the close of the first act in his dialogues with Roderigo, whose foolish vanity has in it a stiffening touch of pride. In the second act Roderigo and incidentally the complacent Montano help to bring into

---

[24] Hence the casualness of Hamlet's allusion to it, testifying to its currency, not to its cursoriness as many have supposed, including Bradley.

[25] For example, in the climax of the first act of *All's Well* Helena's phrase "by grace itself," capping her appeal to "high heaven," echoes the Countess's words "as heaven shall work" (I. iii. 190, 198 f., 226). See the original analysis of this play by Harold S. Wilson in the *Huntington Library Quarterly* for May, 1950, particularly his treatment of the conversion of Bertram.

[26] Hamlet urges his mother to seek the unction of "grace" instead of "a flattering unction" (III. iv. 144 f.). Othello hopes that "heaven and grace" may conquer his wife's arrogant concealment, as he imagines it, of her sin (V. i. 27).

the foreground a personage who from here to the end—with the aid in Act IV of the humorously proud Bianca—plays a leading part in the tragic action: the chivalrous and charming but proudly, and fatefully, conceited Cassio.

Critics have taken at its face value that young gentleman's complacent remark at the close when he learns of Othello's murderous plot against him: "Dear general, I never gave you cause" (V. ii. 299). But in fact he had given cause of a very weighty sort. He is possessed of that resonant sense of honor, in certain respects excellent but always questionable and sometimes very wrong, that Shakespeare along with the other dramatists of the time, notably Beaumont and Fletcher, took delight in dramatically criticizing. To spectators normally aware, as the Elizabethan audience was, of the crookedness of pride Cassio's procedure must appear crooked in the extreme. His curious sense of honor prevents him from honorably confessing to his general his luckless fit of drunkenness. Infinitely worse than that transient insobriety is his fixed intoxication with his honor, his outward repute. This gentleman's improper and very compromising suit to Desdemona is as ungentlemanly, in reality, as it could possibly be. Its sexual purity throws into relief its spiritual impurity, its motive of selfish, blinding pride. Cassio becomes what he unconsciously instigates his best friend, Othello, to be: an excellent gentleman who submerges his better will in a monomaniacal, pride-inspired dream. Romantic tradition to the contrary, Cassio is no less important than Iago as a factor in the tragedy.

But the critics have taken Iago, too, at his word, agreeing with his reiterated claim that the action of the play is mainly the product of his mighty mind. They have missed one of Shakespeare's finest strokes of art, the dramatic contrast, along with likeness of function, between Othello's two friends: Cassio smugly certain, in his refined fashion, that nothing of the catastrophe is due to him; Iago smugly certain, in his coarse way, that all of it is his doing.[27] Moreover, criticism has been

---

[27] Bradley's omission of that contrast is emphasized by his inclusion of the two persons in one chapter, Lecture VI. The contrast is of course not ex-

visibly embarrassed by the seemingly strange fact that Shakespeare chose to make his major villain also a remarkable buffoon. Explanations of this phenomenon have been many and various. The real point is that Iago's pride is at once very evil and very ludicrous; he is "like an angry ape . . . before high heaven"; and the chief of his "fantastic tricks" is his assumption of intellectual omnipotence. His very acute thinking is, from the standpoint of normal humanity, extremely shallow and often apishly, or asininely, so. That which renders him in the upshot more tragic than absurd is his proud, devilish hate; especially, as I have tried to show in my text, his largely subconscious hatred of Desdemona.

Yet his hate is shallow too in comparison with the "loving hate" (*Romeo and Juliet* I. i. 182) that rises more and more in the breast of Othello, like a billow from the dark cosmic deeps. Iago, devoid of love, is incapable of profoundest hate and has no real understanding of it. Not in the least does it enter into his calculations in the first two acts. And when in the opening of the Temptation scene (III. iii) he incites the Moor's suspicions, with the blind aid of Cassio, he is *just as unconscious as Cassio is* of stirring in their master something far deeper than conventional jealousy·[28] a terrific passion of loving hate or hate-full love. When Iago later in the scene becomes, with surprise and dismay, aware of that passion in Othello he sets himself to foment it. And from then on he believes with increasingly fantastic conceit that he is the creator and absolute controller of it—while the great tide of it sweeps him, along with his master, to his doom. Iago is as simple in his way as Cassio is in his[29]—over against Othello, who,

---

plicitly stated by Shakespeare; it is deeply implicit and dramatically displayed, the sort of thing that Bradley tends to overlook. And he follows, though with some qualification, the Romantic tradition that Iago's "intellect . . . is great" (p. 219). But for the most part his view of the villain, unlike his view of the hero, is incisive and excellent. He sees pride at the center of Iago, not of Othello.

[28] The supposedly unconventional Iago is entirely conventional in his conception of jealousy.

[29] Certainly Iago is not so simple as the other personages of the play deem him. But we can better sympathize with them when we realize that Iago is more simple than the modern reader is apt to perceive.

despite the current notion to the contrary, is profoundly complex.

In *Othello* as in Shakespeare's other chief plays the whole design is germinally present in the first act, where, significantly, Iago's active part in the plot is extremely slight.[30] The love of Othello and Desdemona, coming to the fore in the central part of that act, is radiant and harmonious over against the dark background, social and personal, of proud, equivocal, warring intentions. At the same time, however, the dramatist with amazing art makes us feel that the two principals are closely related to the atmosphere surrounding them. Though Othello is not a barbarian and Desdemona far from typical of civic society, they are nevertheless as contrary to each other in their own mode as the Turks and Venetians are in theirs. And the impending warfare that prevents the consummation of their hasty marriage—in modern phrase, a war marriage—adumbrates the fact that the hero and heroine, despite their surface concord, are not wedded in spirit. In basal character, far more than in body and circumstance, they are militantly though tacitly different from each other.

They are opposites in the essential nature of their loves.[31] This veiled but fundamental contrast can be grasped only through a fresh study of Act I, such as I have attempted below. Here be it stated that neither of the two, while pure and devoted, sees and loves the other's *whole being*. Othello loves too outwardly, Desdemona too inwardly. He loves all of her except her very self; she thinks she loves all of him in the light of his very self, but her light is too partial. Each loves an image of the other that is true so far as it goes but fearfully inadequate. In general the situation, like that of young Romeo and Juliet, is human and typical: the heroine is the eternal

---

[30] Far slighter than that of his immediate predecessor, Claudius, in *Hamlet*, Act I, and his successors, Goneril, Regan, and Edmund in the first act of *Lear*.

[31] Coleridge missed that difference entirely and obscured it in the eyes of later critics. His famous summary of the catastrophe, cited at the end of the *Furness Variorum* text of the play, is surely an example of Romantic interpretation at its sentimental worst. While beautifully written and partially true it equates the hero and heroine in a "holy entireness of love" that is wholly ruinous from the dramatic standpoint.

feminine in love, direct and self-giving; the hero, the eternal masculine, romantic and self-involved. But here the situation is extreme and tragic. Desdemona, humble in love, is far from meek in her confidence that she entirely knows Othello; and we feel that if he should turn against her she may (as she does in the second half of the play) become proudly obstinate in refusing to confront the real grounds of the crisis. Still more ominous is the initial bearing of Othello. His pride, entirely justified in his military vocation, goes wrong in his new vocation of love. Considerably aware that his *knowledge* of his wife is deficient, he is *totally* unaware that his *love* for her is far more so, and that this defect is a fateful barrier to an inward knowing of her. In the first act he is serenely (later, dreadfully) confident of the faultlessness of his love for her.

Othello's blind pride-in-love is the central cause of his jealousy and of his wicked concealment of it. In the first half of the play he hides from himself, but reveals to us (*not* to Iago), his growing sense that his wife's devotion *unlike his own* —that is the fatal core of his delusion—is innately infirm. Hence the violence with which his repressed suspicions erupt in the course of the third act.[32] But far more tragic is his violent and yet successful effort, inspired and sustained by pride, to cloak from Desdemona the causes of his fury while trying to make her confess her own supposed sin. Thus he is caught in a hellishly vicious circle. The more he dissembles the more he is sure that she is doing likewise: his refusal to tell the truth prevents him from learning the truth. His diabolic pride far surpasses Iago's: the hero of the play becomes the chief officer and exponent of "hell" (III. iii. 447, IV. ii. 64, 92).[33] In the fourth act, so much greater and more crucial than the third, Othello's pride is both highly fantastical and deeply tragic. And Desdemona in her great misery learns a new humility:

[32] Years ago Professor E. E. Stoll showed conclusively that those suspicions could not have been created by Iago. A very suggestive recent treatment of that character is Frank P. Rand's essay, "The Over Garrulous Iago," in the *Shakespeare Quarterly* for July, 1950.

[33] See S. L. Bethell's penetrating essay on the "Diabolic Imagery in *Othello*" in the *Shakespeare Survey* for 1952.

she undergoes a conversion that prepares for the conversion of her husband in the play's final scene.

That scene is the dramatic acme (the three last books of *Paradise Lost* are the epic acme) of the conversion motif so marked in the literature of the Renaissance, and so foreign to the spirit of humanitarian rationalism. The violent changes of heart evinced by many personages in Elizabethan drama seem very unnatural to the modern reader. In general, however, they exemplify a very human trait: the liability of pride to maintain itself to the last minute and then collapse swiftly, as in Othello. Anticipations and echoes of his case appear in Shakespeare's earlier and later dramas, notably in *Hamlet* and *Measure for Measure, Lear* and *Coriolanus*—Angelo's story reads like a forestudy for the Moor's.[34] But all comparisons serve to throw into relief the spiritual profundity and consummate art of the catastrophe of *Othello*. The "burning hell" (V. ii. 129) of pride, shadowy in the first act, glaring in the fourth, flames out horridly in Othello's repudiation of his dying wife's forgiveness.[35] But soon, at first slowly, then rapidly, that hellish flame subsides—overcome by the heavenly fire, the "flaming minister" (V. ii. 8), of humble love.

Desdemona's love, not completely sacrificial until the end, works upon her husband after her death with the wonderful aid of poor Emilia. Othello goes through a great transformation that appears on the surface precipitous; but actually the process of it began with the beginning of the drama. There Brabantio's treatment of him initiated a series of ever-increas-

---

[34] Note the *functional* parallels between the female characters in *Othello* and *Measure for Measure*, especially in the finale.

[35] Gloucester's cry "down to hell" in repudiating the "pardon" of the murdered King Henry (*3 Henry VI* V. vi. 60, 67) is a crude precursor of Othello's outbreak. Naturally the episode seemed baffling to Bradley; see his strange note O. Missing the pride of Othello, he misses the main point of the final scene. But, interestingly, he advocates (page 240) the First Quarto's very religious version of a climactic line uttered by the humble Emilia, worded as follows in the later texts: "O heaven, O heavenly powers" (V. ii. 218). This wording, with the First Folio's capitals and punctuation, was accepted by me (page 231, below). But now, under Bradley's fine influence (and accepting, incidentally, his inserted exclamation points), I incline to the earlier and stronger version: "O God! O heavenly God!"

ing humiliations. To these the great man reacts with increasing pride—but also, under the surface, with increasing love. Unawares his devotion to the real Desdemona deepens with his hatred of the unreal Desdemona of his imagination, the false image created by his proud and jealous but "great . . . heart" (V. ii. 361). There is a "soul of goodness" (*Henry V* IV. i. 4) in his evil hate. He rightly hates, though he does so with dreadful self-righteousness, all the evil he identifies with his wife, while he loves all the more what he wishes she were, and what we know she really is. In the end she surpasses, awfully, the best that he was able to wish and conceive: *that is his crowning humiliation.* So finally he learns with seeming suddenness what "Heaven" (IV. ii. 47) all along has been schooling him in: the utter humility of true and full love. His wrong pride—not his right self-esteem, as I have emphasized below (page 238)—is as entirely destroyed as the murderer, i. e. himself, whom the justice of love, far more than earthly justice (though this too is a motive), requires him to execute.[36] And his new humility prevents him from seeing what we see: his love, gradually growing and now freed from its egoism, corresponds intimately, in the end, to his wife's love of him. Her love, now so "heavenly" (V. ii. 135, 278), has condemned his sin but has clung to and lifted him. Through death of pride-in-love he and she, strangely and outwardly married in the first act, are at the last wedded in spirit.

Othello is thus a true, and sublime, love tragedy—not a true-love romance with a tragic ending brought about chiefly by a heavy villain. It is *Romeo and Juliet* matured and re-composed. In writing the earlier play Shakespeare was aware, though not deeply aware, that the tragedy of love, when supreme, is also the tragedy of hate.[37] In *Othello* those two

[36] I think the Christian condemnation of suicide would not seem much in point here to the judicious members, at least, of the Elizabethan audience.

[37] In the climax of the first act Juliet exclaims, "My only love sprung from my only hate!" (I. v. 140). But the hate is very extraneous. Othello could have made a similar exclamation with tragic veracity in the climax of the last act. Hamlet's mixed emotions for Ophelia may be regarded as the immediate, though weak, forerunner of Othello's case.

passions, comparatively superficial in all his previous stories, are intensified to the uttermost and deeply interwoven. And the atmosphere is at once tense and cosmic. In *Romeo and Juliet* the cosmic touches are pure and bright; in *Antony and Cleopatra*, spacious and picturesque. In *Othello* the air is compressed cosmic fire.[38] Lucent and dusky flames intermingle; foul things stir and move in lurid darkness; bright gleams and flashes, as from great jewels, come and go in chaos: the "black" fire of "hell" (III. iii. 447) tries to smother, but in the end serves to enhance, the striving "heavenly light" (IV. iii. 65 f.). Universal meanings are not obtruded: they are uniquely implicated here in the common stuff of life. Love, our chief and daily good, working throughout this play in a closely woven pattern of all its main guises—sexual, parental, filial, friendly, duteous, vocational, patriotic,[39] religious—appears as potently ruinous in proportion as it is tainted with our chief evil, the subtly self-disguising demon of pride; which can be conquered only by that same love religiously purged and transfigured.[40] *Othello* is Shakespeare's, and surely the world's, supreme *secular* tragic poem of "human love divine."[41]

[38] See G. Wilson Knight's interpretation of *Othello* in *The Wheel of Fire*.

[39] Probably the most dangerous feature of the world situation at present is patriotic democracy's pride in the excellence of its very imperfect love for country and for mankind. An important though subordinate feature of "Othello, the Moor of Venice" is his devotion to that state and to its mission against barbarism: in the end he commits a barbarous crime against his state and against mankind.

[40] Othello's Christianity, alluded to by the dramatist (as shown in my text) at certain crucial points in his career, is the more striking because of his predominantly mundane outlook. And the secularity of this play as a whole, in strong contrast with *Hamlet* and *Measure for Measure*, renders its underlying religious theme all the more significant. The workings of supernatural powers are completely embodied in human and dramatic action. "Heaven and grace" (V. ii. 27)—as suggested in the passage from which those words are quoted—are important in this play, as in everyday life, only in so far as the person who is aware of them allows them to sway his own conduct.

[41] The phrase is of course adapted from Milton's great image, highly characteristic of the Renaissance outlook: "human face divine" (*Paradise Lost* III. 44).

Note on the Text

The authoritative text of *Othello* is that given in the first collected edition of Shakespeare's works, issued seven years after his death, the First Folio (F1) of 1623. In the preceding year, however, there appeared a separate and independent edition of the play, the First Quarto (Q1). This contains a very few lines peculiar to itself but omits some 160 included in F1. Since, unlike F1, it prints oaths forbidden on the stage by an act of Parliament in 1606, it seems to go back to an earlier manuscript; this may, however, have been retouched by the author before his death in 1616. The Second Quarto (Q2) of 1630 is a reissue of Q1 with corrections derived from F1; occasionally it is suggestive as evincing the leanings of an editor close to Shakespeare's time. Four further quartos and three further folios appeared before the end of the seventeenth century; they are of minor importance.

My main resource has been a negative photostat of *Othello* as given in Copy 10 of F1, obtained from the Folger Shakespeare Library in Washington;* also I have had before me the Praetorius facsimiles of Q1 and Q2. In quotations from the play, italics are mine unless otherwise stated. Often I have reproduced the original punctuation, sometimes the spelling and capitalization, when they seemed significant. Here and there I have substituted a dash (rarely used in Elizabethan printing) for a colon or other punctuation mark in the original. The line-numbering is that of the Globe edition. It is used in most of the recent texts, including G. L. Kittredge's edition of Shakespeare, the *Principal Plays* (twenty in number) edited by Tucker Brooke, etc., and G. B. Harrison's *23 Plays and the Sonnets*.

A definitive edition of Shakespeare's text, supposing that wonder to be possible, can only come about in some pleasant future day when scholars shall be agreed upon the denotation of the term "Shakespearean." Following are two illustrations. In all the early texts of *Othello*, excepting Q1, the reading of a phrase of Desdemona's in IV. iii. 23 is "good father" or "good Father," referring to God. This was accepted by successive editors down to the middle of the nineteenth century. Since then, however, the less obviously Chris-

---

* I am grateful for advice in this matter from two members of that library: Dr. James G. McManaway, consultant in literature and bibliography; and Professor Charlton Hinman, lieutenant commander USNR, who is engaged in notable work upon the text of Shakespeare, particularly *Othello*.

tian reading of Q1, "Good faith," has been preferred. On sheer
dramatic grounds, however, the other reading is far better (see my
footnote 70 to Act IV, page 203 below): in its context it is more
truly "Shakespearean." On the other hand, the very religious version in Q1 of a line by Emilia, "O God, O heavenly God" (V. ii.
218), has been generally rejected in favor of the reading in the other
early texts, "O heaven, O heavenly powers." This reading was
accepted by me too—until at the last moment I changed my mind
(see footnote 35 to my Introduction, page xxxii). I see now that
in Emilia's case, as in Desdemona's, the context, in the finale, requires a *uniquely* religious exclamation (cf. footnote 5 to my Preface).
The two readings which I am advocating seem to me thoroughly
"Shakespearean."

Flaming Minister

Othello's Visage

(a) *poison his delight*   I. i. 1—81

R<small>ODERIGO</small> enters hastily with Iago at his elbow. Both utter rushing, crowded lines. But Roderigo, a very young gentleman, richly attired, has a tone of weak and hurt protest. Iago, a soldier in the prime of life, wearing a uniform that has seen much service, answers with coarse force.

R<small>ODERIGO</small> Tush,[1] never tell me; I take it much unkindly
That thou, Iago, who hast had my purse
As if the strings were thine, shouldst know of this.

I<small>AGO</small> S'blood,[1] but you'll not hear me If ever I did dream
Of such a matter, abhor me.

The "matter" is Othello's marriage to Desdemona (66 ff.),* with whom Roderigo is in love. It has just taken place, in the dead of night. Iago has forthwith and loyally, so he implies, wakened and informed his friend. He claims that he had no foreknowledge nor even a premonition of this "matter." Is he lying?

We of the audience suspend judgment. Roderigo still doubts, but much more weakly. His next speech, quoted below, retreats from the directness of his opening lines, lines sounding that note of urgent suspicion which will pervade this play.[2] After uttering them he is silent for a moment, then resumes. Taking his cue from his friend's last words, "abhor me," he

---

* Arabic numerals in parentheses refer to lines in the scene under discussion.
[1] The initial expletives "Tush" and "S'blood" (God's blood), from Q1, signalize the contrast described above between the tones of the two speakers.
[2] Roderigo's "never tell me" is parallel in function to Bernardo's "Who's there?," the opening line of *Hamlet*, giving the note of *questioning* which pervades that drama.

shifts the subject to Iago's abhorrence of Othello; speaking
slowly now, shaking a wavering finger at his listener.

RODERIGO   Thou toldst me
            Thou didst hold him in thine hate.[3]
IAGO   Despise me
            If I do not. Three great ones of the city,
            In personal suit to make me his lieutenant . . . .

Roderigo's emphatic slowness is far outdone by the hissing,
heavy deliberation of Iago's *de-spise-me*, uttered with right
hand upraised sharply in the darkness, asseverative and threat-
ening.[4] That phrase is the opening dialogue's crest, which now
resolves into the swift-streaming lines of Iago's long monologues (8-65). And that phrase gives the very essence of these
monologues: bitter, mocking, scornful pride nourished on deadly hate.

Iago's hatred of the Moor soon becomes a mystery. He
explains it elaborately, but in so doing he reveals it still more
elaborately: the revelation far outruns the explanation. This
hate is an underground river. Iago confidently charts its
course; hearkening here to the murmur of it, pointing there
to a superficial pool or stream. But just where did it come
from? Whither is it going? And why, we wonder, has it
such volume and power? His answer to these queries is progressively unconvincing.

When did that hate begin? Later we shall be convinced
that it began with Iago's acquaintance with Othello; but early
in the present scene we are made to feel that it antedates, perhaps long, the affair of the lieutenancy. But at present the
important point is Iago's use of that affair to explain his hate:
he tries to show himself, as well as Roderigo, how very rational
it is. At the same time we perceive that Othello's choice of
Cassio for his lieutenant instead of Iago, his "ancient" (i. e.

---

[3] Modern editions, following Q1, print these ten words as one verse, thus
quickening the tempo. Properly the second line takes the full time of a
pentameter verse. Moreover, Roderigo's final "me" echoes that of Iago in
the preceding speech.
[4] In the Elizabethan theater that hand would have for background the
black curtain drawn across the rear stage to indicate night.

ensign), has very rational grounds. The head of the army desired for his second in command an educated gentleman, one who has book knowledge—Iago terms it "bookish" (24)—of military affairs. He desired it all the more because the third in command, Iago, is a rough soldier of wide practical experience (28-30). The two would thus constitute an effective team; supposing that Cassio will be courteous and appreciative in his bearing to Iago, as later proves to be the case; and supposing Iago to be loyal, as both Cassio and Othello like everyone else (except Roderigo) have every reason, it will soon appear, to believe him to be. Of course we see it is possible that Cassio may be not only inexperienced but, as Iago insinuates (18 ff.), unpractical by temperament; and that Othello's "affection" (36) has blinded him to that defect. But it is still more clear that, whatever be the truth about Cassio, Iago is not fit to be second in command: other considerations apart he is far too crude and narrow. That fact must have been apparent to Othello though naturally he would not publish it; hence the circumlocutory evasiveness of his reply to Iago's advocates (8-17).

But Iago's disappointment is also very natural. We would sympathize entirely if he should decide to resign from Othello's service, as indeed he seems about to do when he declares that "there's no remedy" and that he is not "affined To love the Moor" (35, 39 f.). Roderigo speaks *for us* in exclaiming, "I would not follow him then." These words, however, nettle and embarrass Iago. "O sir, content you," he says sharply. He deliberates for a moment; then glances about quickly, comes closer to his friend, and avers: "I follow him, to serve my turn upon him." That assertion is clearly villainous but otherwise it is vague. Just what does "serve my turn" mean? Iago's ensuing explanation is paradoxical; at the same time it is too earnestly confessional to be insincere. If he is trying to fool Roderigo, he is trying still harder to fool himself.

He claims to be an out-and-out materialist. In reaction to his recent painful experience of "the curse of *service*" (35) he will join the ranks of those (50 ff.)

> Who trimmed in forms, and visages of duty,
> Keep yet their hearts attending on themselves,
> And throwing but shows of service on their lords
> Do well thrive by them.
> And when they have lined their coats
> Do themselves homage.

The first three lines are full, smooth, and figurative, like a lasso elaborately thrown; the last three, curt and strict—the noose jerked tight on its object; no image here except "lined their coats." Iago is trying to constrict his "heart" to material gains. Above we learned he was using Roderigo's purse freely; apparently he is determined now to do likewise with the purse of Othello and Venice. Thus serving his "turn" would mean the kind of self-service that would richly line his coat.

But in the sequel he will do nothing of the sort; and we shall not be surprised. For at the very first Shakespeare makes us feel that this man, while pretending devotion to his small material self, is really devoted to a great immaterial self—his hate. We sense his dissembled detestation of Roderigo. We note the imaginative pungency and vigor of his hatred of all "duteous" servants and followers (45-49); a hot emotion far removed from the casual, cool contempt proper to a right materialist. This may help to account for his utter abhorrence above (18-27) of "one *Michael Cassio*,"[5] who may well be an especially unselfish and duteous officer. Our main impression, however, is that Iago is a hater of human beings in general, and of Othello in particular, on deeper grounds than have appeared. In his climax (55-65) he slurs the question of the causes of his hate while pluming himself upon his skill in hiding his hate:

> In following him, I follow but my self.
> Heaven is my judge, not I for love and duty,
> But seeming so, for my peculiar end. . . .

His "self" may or may not mean monetary gain, and "my peculiar end" is just as enigmatic as "my turn" (42) above. His conclusion sums up his ambiguity: "I am not what I am."

---

[5] Italicized in the original texts, as names generally are.

He broods for a moment, proudly but uneasily, gloating upon his consummate hypocrisy but aware of his failure to explain the deadliness of his hate. Roderigo, unconvinced but overawed, will not pursue the question further. He resumes the subject of the marriage. Iago tells him to "call up her father"[6]—then, with sudden bitter intensity, urges him to "rouse" Othello, using that verb in the sense of hunting a wild animal from its lair:

> Rouse him, make after him, poison his delight,
> Proclaim him in the streets. Incense her kinsmen,
> And though he in a fertile climate dwell,
> Plague him with flies: though that his joy be joy,
> Yet throw such chances of vexation on't,
> As it may lose some colour.[7]

Warm, fertile joy, plagued, vexed, poisoned with flies! That is a sort of imagery that will recur in this drama. Another sort appears in Iago's next speech picturing the effect of "fire" outbreaking "by night" in "populous cities"—"populous" recalls "fertile," above, thus connecting the two passages: people swarm in cities like flies in a hot, damp climate. The fiery imagery of the second passage is objectified presently by Brabantio's "tinder" and "taper," below (141-145), and then by the torches moving through the night towards the end of the scene; and in subsequent scenes, in this and every other act of the play; leading up to the torch held in Othello's hand when preparing to kill his wife. This "flaming minister" (V. ii. 8) is the acme of all the figures of fire and heat and flame that appear in this tragedy of consuming love and consuming hate.

At present a mystery of love is beginning to rise over against the mystery of hate we have been watching.

It is clear now that Iago was telling the truth when he de-

---

[6] I have substituted a dash for the colon of F1. Iago jerks his thumb at Brabantio's house—then clenches and shakes his fist at the thought of Othello's "delight." "Rouse" is not in apposition but in opposition to "Call up." Modern editors have destroyed that dramatic contrast by placing a comma after "father" and a colon after "Rouse him."

[7] Compare Satan's ambition to "grieve" and "disturb" the Almighty whom he cannot overthrow (*Paradise Lost* I. 167).

clared that he never "did dream of such a matter" as the union
of the Moor and Desdemona. We perceive that "such a matter" would be an entire enigma to such a person, and, incidentally, that Othello would surely refrain from giving him the least
hint of it beforehand. Othello would refuse him his confidence
in such a matter, despite all his seeming honesty and devotion,
for the same reason that he refused him the lieutenancy, namely
his gross boorishness. And the implication is that Iago resents
the former refusal even more bitterly than the latter. He will
not say that, here or later, in so many words. He will not
confess it to himself, let alone Roderigo or any other, because
of his pride. His clever and convincing show of unselfish "love
and duty" to his commander has not only failed to win him the
lieutenancy: it has failed to lead Othello to give him his confidence even in regard to such a trifle (from Iago's point of
view) as the marriage. Here the wound to Iago's pride is
deep, too deep for words. And it is further deepened by the
fact that, notwithstanding his brainy acuteness, he cannot understand how such a trifle can give Othello so rich a joy. Iago has
perceived that joy but hates to admit its reality; hence the conditional clauses in the passage quoted above: "*though* he in a
fertile climate dwell . . . *though* that his joy *be* joy." The passage as a whole stands out in vivid contrast to the long preceding
monologues on the subject of the lieutenancy. Its compressed toxic passion tells us what Iago will not confess: his
hatred of the Moor owes far less to the matter of the lieutenancy than to his bafflement regarding Othello's marriage
and love and joy. However, the essential cause of that hate
remains still a mystery; Shakespeare so desires.[8] He will clear
that mystery largely in the close of the first act. But now he
turns our attention more and more to the mystery of the marriage.

[8] Hence he does not till much later let Iago, or us, know that Cassio
was Othello's confidant in the course of his wooing (III. iii. 94-100). Of
course this may have been a brilliant afterthought on Shakespeare's part. But
it is certain that this information, if given now or soon, would induce in us
superficial and wrong assumptions regarding the lieutenancy and Iago's mysterious hate.

(b) *Is there not charms ...?* I. i. 82—184

In this murky, clamorous episode the marriage is made to appear to us extremely questionable, and very likely tragic in effect—a "summons" (82) to the dark powers that bring about human misery. But at the same time we doubt that the marriage is absolutely unnatural since the three men who claim that it is are the worst sort of witnesses: Roderigo, a shallow creature and disappointed lover; Brabantio, a bereft, hot-tempered father; above all Iago, hater and deceiver, who leads the chorus. They indeed force us to see that this marriage is extraordinary, even unique. It is strikingly abnormal in all its external features. But why, then, did it occur?

The obvious answer would be lust. But this, though it may have actuated the Moor—that possibility remains open at the end of the scene—is almost if not entirely excluded in the case of his wife. For the more Iago and Roderigo vilify the Moor, as "thick-lips" (66), "old black ram" (88), "gross" and "lascivious" (127), the less likely it seems that, if what they say has in it a grain of truth, he could attract her physically; and still less likely that she, the daughter of a Venetian "senator" (119), would, in addition to eloping with the Moor, *bind* herself to him through the sacrament of marriage,

> *Tying* her duty, beauty, wit, and fortune
> In an extravagant and wheeling stranger,
> Of here, and everywhere . . . . (136-138)

a homeless as well as physically unalluring soldier of fortune; who at this very moment, moreover, is on the verge of embarking for distant "Cyprus wars" (151). The enigma centers in the word "tying." Why would this "extravagant [wandering] stranger" be willing to tie himself to a girl-wife at this time? But far more peculiar is her "tying" herself "in" him—unless, strangely enough, she be extraordinarily devoted to him, and he responsive enough to accept the tie of marriage. Thus the mysterious affair would be accounted for. But that explication, the possibility of which is opened by Shakespeare's art through the words of the three speakers, is not in the least given by them. All are vociferantly hostile to anything like such a view, each in his own way. Their viewpoints come out in ironic and darkly comical conflict with each other—darkly, because of our sense of hovering tragedy while the three proclaim their jealous passions in the night.

Iago, puzzled by and hating Othello's "joy" (71), is intent on wounding it as severely as possible. His pertinent oath " 'Zounds" (God's wounds), twice uttered (86, 108), is the sequel of his "dire yell" (75-81) and the prologue to grossly sexual depictions of the Moor; which, incidentally and covertly, asperse also the motives of the Moor's wife. The note of intenseness in his melodramatic blatancy tells us that he would love to believe utterly, though he cannot, every word he is saying. His words overshoot their immediate aim: his effort to enrage Brabantio against Othello has the primary effect of awakening a righteous anger against himself. The old man, peering down from his window in the direction of his hidden interlocutor, and speaking with an unwitting meaningfulness, pronounces him a "profane wretch" and "a villain" (115, 119). Profane villainy is at work in the darkness, from the beginning to the end of this play.

Brabantio is also prophetic when he declares to Iago's companion: "This thou shalt answer. I know thee, Roderigo" (120). We too know him pretty well and foresee that he will have to "answer" terribly for his subservience to a profane, revengeful, and hypocritic villain. He and he alone knows of Iago's secret disloyalty to the Venetian general. Roderigo is therefore a key figure in the plot. A word from him to the authorities could expose the machinator and forestall impending evil. But that word, we now perceive, will in all probability not be spoken, for he fails to take his present inviting opportunity to dissociate his purposes from those of Iago. He wins Brabantio's credence and approval by his full and sufficiently reasonable account of Desdemona's elopement (121-141). Inspired by his affection for the girl and his respect for her father, the "reverend" and "grave" signior (93, 106), Roderigo is here at his very best. His real "sense" of "civility" (132) comes out in strong contrast with the grossness of his concealed companion. Properly that sense would lead him to expose Iago, in some degree, when he is left alone with Brabantio in the final episode of this scene (161 ff.). But his civility and prudence are too weak. His three brief speeches in the final dialogue are feeble and hesitant. Waveringly he says of the Moor, "I *think* I can discover him . . . " (179), though Iago had told him where the Moor was "surely" (158) to be found. He knows that to "discover" (unmask) Iago to the senator is much more urgent than to "discover" the Moor. But the dark power of the absent Iago prevails with him. Not a single revealing word about that evil fellow is uttered here by the "good" Roderigo (184).[9]

Meanwhile Brabantio has revealed his violent heart to us. His daughter's misconduct, not the Moor's, is here his main theme. Later we learn that he himself had provided occasion for the strange love affair (I. iii. 128), which, he now confesses, "is not unlike my dream, / Belief of it oppresses me already" (143). In modern terms his subconscious mind was aware of a possibility which his will rejected absolutely; and now he will not allot to himself the least jot of blame. And his suppressed sense of responsibility makes him all the more violent in his blame of her. His love of her is intense but extremely selfish. When he finds that his "dream" has turned out to be "too true," the "evil," as his ensuing lines show, is mainly his own bitter unhappiness (161 ff.). His "girl" is "unhappy" mainly in the fact of having "made a gross revolt" (135) from her duty to her father. He had assumed her complete subjection

[9] He had suppressed the fact that it was Iago, not himself, who saw Desdemona transported to the Moor by "a gondolier" (126). And when Brabantio, alone with him, cross-questions him about the elopement (163-166) he gives no answer instead of confessing that all his information came from Iago. His embarrassed behavior (if the part is well acted on the stage) tells the audience that he knows he ought now to inform Brabantio of Iago's villainy. (To suppose that Roderigo himself witnessed the elopement is to spoil Shakespeare's story in several important particulars.)

to his will and to his impregnable race prejudice[10] in regard
to marriage. "Oh, she deceives me / Past thought." Certainly
her dissimulation strikes us, here, as ominous: it is a climactic
touch in a scene of darkness and deceit. Yet we see that it
was induced by her father's imperiousness; if she had given
him any inkling of her intention he would have sequestered
her, as he later intimates (I. iii. 195-198). Also it is clear that
she need not have been in the least an *artful* dissembler—like
Iago: no father would be blinder than hers to what he did not
wish to believe. His egoism, however, blinds him to his own
blindness. In the following lines (170 ff.) he classes himself
with normally perceptive fathers, to the amusement of those
in the audience who consider themselves such:

> Oh heaven: how got she out?[11]
> Oh treason of the blood.
> Fathers, from hence trust not your daughters' minds
> By what you see them act—Is there not charms
> By which the property of youth and maidhood
> May be abused? . . .

His mind leaps to the notion of charms to account for his own
blindness and, more suggestively and pathetically, for his
daughter's infatuation. Abnormally ignorant of her mind,
he has at least the intuition that her "blood" (171), her heart,
is devoid of the gross lust insinuated by Iago above: surely she
has the purity proper to her young "maidhood." It must be
that she "abused" (deceived) her father because she herself
was "abused" (corrupted) by magic employed by the Moor.

That is improbable to us; but it stresses strongly the mystery of this strange love-and-marriage. For us the two principals are still remote—remotely vivid. They have been pre-

---

[10] In America at the present time the contrast between the older and
younger generations regarding this matter is often very striking.

[11] He pauses here, hoping in vain for some light from Roderigo; hence
the shortness of the line. The next line is equally short because it announces
a theme of great importance for the whole tragedy. Incidentally the actor
of Brabantio's role must have time to turn from Roderigo to the "Fathers"
in the audience. After "act" in the fourth line he turns again to his companion; here I have substituted a dash for the period of F1.

sented to us graphically but distantly through the alien minds
of three others, who, as though of set purpose, have refrained
from speaking their names. So far the two are types or species
rather than individual persons; and very unusual species they
are, especially Brabantio's daughter. The scene leaves us with
the feeling that her Moor exerts upon her, and perhaps tragically, certain strange, compelling "charms." What may these be?
That question is foremost in our minds when now he appears
in person.

(c) *my unhoused free condition*   I. ii

Othello enters silently with firm step, unlike Roderigo at
the beginning; but, like him, with Iago gesticulating at his
elbow: that parallel is significant. The Moor's dark face in
the torchlight—a face not unhandsome, that of a gentleman
of distinguished character and ability, in early middle age[12]—
is serenely, radiantly happy. He scarcely glances at his companion, whose every word is carefully "contrived" (3) to
"poison his delight" (I. i. 68). To us the villain's mien says
"I do hate him as I do hell pains," while showing out "a flag
and sign of love" (I. i. 155-158) by pretending that the one he
hates is Brabantio. "I had thought t'have yerked him here
under the ribs"—he makes a checked stabbing gesture towards
his master's breast, then fingers his own ribs. Othello laughs
quietly: " 'Tis better as it is." That is all he will say. He
stands still with arms folded on his breast.

Iago, further embittered by his failure to disturb him, re-
doubles his efforts (6-17, 29-30). These naturally seem to the
amused Othello the crude, honest expression of a coarse soldier's devotion to his commander. Therefore as a gentleman
he responds by addressing the fellow with a new though very
strictly limited intimacy (17-28, 30-32). He condescends
smilingly to justify his marriage in terms which his earthly
ancient can understand and appreciate. To him, and to him

---

[12] Like Richard Burbage, who created the part. See his picture and
imagine it with the skin darkened. As to age, Othello is not "old" as Iago
said (I. i. 88) but no longer youthful (I. iii. 264 f., III. iii. 265 f.).

only, and only here, Othello declares that he has in his veins "royal" blood and that his deserts ("demerits") are equal to "as proud a fortune / As this that I have reached": in vulgar terms, the hand of the heiress of a senator of mercantile Venice. But such a "fortune" was not his motive any more than the lust attributed to him above by Iago and Roderigo. His whole demeanor tells us the contrary. It also tells us that the word "love," which he now utters casually, has for him a fineness of meaning which he could not and would not express to his present auditor:

> . . . . For know, Iago,
> But that I love the gentle Desdemona,
> I would not my unhoused free condition
> Put into circumscription, and confine,
> For the sea's worth.

The very movement of that simple-flowing second verse, culminating in the lovely name, here for the first time uttered, conveys the gentility of the speaker as well as of his "gentle Desdemona."

That, however, is a frail though fine ground for so unusual a union. And before we learn of stronger ties we are made to see the strength of the Moor's attachment to his free life as a soldier. At the outset Iago pictured him "as loving his own pride and purposes" (I. i. 12); Roderigo termed him "an extravagant and wheeling stranger / Of here and everywhere" (I. i. 137 f.). But afterwards Iago had to admit reluctantly that "the State" had not "another of his fathom . . . To lead their business" (I. i. 148-154). And now Othello shows himself well aware of that fact, while he eschews "boasting" (20). His modest allusion to "my services" (18) evinces, along with firm loyalty to the state, a strong self-trust. Certainly he does not *love*—not here, not yet—"his own pride and purposes": that is precisely what the boastful Iago does, and he eagerly tries to read his own egotism into his hated captain. Othello has a decorous pride in his past deeds and in his capability for future achievements. His pride, so far, has no touch of ignobility or undue confidence. Nevertheless in the passage quoted above, stressed as it is by the interrupting entrance of others, his intense satisfaction in his unconfined, uncircumscribed existence is somewhat ominous. Certainly he is not a "wheeling stranger" and, as already noted, his confession to Iago of his love for his newly wedded wife is restrained in tone because of his refinement. Yet we are dramatically warned that his love *may* be too refined, too "gentle," in comparison with his imaginative passion for his "free condition." This he loves more than the wide-wandering "sea"; and his marriage puts his life into an uncongenial "confine" (confinement). Othello has two loves: one, old and innate; one new and pure and fine—strong enough, too, to rival the other. But we wonder as to the *quality* of its strength: how deepgoing is this new love?

In the rest of the scene his old love holds the foreground while his new love remains an occult and somewhat dim presence. Othello's quiet joy in it suffuses his greeting to the first newcomers:

> The servants of the duke?
> And my lieutenant?
> The goodness of the night upon you, friends—
> What is the news?

While uttering the two opening lines[13] he peers through the dark, recognizing first the "servants" by the "lights" (28) of the torches in their hands. This night, so grim and lurid with hate and suspicion, hurry and alarm, has for the Moor a happy "goodness." It emanates from the unseen Desdemona as well as from himself. But now it is heightened by the general's eagerness for "news" of the state and for action in his profession. Others are disturbed by the prospect of war; not he. With cool intentness and calm delight he listens to Cassio's hasty account of the "business of some heat" (40) and of the hot "quests" for "you" (44, 47).

---

[13] Printed in Q1 as a single line with no question marks. In the third line "the goodness of the night" is stressed by forming an exact rhythmic parallel to "the servants of the duke."

Incidentally the urgent "galleys" from "Cyprus" (39 f.,
I. i. 151) remind us of Venice's sea empire, reflected also in
Othello's words of "the sea's worth" above (28). And his
love of his *"unhoused* free condition" (26) is recalled when he
replies to Cassio, "I will but spend a word here in the *house"*
(48). This is the "Sagittary" (I. i. 159), an inn of warlike
name. There, throughout this scene, with intense suggestiveness, Desdemona remains hidden, hidden as is, still, the essential meaning of her and Othello's love. During the Moor's
brief secret "word" with her Iago contrives a coarsely humorous image for their union (50-52) which contributes to the
rising atmosphere of sea battle and hints at the violently abnormal aspect of the sudden marriage. This aspect is also be-
tokened by Cassio's pointed ignorance of the event. Disturbing
for us is his abrupt surprise at Othello's wedding—"To who?"
(52). It is hard for him to conceive that such a quick, secret
bond has been accepted by the warrior who so much loves the
urgent present call (44) to battle at sea.[14]

Great in real battle, Othello is just as great in the petty
war with Brabantio. Not waiting to be accosted, he sings out
genially, "Holla, stand there!" And the incipient fray
with the old man's "officers of the night" (I. i. 183) is
stopped less by the general's words than by his strong, bright
air of command: "Keep up your bright swords, for the dew
will rust them!" For Othello the swords gleaming in the
torchlight and darkness are luminous with the happiness of
his marriage and radiant with the renewed joy of his profession.[15] Othello is genial and magnanimous. This Moorish
soldier of fortune justifies his "royal" descent by showing in his
own "life and being" (21-22) a royal gentility,[16] over against

[14] If Cassio knows of his master's love (see note 8 above) he is nonetheless startled by his marrying *at this time.* "To *who?"* may imply: how
could Othello be so inconsiderate to Desdemona?

[15] The actor will have in mind the fact that Othello has been out of action
for some nine months (I. iii. 84).

[16] In sixteenth-century thought noble birth was considered a real but far
from inalienable advantage. It rendered a person predisposed to be a gentleman but could not make him one. Often in the literature of the time titular
gentlemen are boorish and persons of low birth gentle.

an influential Venetian "signior" (60) who appears here a scurrilous boor, akin in that point to Iago.

Above, Iago lied when he said he had heard Brabantio speak "scurvy and provoking terms" (7) against Othello; but he lied, as so often in the course of this play, with insight and lucky foresight. In the first scene Brabantio did not speak those terms. But Iago perceived that the old man, impelled by his own temperament and by the tempter's gross words, for the present rejected (I. i. 115 ff.) but bound to work in him subconsciously, would doubtless use such terms when he encountered the Moor; and this proves to be the case. Brabantio, having brooded fruitfully upon his notion of "charms," screams out now:

> Oh thou foul thief,[17]
> Where hast thou stowed my daughter?
> Damned as thou art, thou hast enchanted her. . . .

Othello, protecting his wife from her father's rage, will not reveal that she is "stowed" close at hand; and Iago dare not do so, though he glances suggestively (I think) in the direction of the Sagittary. Brabantio, however, is now less anxious to "apprehend her" (I. i. 178) than to convict the Moor, the "foul thief," of using "foul charms" (73). Othello's complexion, hitherto not mentioned by Brabantio but in his hearing termed "black" by Iago (I. i. 88), is now made "sooty" (70) by the old man's dire suspicion and rage. The Moor's soul is "damned," in the lines quoted above, damned and blackened by the sin of practicing black "arts" (79):[18] hence his visage, too, must be "foul" (ugly) and grimy as soot.

In the course of his diatribe the old senator gives us new information regarding his daughter:

---

[17] The shortness of the line allows the speaker to regain his breath, lost in his recourse to weapons (61), and throws heavy emphasis on these four words, paralleling his previous line, "Down with him, thief" (57). The next line too is short because the speaker pauses slightly for an answer to his question.

[18] Shakespeare in using here the phrase "arts inhibited and out of warrant," expressive of Brabantio's legalism, knows that the term "black art" will be in the minds of the spectators, along with the old belief that a "damned" soul is "black," as in *Hamlet* III. iii. 94.

> . . . a maid so tender, fair, and happy,
> So opposite to marriage that she shunned
> The wealthy curled darlings of our nation. . . .

Her father finds it utterly inconceivable that such a maid, "unless enchanted" (63), "Would ever have—t'incur a general mock— / Run from her guardage" (69 f.) to such a person as the Moor. But this view is paradoxical. For a girl unconventional enough to refuse highly approved suitors would be the less likely to mind the amused scorn incurred by an elopement with Othello: her egoistic father attributes to her his own susceptibility to the "general mock" of Venetian society. Nor was her repugnance for a marriage of convenience synonymous, as he believes, with aversion to the very idea of marriage. Her father reveals unwittingly that what she was mainly "opposite to" was probably his own vulgarity.[19] Of course her very gentility would keep her from displaying that distaste: her bearing to him was "tender" and "happy." But the present scene makes us see that she would have a not unnatural inclination to "run from" the "guardage" of such a parent. His crude talk of "wealthy and curled darlings" would repel her, invisibly to him, even more than the "darlings" themselves would repel her visibly. By contrast the gentility of Othello would be very attractive to the "gentle Desdemona" (25).[20]

His homelessness, however, would be the reverse of attractive to her. This, not his age and complexion, would be the chief barrier. His "unhoused free condition" would be for her, far more than for him, an obstacle to their marriage. For Shakespeare has subtly made us feel that she is strongly, quietly home-loving despite the uncongeniality of her present domestic scene. Othello's devotion to his wandering life would be "a

---

[19] This particular contrast between parent and child is common in Elizabethan literature, e.g., Old Capulet and Juliet, Polonius and Ophelia. Its dramatic quality, not the question of its grounds in nature, intrigued the dramatists.

[20] The reader of Elizabethan literature must bear in mind that the word "gentle" is constantly, though not always, synonymous with our adjectives "gentlemanly" and "gentlewomanly."

thing" to arouse in her a "fear," not "delight" (71), a fear
to be overcome only by a love as mighty as "chains of magic"
(65)—and equally inscrutable to us, so far.

And now we see the strange marriage becoming more and
more overshadowed by "the present business of the State" (90)
so engrossing to the Moor. He will let nothing hinder it. The
renewed and now importunate threat of a street battle, due to
Brabantio's effort to "apprehend" him by force (77 ff.), brings
out in Othello the stern commander. Gone is all his previous
geniality. Above the noise he shouts (81 ff.): "Hold your
hands, / Both you of my inclining, and the rest." To Iago
he adds in a tone of austere kindliness, "Were it my cue to
fight, I should have known it / Without a prompter." The
villain had again advanced his sword against Roderigo, his
halfhearted fellow conspirator, as at the outset (55-58). Meanwhile his looks and gestures have fomented surreptitiously the
spirit of strife. Beneath his assumed wrath at his master's
opponents we discern his hot hatred of his master's dispas-
sionateness. Throughout this scene not a single unbecoming
word or motion escapes Othello despite steadily heightening
provocation. The provocation culminates, and so does the
Moor's self-control, when Brabantio furiously threatens him
with "prison" (85), most hateful of all words to one who hates
"confine"(27). Othello's final words to the old man (87-91)
reach the acme of dignified simplicity and reasonableness. Brabantio's chief officer is completely overswayed. The terms
"most worthy" and "noble" (91 f.), with which he deprecat-
ingly addresses his employer, are dramatically ironic: they
really apply to Othello, epitomizing his demeanor during this
scene. The upshot, however, is that we are made to feel that
"the duke's council / In this time of the night?" (93 f.) con-
stitutes for the soldierly Othello a problem more vital at present than the question of his marriage.

(d) *my traveller's history*   I. iii. 1-170

DUKE   There's no composition in this news
                    That gives them credit.
FIRST SENATOR   Indeed, they are disproportioned. . . .

For us those opening verses mean far more than the speakers
intend. The "news" given in the first two scenes about the
strange marriage lacks "composition" (consistency) like the
tidings now arriving of the Turkish fleet; and the word "disproportioned," peculiarly used here,[21] harps upon an outstanding fact. For we know that whatever else may be false, Othello's "condition" (I. ii. 26) is extraordinarily "disproportioned"
to that of his wife. Nevertheless their union *may* be essentially sound and right: that "is possible enough to judgement"
(9), like the supposed intention of the Turks to attack Cyprus.
News arrives, however, that they are now steering for Rhodes
(14). But this may be, and indeed presently proves to be, "a
pageant / To keep us in false gaze" (18 f.).[22] Such pageants
have been enacted in the preceding scenes in regard to the marriage. The mood of those scenes, doubt, suspicion, haste, discomposure, is maintained in the opening dialogue here (1-46),
though in a muted key. Intensity is resumed and heightened
when Brabantio, entering with Othello and others, addresses
the duke and senate.

Here the old man's "grief" (55)

> Is of so flood-gate and o'erbearing nature
> That it engluts and swallows other sorrows,
> And it is still itself.

He sobs out passionately, "My daughter—oh my daughter!"
Here our sympathy for him, like that of the duke and senators
—and that, too, which appears in the face of the silent Othello—
is at its keenest. Thus we are rendered susceptible to a very

---

[21] See this word in Onions's *Shakespeare Glossary*. Later Iago will urge
the "foul disproportions" (III. iii. 233) involved in Desdemona's desire to
marry the Moor.

[22] The atmospheric effect of these words would be heightened for the
Elizabethan audience by their awareness that "pageant" denoted a scene in a
medieval mystery play.

significant theme which he now proceeds to emphasize, the
theme of "nature." This word is not used in the play until it
appears casually in the passage quoted above, in relation to Brabantio's grief. In the sequel he employs it thrice (62, 96, 101) in
relation to the emotions of his daughter. And the net effect is to
accentuate tragically the mystery of her character and of the
nature of her love.

Mastering his sobs he declares that in her case "nature,"
not being in any way abnormal, was not able "so preposterously
to err" (62) unless illicitly swayed. We reject his repeated
claim that she must have been "corrupted" (60) by magical
means. But of course he may be equally mistaken in his belief
that her nature is not in any way "deficient, blind, or lame of
sense" (63). In "sense," i.e. in perception, feeling, discernment, understanding, she may have erred "preposterously."
And she may, however innocently, have been, in the duke's
phrase, "beguiled . . . of her self" (66). Such possibilities are
open. They strike us here sharply because of the simple intensity of her father's grief for her. He speaks now more in
sorrow than in anger, not repeating his grossly personal asper-
sions of Othello. The esteemed "signior" Brabantio (50 f.)
has, along with his sorrow, the discretion to refrain in the presence of the senate from terming their distinguished general a
"foul thief" with a "sooty bosom" (I. ii. 62, 70).[23] At the
first he even refrains from revealing the identity of the supposed malefactor. So that when, after winning the duke's
warm and unqualified sympathy for his cause (65-69), he declares simply "Here is the man—this Moor . . . " the effect is
tremendous:

ALL   We are very sorry for't.
DUKE (*to Othello*) What in your own part, *can* you say to this?
BRABANTIO   Nothing, but this is so.

Brabantio and Othello look around upon the perturbed, mur-
muring assembly, Othello still maintaining his silence. Bra-

[23] In the present scene the word "foul" is uttered by the duke and Othello
(65, 117), not by Brabantio as previously (I. ii. 62, 73).

bantio's five staccato words, above, evince the assurance given him by the duke's doubtful question to the Moor, a question expressing the mood of the whole council. All of them believe, though "very sorry" to do so, that their great general "can" scarcely clear himself entirely of the charge brought against him.

Nor do his ensuing replies do so. They establish his honesty; but they do not convince the senate, nor us, that he has not, in all honesty, exerted an undue influence upon Desdemona. Othello's exordium, beginning

> Most potent, grave, and reverend signiors,
> My very noble, and approved good masters . . . .

is "very noble" throughout and, at first, "most . . . grave." He pleads for continued confidence on the part of his "good masters," reminding them tacitly and modestly of all his "services" (I. ii. 17) to them. His reference to Brabantio as "this old man" (78) is respectful and sympathetic in tone even while echoing the plainness of his accuser's reference to him, above, as "the man, this Moor." But gradually the formal dignity of the speech yields to a warmer mood when Othello speaks of the life he loves "in the tented field" (85) and, finally, of his new "love"(91). With the words "grace" and "gracious" (88 f.) a peculiarly gracious smile begins to light up his visage. It becomes entirely radiant when at the close he proposes to reveal—parodying Brabantio's "spells . . . medicines . . . witchcraft" (61, 64)—by means of

> What drugs, what charms,[24]
> What conjuration, and what mighty magic,
> (For such proceeding I am charged withal),
> I won his daughter—
>
> BRABANTIO (*breaking in*) A maiden, never bold:
> Of spirit so still, and quiet, that her motion

---

[24] These four words are uttered with emphatic slowness while Othello turns towards his accuser. But Q1, by combining these words with the preceding line, also short, to form one pentameter verse, spoils the dramatic effect of both lines.

> Blushed at herself—and she, in spite of *nature*,
> Of years, of country, credit, everything,
> To fall in love, with what she feared to look on!

Thus the old man resumes his theme of "nature" before Othello can try to explain what innocent "mighty magic" he used. And the interruption greatly complicates the Moor's task. For certainly the kind of life he has just confessed to having lived, a life of "broil and battle" since the age of "seven years" (83, 87), would be very likely to repel a maiden with a "spirit" so extremely "quiet" and bashful. Previously we were encouraged to believe that she was unconventional enough to choose an unconventional husband (I. ii. 67 f.). But now the very "spirit" of her life seems entirely contrary to that which has animated Othello's life. Her father proceeds to intimate that the retiringness of her nature is her "perfection" (100), her characteristic excellence. And we feel that Othello's career, so publicly violent as well as wandering and "unhoused," would, far more than his age and complexion, render him a being that "she feared to look on"—unless her "spirit" experienced some "motion," still obscure to us, which transcended the "rules of nature" (101).

Here Brabantio shouts out that she must have been corrupted by "practices of cunning hell." This phrase, the acme of his accusation, the word "hell" being new in his vocabulary, goes wide of Othello. For us, however, it strikes Iago. He is a silent, eager listener throughout the present ensemble, sending now and then to the equally silent Roderigo a look that recalls to him and to us his hell-like "hate" of Othello (I. i. 155). Just now the villain's mien shows him gloating upon Brabantio's appeal to "nature," a theme which he will later distort against Desdemona by "practices of cunning hell" to arouse hellish jealousy in her husband.

And here, already, perplexity appears in the Moor's face, that visage so dark, and so bright, in contrast with Iago's. Othello is silent. To encourage him the facile duke, reversing his previous attitude (65-70), terms Brabantio's charge a "poor likelihood" (108). The First Senator, realistic and decisive, as above (17-30, 36), exhorts the commander strongly:

> But Othello, speak,
> Did you, by indirect and forced courses,
> Subdue, and poison this young maid's affections?
> Or came it by request, and such fair question
> As soul to soul affordeth?

Normally the soldierly Moor would, in a tone still more forceful than that of his inquisitor, give a definitive answer: No, for the first question; for the second, Yes. But he does not do so; and the smile with which he spoke of his "mighty magic," above, has faded utterly. He is absolutely certain of his own "perfect" sincerity (I. ii. 31) and, at least in his conscious mind, of Desdemona's. But he is deeply disturbed by the mystery of this "young maid's" love for him in the face of her extreme difference from him in "nature." This problem would not so perplex him now if it had not been in his mind all along. It confronts him now, however, with novel power and inescapable importunity. He is enjoined to make clear to his respected "masters" and "potent" judges (76 f.) just how he won this girl's love, despite all obstacles of "nature," without employing any "indirect" means or exerting any influence that could possibly seem in any way not "fair." And he who has always obeyed the senate so well, finds this command far too difficult. Without making any reply to the First Senator he turns to the duke with considerable agitation and beseeches him to

> Send for the lady to the Sagittary
> And let her speak of me before her father. . . .

Not he but "the lady," as he terms her formally here—presently "this fair lady" (125)[25]—can clear up the mystery. Previously he was determined, as shown in scene ii,[26] to shield

---

[25] The formality is accentuated by the duke's terming her, in contrast, "Desdemona" (120)—the first time her name has been uttered since Othello himself introduced it in the preceding scene (I. ii. 25). And the term "fair" seems to echo the First Senator's suggestive use of it above (113).

[26] There he was certain that he could present his case to the senate successfully (I. ii. 17 ff., 84 ff.) without producing his wife.

his wife from her father's presence in accordance with her own
desire: every allusion to her and her marriage, from the fifth
line of the play on, has implied her craving for the maximum
of secrecy and seclusion. But now Othello, "perplexed in the
extreme" (V. ii. 346), requires her public aid. His perturbation appears through his grave words to the senate regarding
his "office" and his "life" (117-120) and, finally, his religion
(122 ff.):

> And till she come, as truly as to heaven
> I do confess the vices of my blood,
> So justly to your grave ears I'll present
> How I did thrive in this fair lady's love,
> And she in mine.

That second line, declaimed with hand raised solemnly to
"heaven," strikes us very forcibly.[27] It is extremely different
from all his previous utterances. The distinguished general
and gentleman, proud of his past "services," his "royal" blood,
and his effectual strength in emergencies (I. ii. 17 ff., 82 ff.),
seemed the last person to harbor or, at the least, publicly confess
harboring any inordinate passions; such as Iago's jealous hate
and Brabantio's blind rage. Clearly Othello has for the present been remarkably humbled, as well as deeply disturbed, by
being forced to face in public the mystery of "this fair lady's"
extraordinary devotion to him. He will try religiously, "truly,"
and "justly" to "present" the matter to the senate from his own
standpoint. But his tale will be not only simple, as he declared
above (81-90): he intimates now that his account will be merely
provisional and interim—"till she come."

"Her father loved me, oft invited me. . . . "[28] This lovely
verse is sensational, theatrically speaking: a flash of illumina-

---

[27] An academic reader may of course regard this verse as merely an old-
time, conventional Christian asseveration instead of a masterstroke of dramatic
revelation on the part of Shakespeare.

[28] Every single one of the seven words goes quietly to its goal, borne on
an even tide of rhythm and assonance. Try speaking the vowel sounds only,
omitting or whispering the consonants, noting particularly how "loved" prepares for "oft." The first "me," unstressed, intimating Othello's dignified
reserve, wins an emphatic quality from the long vowel, the caesura, and the
repetition of "me" (with slight increase of stress) at the end of the line.

tion, a prepared surprise. Consciously or not the audience has been wondering how the Moor got access, at the outset, to the very shy daughter of a very race-prejudiced Venetian "magnifico" (I. ii. 12). The answer, as suggested above (page 11 f.), is Brabantio's self-centeredness. He would not see that his own warm friendliness for the Moor, despite the color line, "invited" a similar feeling on the part of his daughter; and that his keen interest as a sedentary person in Othello's "traveller's history" (139) might well be reproduced with intenser emotion in a woman not only reclusive but, unlike himself, very young, inexperienced, and above all unselfish. We know that Brabantio must have listened to Othello's story for what it meant to Brabantio. His daughter, we are now shown, listened to it for what it meant to Othello.

Her love, however, was a very gradual growth; the while Othello visited her home "oft," in the course of "nine moons" (84), and repeated or enlarged his narratives as he was "still [continually] questioned" (129) by her father. At the first no doubt she "feared to look on" (98) the Moor. And her natural pity for his "disastrous chances" (134-139) would have to struggle with the terror inspired by his account of dreadful sights (140-145), from the vague "antars [antres] vast" to the horrid particularity of "men whose heads / Grew beneath their shoulders." Her initial and dubious response is exquisitely denoted by the phrase "seriously incline" in the opening of the following passage, wherein we sense the gradual intensifying of her pity up to the final word "suffered":

```
. . . . These things to hear                          145
Would Desdemona seriously incline:
But still the house affairs would draw her hence;
Which ever as she could with haste despatch,
She'ld come again, and with a greedy ear
Devour up my discourse. Which I observing,          150
Took once a pliant hour, and found good means
To draw from her a prayer of earnest heart
That I would all my pilgrimage dilate,
Whereof by parcels she had something heard,
```

But not instinctively. I did consent,   155
And often did beguile her of her tears,
When I did speak of some distressful stroke
That my youth suffered. . . .

At first she would enter the room bashfully and listen "seriously" with downcast eyes. Later she came hastily, to hearken with
"greedy ear," her eyes fixed on the Moor. Eventually, in her
father's absence, and after gently powerful words of encourage-
ment from her visitor—such would be his "good means" (151)
—this maiden "so still and quiet" (95) speaks with a sudden
passionate intensity.

She yearns with "earnest heart" to hear his whole "pilgrimage"—all the travel and travail that have brought him religiously to this great moment with her[29]—told to her alone,
his gaze given solely to her. She watches "Othello's visage"
(253) during his narrative more intensely than she hearkens
to his words. She listens to him now not just attentively but "instinctively" (155),[30] i.e. with all her soul, trying to fathom all
the soul of him. For her the external details or "parcels" of
his history are of minor interest: she wants to know his "por-
tance" (139) throughout it all, his own behavior and spirit.
This he had barely mentioned when speaking to her father
with a soldier's reticence; but now, speaking as a lover, he "instinctively" stresses it. Love's "witchcraft" (64, 169) leads
him to tell her of the miseries he endured *when he was young
like her*. To her father he spoke of the "disastrous chances" that

[29] In Shakespeare's time the words "travel" and "travail" were closely
associated; and the lover was often figured as a religious pilgrim; see *Romeo
and Juliet* I. v. 95 ff., II. ii. 55.
[30] The folios excepting F1 read "distinctively," which is hopelessly bad.
The quartos have "intentively," i.e., intently or attentively; but this is anticlimactic to the "greedy" and devouring "ear" above. I think Shakespeare's
ultimate choice was "instinctively," giving the word an exceptionally comprehensive sense·by means of the context. The implication (which Desdemona,
Othello, and Shakespeare are too "gentle" to put into blunt words) is that
she could not finally make up her mind about her lover until she had heard
him tell his story solely to and for her. She had devoured and brooded upon
the "parcels" she had heard, addressed mainly to her father; but her feminine
instinct could not thus have full play: "she had something heard, / But not
instinctively." Now she will listen with "earnest heart," using all her re-
sources of intuition and divination, her whole woman's instinct.

studded his career as a whole; to her he speaks of one and
another "distressful stroke" that his "youth suffered." These
two words, neither of them used by Othello hitherto, allude
more vividly to his hearer's present state than to his own past.
His own youth and suffering are gone. She in her "youth and
maidhood" (I. i. 173) found in this middle-aged man a pure,
perpetual youth—simplehearted, "unvarnished" (90), utterly
untainted by the "great world" (86) of Venice. In him she
found the antithesis of the "wealthy curled darlings" who
sought her hand (I. ii. 67 f.); a man not selfish, though self-
centered, naïvely, modestly proud of his career; devoid of
pity for himself but eliciting all of hers. And so she intensely
"suffered."

But the *inmost* quality of her love is still not clear to us,
much less to Othello; that is the point of the rest of his great
monologue (158-170). The new world he had opened to her
produced in her "a world of sighs":[31] solemnly she whispered
that his story was for her not only surpassingly "strange" but
wonderfully "pitiful." Pity, however, is one thing; sexual love
is another.[32] Her father "loved" Othello; she herself had conceived a far deeper affection for him, such love as would be
given him by a friend, sister, daughter, mother; all absent from
his "traveller's history," all present (as we may here divine and
later shall see fully) in her regard of him. But now she knows
that her love is more, very much more. And she knows that
her love for him is more than his for her. Certainly she sees
he loves her and wishes she could be his wife; moreover, she
sees that under the circumstances he as a gentleman must be
cautious and restrained in his advances. But also she knows
that his love, unlike hers, and unlike his devotion to his military life, is not a consuming passion defiant of all obstacles
and "disastrous chances" (134). And so she now makes a
crucial decision, long prepared but nonetheless momentous and
even desperate. Mastering her sighs she declares, simply and

[31] From Q1. F1 has "a world of kisses," which the audience would
enjoy, for the moment, but which does not fit the dramatic context.
[32] Hence the importance of the period after "pitiful" in F1.

strongly: "She wished she had not heard" the story of his life
—it means so violent (250) a change in her own—"yet she
wished / That Heaven had made her such another man . . . "
(163). She intensely desires him as her man, her husband, and
believes that "Heaven" so wills. In the strength of her love,
incidentally with that instinct of a true "lady" (115, 125) which
Othello perceives in her far more fully than he apprehends the
quality of her love, she puts away the ingrained shyness of her
"nature" (96) and offers, with indirect directness, to be his
wife if he will "woo her" (166).[33] Only upon this full, this
gently bold "hint" could Othello feel justified in speaking out.
He does not tell us what he "spake"; his failure to do so establishes our impression of the comparative mildness of his love.
Instead, he sums up simply:

> She loved me for the dangers I had passed,
> And I loved her, that she did pity them.
> This only is the witchcraft I have used.
> Here comes the lady. Let her witness it.

Those four lines, so conclusive for his own love story, are
very inconclusive for hers, as he is well aware. He is just as
relieved by her arrival as he was anxious beforehand to have
her come. She will not only "witness" to the truth of his
narrative, so far as it goes: she can throw light upon its crucial
enigma, the nature of her love for him. The first of those
four lines is strikingly anticlimactic. Certainly she loved him
for his "dangers" in the sense that these aroused her pity and
affection. But why her *passion* for him? Why was she so
desperately desirous of marrying him in spite of all the "dangers" to *her*? His desire for her was far from desperate: if
she had refused him he would have continued to be happy in
his other love, his military profession. He has displayed an
elaborate interest in his own life in contrast with his very meager interest in hers. He noted her "house affairs" (147) vaguely and passingly, as interfering with her attention to his de-
tailed accounts of the incidents of his own "unhoused free"

[33] Compare Juliet in *Romeo and Juliet* II. ii. 142 ff.

(I. ii. 26) career. He loves her because of her pity and affection for him. His love though genuine is self-centered and
romantic. Is her love, too, romantic, but much more so than
his because not self-centered and far more intense? In other
words is her love for him essentially the same as his for her?
That may be the case, so far as his story goes; but he, and we,
are aware that it does not go far enough. He has revealed
the inside of his own love—only the outside of hers. Nevertheless it is possible that her story, when she tells it, will be
the counterpart of his though much more romantic.

(e) *the very quality*   (I. iii. 171-301)

That is what the good duke anticipates when she enters.
He caps Othello's story with the sentimental exclamation, "I
think this tale would win my daughter too!" But would she
stay won? That is the pressing question. If her passion were
sheerly romantic it would soon begin to weaken. Othello,
while apparently certain that Desdemona will not weaken in
the severe trial just ahead of her, has been unable to state
any firm ground of his confidence. So far she has clung to
secrecy and retirement, above all avoiding her father. Can
she now face him in public without any wavering? The least
sign of it will assist his purpose of nullifying the still uncon-
summated marriage; he will exert all his influence to effect
a separation (I. ii. 11-17). Hence he interrupts the duke's
facile adjuration (172-175) with the loud, rising-tone demand,
"I pray you hear her speak?"[34] Will she confess, in public,
that she was "half the wooer" (176)? Above all will she
dare, in this "noble company" (179), to refuse *absolutely* the
filial "obedience" required of young ladies in good society,
never hitherto withheld by her, and now solicited crucially by
her father?

Our great suspense, prepared by Shakespeare in every pos-

---

[34] The interrogation point of F1 is thus important. But modern usage
would place a dash at the end of the preceding speech of the duke. If not
interrupted he would have proceeded to utter such trite consolation as he
gives below (199-209).

sible way, is accentuated now by the girl's bashful bearing. She
has entered the scene slowly, with downcast eyes, a slim figure
in white midst the glare of the torches, her gentle mien set off
by the bold, ironic face of her escort, Iago, close behind her.
She comes to the front timidly when summoned by her father;
at his command she lifts her head and surveys the assembly.
And his gently firm question, to which person present does
she "most . . . owe" obedience, is artfully and exactly designed
to induce her to falter; at the least, surely, she will evince some
slight perturbation. But no. Her reply is entirely void of
the distress shown by the Moor above (110-119); and void,
far more remarkably, of the romantic emotion of her love
confession reported by Othello (158-166). Her gaze, after
resting for a moment on the visage of the silent Moor, returns
to her father. And now she speaks, speaks with a firmness far
surpassing his, electrifying all the hearers. Repeating his words
"perceive" and "noble" (179) she shifts their implication from
conventional-social to plain, downright ethical:

> My noble father,   180
> I do perceive here a divided duty.
> To you I am bound for life, and education:
> My life and education both do learn me
> How to respect you. You are the lord of duty;
> I am hitherto your daughter. But here's my husband;   185
> And so much duty as my mother showed
> To you, preferring you before her father,
> So much I challenge that I may profess
> Due to the Moor my lord.

After a moment of dead silence her father exclaims huskily,
"God be with you:[35] I have done." But presently the bitter,
tyrannical temper which he has been restraining breaks out
again (191-198). He endeavors to divorce his daughter from
his heart in lieu of divorcing her from the Moor. His terribly
"bruised heart" (219) is his own fault, mainly, but far from
entirely; his incentive is rare and heavy. By contrast the duke's
rhymed sentences of moralizing condolence (199-209) are pain-

[35] A deliberate and solemn "Good-bye." Q1 has "God bu'y."

fully shallow; we sympathize keenly with the old man's acid rejection of them.[36] His loss of his daughter to the Moor is indeed comparable to Venice's possible loss of Cyprus to the Turk (210). In fact his biased view of the marriage is far less biased than the oily view of the politic duke, so very anxious to "proceed to the affairs of state" (220 ff.). For us, as for Brabantio, the effect of Desdemona's speech is to make her marriage appear more extraordinary than ever, though more real. It is not the speech of a secluded, dreaming girl whose romantic passion for a romantic foreigner made her an hour ago elope to him in a gondola (I. i. 126). It is the assured utterance of a mature married woman delivering an ultimatum not only to her father but to the whole society in which she has been bred— a firm, serene farewell to all her local "life and education" (182 f.). Love has matured her swiftly and, so to speak, against the grain; as her closing lines (186-189) make us feel acutely. For her "mother," whom she cites so boldly, did not, in defiance of "nature" (96 ff.) and "education," choose such a one as "the Moor" for her "lord." We understand fully why the Moor was exactly the person to arouse in Desdemona a romantic, passing infatuation. But far from fully do we yet see just why he, rather than some other and *less foreign* foreigner, should inspire in her a conjugal devotion so intense and sacrificial in contrast to his for her.

And now that contrast comes out vividly in the climactic episode. The suave duke prepares Othello for a great self-sacrifice (221-229). The Moor is the sole commander who can be relied on to save Cyprus from the Turk: "you must therefore be content to slubber the gloss of your new fortunes with this more stubborn and boisterous [rough] expedition"— a euphemistic way of saying that love-making must at once yield to making war. But Othello overrides the euphemism with an imagination kindled by his other love, the military life. In verse (230-235) whose gleaming hardness pinnacles the duke's smooth prose he devotes himself to "the flinty and steel couch of war" instead of the marriage bed; which, implied

---

[36] Compare Leonato in *Much Ado* V. i. 34-38.

in the duke's words, is now relegated into a cold distance by Othello's metaphor of the "thrice-driven bed of down," a phrase that might well have been uttered by a confirmed bachelor. Indeed, that "soft phrase of peace" intimates that the Moor, in his joy at resuming his "dearest action" after "some nine moons wasted" —his sole period of inaction since the age of "seven years" (82-85)—regards regular married life merely as one among all those unaccustomed comforts of civilization which "tyrant custom" (230) has rendered him entirely ready to eschew. That which confronts him now is not, in his view, a "stubborn and boisterous" duty supplanting the sweet "expedition" to a wife's embraces. He does "undertake / These present wars" with a "natural and prompt alacrity"—so "natural" as to make the marriage seem still less accordant with "nature" (96, 101).

And that impression is confirmed by the rest of his speech (236-240). The driving reality of his military diction is succeeded by a coolly conventional period requesting of the duke "fit disposition for my wife . . . . " The tone and language are those of a high Venetian dignitary for whom all domestic emotion is totally eclipsed by the call to great public service abroad, and who with stately propriety requires for his lady "such accommodation and besort / as levels with her breeding." Accordingly the conventional duke rejoins at once, "Why [i.e. obviously] at her father's?"[37]   This plan is rejected violently by Brabantio, equably by Othello. Then Desdemona says with mournful considerateness,

> Nor would I there reside,
> To put my father in impatient thoughts
> By being in his eye. . . .

Those words win the sympathy of the senate and draw all eyes again to her, above all the duke's. And now her tone changes. She has listened with deep concern to Othello's speech. And so with clasped hands and flushed face she utters her extraor-

[37] The effect is ruined by Q1's substitution, "If you please, be't at her father's."

dinary petition; speaking at first with shy confusion, then with
clarity and growing power; unveiling, publicly and perforce,
that which we have been waiting for all along, the very heart
of her love:

> . . . . Most gracious duke,
> To my unfolding lend a gracious ear,[38]   245
> And let me find a charter in your voice,
> And if my simpleness—
> DUKE   What would you?—Speak.
> DESDEMONA That I love the Moor to live with him,
> My downright violence and storm of fortunes   250
> May trumpet to the world. My heart's subdued
> Even to the very quality of my lord:
> I saw Othello's visage in his mind,
> And to his honours and his valiant parts
> Did I my soul and fortunes consecrate.   255
> So that, dear lords, if I be left behind,
> A moth of peace, and he go to the war,
> The rites for which I love him are bereft me;
> And I a heavy interim shall support
> By his dear absence. Let me go with him.   260

One fact, however, she cannot put into words. She could
not tell it to Othello when alone with him; doubtless she could
not express it clearly to herself. But it is implied in her
speech as a whole, and all of Othello's utterances have prepared
us to perceive it. She intensely desires to "go with him," to
share his "flinty and steel couch,"[39] *because she hopes thus to
win his full love.*

So far his affection for her, though fixed and true, is comparatively superficial. The dozen lines in which she has now
fully uttered her passion for him stand out in smiting contrast

[38] Lines 245-248, including the two dashes, are from Q1. The folio
version, generally preferred by editors, is smoother but less true to Desdemona's
present state of mind.

[39] The reader must banish from his mind the peace that ensues in Act II.
In Act I all the indications are that the Moor's wife, if she goes with him,
will be subject to "disastrous chances" and "moving accidents by flood and
field" (134 f.). Thus the strength of her determination is thrown into high
relief.

to the forty lines, above, in which he told of his love for her. To be sure the two speeches are differently occasioned. But under any circumstances we cannot imagine *her* declaring with finality that she loved him for the dangers he had passed (167); nor *him* declaring that his "heart's subdued" to her "very quality," her inmost nature and character.[40] He loves her "visage," her mien: her beautiful gentility (I. ii. 25), her pity for him, and her "simpleness" (247) so correspondent to his own. Above all he loves her love for him, in its romantic aspect, akin to the strange adventurousness of his own life, yet so utterly and charmingly different—*and to be kept just that*. His career is one thing; his married life another, and at present irrelevant. She realizes with a deep pang that he envisages her as "a moth of peace" (257), a rare and lovely one, to be admired and enjoyed in the intervals of his warfare; and that he is now so obsessed by his other love that he has determined without a pang to postpone, perhaps for very long, the bodily "rites" (258) of their union; in other words, to leave their sacrament of marriage indefinitely uncompleted.[41] Each of the two has a passionate devotion: he, for the martial life, all of it; she, for all that she knows of him. And therefore her devotion, like his, is not just a present feeling but a large growth from the past. At the first she began to see "Othello's visage in his mind"; and more and more perceiving his noble "parts" (254), his virtues and capacities, "did . . . consecrate" (contrast his expression "did pity," above) all her life and being to all of his, particularly to his military career; that is intimated by her military images, "downright violence and storm . . . trumpet . . . subdued." She implies that her extraordinary and very questionable marriage is as militant, in its way, as his adventures in the "imminent deadly breach" (136). Her

---

[40] A secondary meaning of "quality" was professional occupation. Doubtless Shakespeare had that also in mind though very subordinately; he loves to work a word to its utmost in crucial passages.

[41] Consider the terms "rite," "holy," and "rites" in *Romeo and Juliet* II. ii. 146; II. iii. 52, 61; II. vi. 1, 37; III. ii. 8. In *Much Ado* the words "married" and "church" lead up to the phrase "all his [i.e., love's] rites" (II. i. 369-373).

courage corresponds to his, and aligns itself with his, in the spirit and rhythmic march of her verses (249-255).

Courage and duty are basal in her love. Her sense of "duty . . . . to the Moor my lord," expressed so strongly in her opening speech (185-189) and subsumed in the present passage, is the moral principle, so to speak, of her conduct throughout the whole drama. For her, however, it is nothing apart from her love. She stressed it in her first public utterance because it was the thing that could most clearly and easily be made public. But it is just a part, though fundamental, of her *religion of love*. In her solitude she came to the belief that "Heaven had made" this "man" for "her" (163). And now a crisis has forced her to disclose in public her faith that she was made for him: she implies it in declaring religiously that she did "consecrate" her "soul and fortunes," all her inner and outer being, to him. She, unlike him, has now no vocation, no real life, apart from her mate. Her first and last lines give the essence of her love: "I love[42] the Moor to live with him . . . go with him." Her tacit, deep yearning is that he will learn to love her with the same fulness, loving to "live" and "go" with her, every way and all the way.

In the event, he does not learn to love her thus until her way on earth is ended; that is the blackness of the tragedy. Its sublimity is that he does so learn, inspired by her spirit, at "journey's end" (V. ii. 267).

His present speech (261-275) in response to hers is ominously anticlimactic; all the more so because its mood is perfectly sincere. Her speech, so frankly though subordinately sexual, was entirely pure. His speech, disavowing sexual "appetite" (263), is entirely coarse, despite his own innate refinement; for here he is misled, as he will be far more dreadfully later on, by his pride. Here he speaks indeed "as loving his own pride and purposes" and "with a bombast circumstance" (I. i. 12 f.). Of course he wishes to dispel any possible notion

---

[42] The "I did love" of Q1 ruins the emotion in order to fill out the meter of pentameter verse. Desdemona is speaking, urgently, in the present tense, here. Only at "I saw" (253) does she cast back for a moment into the past.

that lust on his part was a motive of his hasty marriage; but
that purpose was sufficiently accomplished by his steel-like
previous speech (230-239). And a sense that his present dis-
claimer is somewhat supererogatory leads him into jocose "bombast" concerning the "light-winged toys / Of feathered Cupid"
etc. But this jocosity, so entirely out of character (he never
shows it elsewhere), is brutally though unwittingly at variance
with the spirit of *her* lovely speech. His phrase "my disports"
(272) is a painful contrast to her "rites for which I love him."
And his affectionate, kindly, patronizing desire "to be free and
bounteous to her mind" (266) indicates pointedly that he does
not know her "mind" as she knows his (253): he misses the
very spirit of her speech, and of her. He is too elaborately
anxious—later he will be tragically anxious—to let nothing,
as his final and summary verse puts it, "make head against my
estimation" (reputation).

That extraordinary speech affects his hearers variously.
Murmurs, noddings, headshakings ripple through the senate.
The faces of the silent Brabantio and Iago, especially the latter,
are darkly cynical. The kindly duke is embarrassed and, now
at long last, impatient. The realistic First Senator is grave
and somewhat grim: he commiserates the Moor's young wife
but is resolved that Venice shall take full advantage of the
Moor's attitude. Desdemona is, more than ever, deeply concerned.

DUKE (*hastily*) Be it as you shall privately determine,   276
　　　　Either for her stay or going: the affair cries haste,
　　　　And speed must answer it.
FIRST SENATOR (*deliberately*) You must away tonight.
DESDEMONA (*to the duke, imploringly*) Tonight, my lord?[43] 280
DUKE (*conclusively, swayed by the First Senator*) This night.
OTHELLO (*simply, proudly*) With all my heart.

The profound irony of the Moor's four words is felt by the
First Senator as his next speech will show. But meanwhile the
irony is sharpened. Othello, replying to the duke's command to

[43] This and the next line are from Q1.

"leave some officer behind" to "bring our commission . . .
With such things else of quality and respect / As doth import
you," designates Iago and adds:

> To his conveyance I assign my wife,
> With what else needful your good Grace shall think
> To be sent after me.

Thus with proud nonchalance Othello waives the possibility
that his wife would "privately determine" (276)—as she un-
doubtedly would—to embark with him.   Publicly and irre-
vocably he determines that she shall come later, "with such
things else . . . " (238), "with what else needful . . . " (287),
his "with" paralleling the duke's significantly.[44]   Desdemona
silently submits with downcast looks: further, and fruitless, ob-
jection from her would wound his pride and signalize the gap·
between them.   But now the First Senator says penetratingly:
"Adieu, brave Moor, use Desdemona well."

His bravery is indeed outstanding; so is his liability in a
crisis to "use" his wife *not* "well."   And here Brabantio, stung
beyond endurance by further words of fatuous comfort from
the duke (290 f.; cf. 199-220), caps the First Senator's line
with a revengeful, deadly couplet:

> Look to her, Moor, if thou hast eyes to see:
> She has deceived her father, and may thee.

Othello, pierced to the quick, but too proud and self-controlled
to display his wound, stands rigid for a moment, while the
senators, rising, begin to move away; his dark face is grim in
the stirring torchlight.   For us, too, her complete deception of
her father (I. ii. 166 ff.) becomes ominous here but mainly
because of the fateful parallel[45] between her husband and her
father in the shallowness of their insight into her.   Brabantio
was easily deceived by her because of the proud self-centeredness

[44] Hence F1's reading of "and" for the first "with" is inferior. These
two initial "with's" echo ironically the initial one of Othello's line above,
"With all my heart."
[45] This is aided by the couplet's caesura coming, first, after "Moor" and
then after "father."

of his love: he had not "eyes to see." For the same reason
Othello might be deceived by someone who could cleverly
enough asperse her: he has keen "eyes to see" the "very quality" of war—not of her. Indeed he is beguiled at this very
instant by Brabantio.[46] For the obvious answer to the old man's
thrust is that his daughter's entire deception of him, whether
right or wrong, was inspired by the entirety of her love of
Othello. But (as appears fully in Act III) Othello does not
consider that fact: he is preoccupied with his own honor. In
a moment he proudly repudiates, *without inwardly confuting*,
Brabantio's poisoned words; which therefore lodge deeply in
his subconscious mind. "My life upon her faith!" he declares
with an *air* of militant nonchalance belied by the extreme gravity of the *substance* of those words. His visage clears completely
as he turns and takes the outstretched hand of her whom here
for the first time he calls *"my* Desdemona," looking into her
clear eyes. The rest of his speech (295-301) tells us that he
will, proudly and fondly, and very fatefully, refrain from any
reference, even when alone with her, to her father's vicious al-
legation.[47]

Portentous also is the fact that Othello's crucial failure to
be *inwardly* assured of his wife's absolute "honesty"[48] is preceded
and followed by asseverations of his entire faith in the "honesty
and trust" (285) of "honest Iago" (295). Here too he is
blinded by his pride and also by his preoccupation with his
"own" very high professional "purposes." A general less noble
and brainy but more humble would certainly have some slight
inkling, at the least, that he had fatefully offended his very
capable "ancient" (I. i. 8-33); but Othello has none. He is
always courteous to and appreciative of Iago but at the same

[46] Surely Shakespeare has made clear that Brabantio has sufficient understanding of his daughter's nature, particularly her purity, to be sure that she
would *not* be unfaithful to her husband. Therefore his present thrust is
sheerly revengeful, an immediate prelude to Iago's revengeful design in the
next episode. Probably Desdemona makes some silent gesture of appeal and
farewell to her father, and is harshly repulsed by him.

[47] In this speech the initial "my" of the first two lines and the three subsequent "I's" indicate the speaker's self-centeredness.

[48] In Shakespeare's time chastity was one of the meanings of "honesty."

time, thoroughly patronizing. That, though on a much higher
level, is precisely his attitude to his wife. And she, a gentlewoman, in love with him and with his essential nobility, en-
dures that attitude with humble patience. But it maddens the
proud boor Iago, as we shall see conclusively in the ensuing
episode. Meanwhile as Othello moves off, hand in hand with
his wife, he leaves with us the impression that he knows her
"very quality" no more than he knows Iago's. It is with gently
patronizing though very real tenderness, and with profound
tragic irony, that he says to her: "I have but an hour / Of love
. . . to spend with thee . . . . "

(f) *this that you call love*   I. iii. 302-410

"Of love . . . . " Iago grimaces. He watches the retiring
lovers with a brooding, baffled fascination till roused by the
sound of his own name uttered with tearful entreaty[49] by the
frustrate lover, Roderigo. Iago responds with a leer: "What
sayst thou, noble heart?" That title for the "silly gentleman"
(308) gives us a relieving laugh. At the same time we see that
Iago is relieving his own hurt pride. Patronized by that "noble
heart," that lofty gentleman, Othello, he patronizes with a
vengeance the flimsy gentleman Roderigo. Vexed by his failure to impair Othello's joy and chagrined by his incapacity to
understand the love he has just witnessed Iago sets himself by
way of self-amends to destroy whatever validity there is, or
seems to be, in Roderigo's affection for Desdemona. He will
turn this love into lust; or rather he will demonstrate, to his
own satisfaction, that such is what it essentially is.

"Oh villainous!" he exclaims of his friend's romantic inclination to die for love. There is real wrath in this speech
(312-318), out of keeping with the attitude of a sheer materialist, as in his hot condemnation of dutiful servants at the first
(I. i. 44-49). He declares now, in serious parody of righteous
indignation, "I never found a man that knew how to love him-

---

[49] Instead of the suspicious petulance with which the name "Iago" was
initially uttered (I. i. 2). Watch the shift and play of tone upon that very
vocalic name in the course of the drama.

self." That is Shakespeare's testimony to the human average: normally our selfishness is never perfect. But Iago, a satanic idealist, proceeds to explain how it can become perfect—indeed how it continually tries to become so—namely *by the use of morality in the service of self-love* (322-337).

This prose passage is dreadfully excellent. The diction, rhythm, and structure are superb; the image of the human will as a gardener is exact and captivating; the healthy will's dependence on reason and temperance is ancient and approved doctrine. Thus indeed it is that real "humanity" rises above the "baboon" (318), that each one of us can learn to "be a man" (340). The ethic of the passage is true and complete if we accept the hypothesis, so alluring to civilized man, that our destiny lies entirely "in ourselves" (322), "in our wills" (330). But that ideal, as Iago (like Shakespeare) sees very clearly, demands that the vast and variable power called "love" shall be regarded, whenever it is anything other than *self*-love, as something far below the level of valid will and reason: "we have reason to cool our raging motions, our carnal stings, our unbitted lusts; whereof I take this that you call love to be a sect or scion."

"It cannot be." These words well up suddenly in Roderigo from the depths of human nature. But his protest, simple and profound in meaning, is utterly weak in will. For previously (316-321) when assailed by Iago's pungent ridicule he had confessed "shame to be so fond" in his love for Desdemona, and he delivered himself into the villain's hands by asking "What should I do?" Weakly good, he admires Iago's evil strength; secretly he yearns to share it. He is no more convinced by the other's reasoned degradation of love than he was by his reasoned idealization of hate in the opening scene. But he does not see the contradiction between Iago's advocacy of sheer self-love and his avowal of "love" (307) and esteem for his "friend" (342) Roderigo. He is blinded by the flattering insinuation that he too can be a strong one. Therefore he does not repeat his protest when Iago asseverates that love "is merely a lust of the blood and a permission of the will" (339 f.). Roderigo knows this is not true; but his vanity conceives that he can become a real "man" (340) by using his "will" to substitute for hopeless love a flourishing "lust of the blood."

And surely it is bound to flourish: Iago demonstrates that. Vividly he represents the love of the Moor and Desdemona as merely a romantic lust which is certain to subside—especially on her part: "She must change for youth."[50] Here Roderigo is visibly shocked; and the cunning Iago at once alters his tactics (360 ff.). Entering into his companion's ineradicable feeling that lust is a sin, while at the same time appealing to his longing for strength, he cries with robust jocosity, "If thou wilt needs damn thyself, do it a more delicate way than drowning." Certainly lust is more "delicate" (delightful) than suicide, and also more manly, if the seduction of Desdemona may be so regarded. Iago submerges that consideration by hastily assuming, in vague but confident terms, all the responsibility of scheming against the "sanctimony" (sanctity) of marriage while promising Roderigo all the "joy."

Incidentally Iago appeals throughout to his dupe's single powerful "virtue," his wealth. The incessant iteration of "Put money in thy purse," so amusing to the audience, is enheartening to Roderigo. His "purse," flaunted *by* him to Iago in the opening of this act (I. i. 2), is flaunted *for* him by Iago in the close. Thus the villain gilds his subjugation of the gull. Roderigo's conceit is soothed by the constant reminder of his one superiority to his strong friend and by the romantic prospect, so beautifully vague, of "many events" that his "money" will do much to bring about (377-380). Of course the money must be ready money. Continually suggesting that fact Iago leaves to Roderigo the important decision to sell all his land. With all his wealth about him, yet masquerading in "usurped beard" as a common soldier (345-347), he will be a new, strong

---

[50] Instead of this sentence Q1 has: "She must have change, she must." Perhaps the right reading, effectively transitional and climactic, is: "She must have change, she must—she must change for youth."

person, entirely a "man" instead of a "silly gentleman." At the first he was ready to drown his foolish self for pure, weak love. In the end, through Iago's wonderful art, he is led to inflate that same self with cash and lustful "hopes" (369): he puts it all in a pregnant word when he declares enthusiastically, in the final dialogue, quoted below, that he is "changed."

RODERIGO	Where shall we meet in the morning?
IAGO	At my lodging.
RODERIGO	I'll be with thee betimes.
IAGO	Go to, farewell—Do you hear, Roderigo?[51]
RODERIGO	What say you?
IAGO	No more of drowning, do you hear?
RODERIGO	I am changed.
IAGO	Go to, farewell, put money enough in your purse.
RODERIGO	I'll sell all my land. *Exit*
IAGO	Thus do I ever make my fool my purse. . . .

Iago's soliloquy, closing the act, demonstrates conclusively what the dramatist has been suggesting from the first. Roderigo is a rich fool: Iago is far richer in folly. Patently Roderigo is, as the villain says above, "my fool"; but really Iago's chief fool is his own self. The more smartly he beguiles Roderigo the more subtly, we are intended to see, he deludes himself. At the root of the matter is his egregious belief in the infallibility of his own insight.

His firmest ground is his experience and ability, recognized by all, in the field of practical "soldiership" (I. i. 27). But that very field affords the most striking instances of the realness of human loyalty and duty; as everyone knows, except Iago. He has learned to imitate those two virtues perfectly while inwardly disdaining them. But thus he has put himself in the grip of a painful paradox. In his creed reality is practicality; but his

---

[51] The dash in this line is from Q1; so are the ensuing four lines. The customary arrangement of this dialogue, from the present line to the end, does violence to the two original texts and to the dramatic evolution. Iago's significant "enough" (from Q1) instigates Roderigo's final line (from F1), which caps the climax of his preceding speech. His decision, after a moment of hesitation, to sell "all" his land assures himself, even more than Iago, that he is completely "changed." His soul and the land, so closely related to each other, shall both have been *converted*.

military vocation has forced him to recognize the great practical necessity of virtues which he deems unreal.[52] Accordingly
he is in constant danger, though his pride will not confess it,
of finding in those virtues some touch, however slight, of reality. Hence his incessant, elaborate efforts to discredit every
evidence of altruism, in favor of his claim that self-love alone
is real. His philosophy of egoism is more unrealistic than the
"bookish" theories of warfare which he despises (I. i. 24).
Centrally, Iago is unpractical.

The normal practical man has a natural pride in his own
knowledge and ability together with a prudent sense, sometimes
large, sometimes small, of their limitations. Such plain prudence is essential to real practicality. But Iago has not a jot
of it. He has indeed the prudence to conceal from others his
abnormal self-conceit; but only to indulge it, fully and imprudently, in solitude and in machination—to his own eventual
ruin; which even Roderigo will help to bring about. Iago
believes he can fathom all human beings; but the event shows
that he fathoms no one in the play, not even "such a snipe"
(391) as Roderigo. The first act shows how far Iago is from
fathoming himself.

In his closing soliloquy he lays bare his preposterous idealization, even worship—the verb "profane" (390), antonymous
to worship, is masterly on Shakespeare's part— of "mine own
gained knowledge," of his own brainy and shrewd but extremely limited insight. In the very same sentence he fools himself
by asserting that his large occupation with Roderigo is merely
for "sport and profit." In reality, as stated above, he uses the
fellow as a very important means of bolstering his own pride,

[52] Iago, unlike Othello, has not been a soldier from childhood, and never
from conviction. Note the antiphonic contrast between his and his commander's use of the words "world" and "seven" (83-86, 312-316). Othello,
devoted to soldiership from the age of "seven years," admits he knows little
of the "world" in general. Iago has "looked upon the world for four times
seven years" and believes, arrogantly and foolishly, that he knows it through
and through. In his childhood, probably spent in cities, he learned to "dis-
tinguish between a benefit and an injury." Later he entered the military
service of Venice and Othello (I. i. 28-30), hoping for more "benefit" than
he had so far found, and discovering that self-love must be concealed in the
army.

so heavily injured by "the Moor" (392),[53] of whom Iago now remarks, suddenly and absurdly:

> And it is thought abroad that 'twixt my sheets
> He has done my office. I know not if't be true,
> Yet I, for mere suspicion in that kind,
> Will do as if for surety.

The audience laughs and, at the same time, discounts the villain's sense of humor along with his "own gained knowledge" of which he has just bragged. "I know not," says Iago with prodigious seriousness. Thus the dramatist gives his audience a definitive and pleasing sense of superiority to the clever villain; for even the dullest spectator knows enough of Othello by now to sense the ridiculousness of that cheap camp rumor.[54] Iago snatches at the rumor, in sequel to his pronouncement above upon "these Moors" (353 ff.), in order to depreciate the quality of Othello's love for Desdemona, thereby reassuring himself of the soundness of his theory that all sexual love is reducible to lust and selfishness.

His assurance on that point has been far more heavily shaken by Desdemona than by Othello; though it has been shaken by both; and even, in some degree, by Roderigo. At the first Iago claimed that he himself was merely "one" of a number of persons animated by self-love (I. i. 49-55). But after watching and hating the unfolding of the story of Desdemona and her two lovers he proclaims himself, in hot self-justification, the one and only real self-lover—and her, a "guinea-hen" (312-317). This term, used of old for a strumpet, connotes folly. She must be at the least a fool, like the "duteous knave" of I. i. 44-49, because of her self-sacrificing love; but Iago hopes against hope that she may become an adultress also: "It cannot be that Desdemona should long continue her love to the Moor"

---

[53] The colon after "profit" in the original texts indicates that the following statement, "I hate the Moor," is causally related to Iago's treatment of Roderigo.

[54] The rumor is of course just the kind that would flourish among crude, jocular soldiers in the field: it would humanize for them their beloved but lofty and rather austere commander.

(348). His profoundest hatred, as will fully appear later, is for her "goodness" (II. iii. 367).

To that goodness he now gives unwilling testimony by tacitly admitting he has no real belief that Roderigo can seduce her (389 ff.) and only the very faintest hope that Cassio either can or will (398 ff.):

> Cassio's a proper man: let me see now,
> To get his place, and to plume up my will
> In double knavery. How? How? Let's see.
> After some time, to abuse Othello's ears
> That he is too familiar with his wife:
> He hath a person and a smooth dispose
> To be suspected: framed to make women false.[55]

The last five words, especially the plural "women," give Iago away. Cassio is so attractively "framed" by nature that the other sex, generally regarded, is likely to yield to him. But whether he wishes to seduce any woman in particular, notably his commander's wife, is very doubtful. And that the particular woman Desdemona would be "false" to her husband is unbelievable from a coolly rational standpoint. And so Iago, the would-be rationalist, cloaks the whole matter in the vague generality of those five final words. He tries to fool himself, regarding the seducibleness of Desdemona, with hopes as vague and unfounded as those with which he fooled Roderigo.

Probing for evil in those persons and unable to find any "surety" (396) of it, Iago is driven to face, with deepest reluctance, the goodness of Othello and to found his plot on that. He vows with utmost bitterness:

> The Moor is of a free and open nature   405
> That thinks men honest that but seem to be so,
> And will as tenderly be led by the nose
> As asses are.

[55] The last two lines enlarge upon and clarify the point of the cryptic verse, "A fellow almost damned in a fair wife" (I. i. 21). In relation to any attractive woman, to the fair sex in general, Cassio's mien, merely, is "almost" enough to damn him in the eyes of others. This is demonstrated in the next scene, so Iago will claim.

The first line shows Iago hating and scorning the "very quality" (252) of Othello admired and loved by others, above all by his wife. Thus the heroine and the villain of the play agree, from opposite viewpoints, in their reading of the hero's "visage." And the clarification in the Senate scene of the mystery of Desdemona's love is followed now by the clarification of the mystery of Iago's hate. He does not dislike Othello *primarily* as an individual but as a type.[56] He hates the magnanimous, the large, virtuous, candid, loyal "nature" (405) which is the direct contrary of his own. "Instinctively" (155)—his instinct being the horrid counterpart of Desdemona's—he hates Othello as a great embodiment of that type; loathes him as his commander in their chosen profession; hates and loathes him as a successful and happy lover. The last motive has now become supreme. The affair of the lieutenancy, so prominent in Iago's thoughts at the beginning (I. i. 8 ff.), is barely mentioned by him here (399). He devotes himself to the ruining of Othello's marriage, rightly perceiving it to be a singular demonstration of "this that you call love"—a significant fruit and validation of the "nature" which Iago hates.

His bitter scorn of that "nature" culminates here. The words "honest" and "asses" in the lines quoted above echo his use of the same words in his initial attack upon simple, devoted persons (I. i. 47, 49). But here he condenses all his venom into the image of Othello, with "ears" (401) full of Iago's lies, being led along with ease by his asininely soft "nose" (407). Again the audience laughs; and, more than before, the laugh is against the villain, who has signally failed in Act I to influence his commander. Soon he will indeed succeed in deceiving Othello's ears and eyes. But in the upshot, as will be shown below, it is Iago himself who will be led by the nose.

Here his sanguine fancy is relegating Othello, ridiculously, into the same class with the ass Roderigo. Iago is trying to assure himself that his future career will continue the easy and

[56] The antecedent of the initial "That" (406) is of course "nature," not "Moor"; though these two nouns may be taken as the compound subject of the verb "will"—so artful are Iago's (and Shakespeare's) grammar and syntax here.

full success he has had with that fellow, his sole success so far. Thus his elaborate beguiling of his dupe has been, and will in the ensuing acts continue to be, his main practical means of duping himself. In the beginning of his present soliloquy he depreciates his victory over Roderigo; his acute intelligence forced him to do so. But at the same time we divined, and now we see fully, that he unconsciously and inordinately plumes himself upon that feat, trying to make himself believe that not only Roderigo but all simplehearted persons, notably Othello, are "asses." Iago must continually bolster his own egoism. The underlying, chief aim of his life, and of his present speech as he informs us at the center of it, with great suggestiveness, is "to plume up my will" (399). The feathers of his will to believe in selfishness have been continually ruffled in the past (312 ff.) and, during the present act, heavily depressed by all the love and loyalty, particularly Desdemona's, he has had to witness. So now he must make a unique effort to refurbish those feathers. That is really the main purpose of his new and, in his own regard, very great and wonderful plot. And that is why this plot, as it develops in the following acts, will turn out to have a number of ruinously weak spots. The evil success he aims at is far more spiritual than material; therefore he is heedless of certain material factors. *He wills to hate love and to love hate,* an ideal at once dreadful, ridiculous, and difficult. It entails a solitary, arduous flight in the void: certainly he has need to "plume up" the pen feathers of his "will."

In particular Iago has two hard tasks: to suppress his conscience entirely, and to conceal from himself entirely his envy of the beauty of goodness. His second task is accentuated by the very nature of his plot regarding Cassio. This requires him to recognize and keep constantly in mind the lieutenant's charm and to perceive, increasingly, that this charm is not what he at first considered it, merely a thing of the senses. Despite every temptation to the contrary and his own signal weaknesses Cassio's affection for Othello and his purity in re-

gard to Desdemona remain firm. So that Iago is finally compelled to admit (V. i. 19):

> He hath a daily beauty in his life
> That makes me ugly. . . .

The sudden, simple intensity of those words shows that they
have forced their way up from the depths. Obviously that
dictum applies far more to Othello, before his fall, than to
Cassio; and it is true uniquely of Desdemona. But to confront
so plainly his jealousy of those two great persons would be
ruinous for the villain's self-esteem. The case of Cassio, and
this alone, is such as to cause a momentary plain eruption of
that hidden bitter envy of the "beauty" of goodness which is
the "daily" and "ugly" motive of Iago's "life" and being.[57]

As to his conscience, Iago's most obvious way of smothering it is to play the villain,[58] very histrionically, in glaring contradiction of his reasoned rejection of the difference between
right and wrong. In his theory nothing is really "villainous"
except failing to love oneself; "virtue" so called is "a fig"
(312, 322). Nothing overtly out of keeping with that view
escapes his lips before the final fifty lines of Act I. Here, however, as his evil schemes develop, he feels the need of submerg-
ing his sense of guilt by a jocular assumption of wickedness.
Mostly for Roderigo's sake, as stated above, he employs the
conventional phrase "damn thyself" (360); but also for his
own sake he proceeds at once to laud the powers of "my wits
and all the tribe of hell" (364 f.). When alone he confesses
leeringly to himself, and us, that he is guilty of "knavery"
(400)—unlike the "honest knaves" (i.e. servants) at whom he

---

[57] The three "y's" and three "l's" in the four quoted words serve, along
with the whole movement of the passage, to weave those words into a suggestive pattern.

[58] So do many other evil persons in Elizabethan drama, one of the most
remarkable cases being that of Macbeth in II. i. 49-60. Iago and Richard III
stand out among Shakespeare's villains in their accomplished art of downing
their consciences with rich and often blasphemous jocularity. But Iago's case
is of course far more subtle than the other. Richard's conscience, entirely
quelled from the start, apparently, breaks out in the dreams and ghosts of
the last act. But Iago's at the last is remarkably quiescent just because he
has so carefully and subtly submerged it throughout the play.

loves to rail (I. i. 49). And when he has conceived his devilish
plot against Othello he stifles his conscience, first by classing
the Moor with "asses"—sequel of the "guinea-hen," "baboon,"
"cats and blind puppies" above (317 f., 341)—then by exclaiming with facetious melodramatic zest:

> I have't; it is engender'd: Hell, and Night,
> Must bright this monstrous birth to the world's light.

"I have't" is shrill staccato accompanied by an upthrust finger,
with which he taps his forehead while he speaks the ensuing
three words. Then, slowing and deepening his tone,[59] he peers
down to "Hell," up and around into "Night," the black night
of Act I, to which he lifts his open hands. His hellish pride
craves all the credit, while his tacit conscience waives the full
responsibility, for the "monstrous" thing he has conceived.
Hence the initial "I" is not iterated in those two final verses
as it was in the first half of the soliloquy and in many preceding speeches of his. The strident possessiveness of the opening
clause, "I have't," is softened by the passive mood of the next
clause, and submerged in the long last sentence. From the
standpoint of the cool, amoral rationalism that Iago professes,
there is nothing "monstrous" in his clever plot, and he himself
is the only begetter of it and its future accoucheur. But his
outraged conscience makes a climactic hidden protest. And
he pacifies it by making himself feel that "Hell" and "Night"
have taken part in the engendering, indeed are the real parents,
of the design that he cannot help regarding in his heart of
hearts as an immoral monster—just as the fool Roderigo could
not help regarding lust as something different from love (338).

Certainly the powers of hell and night, in a sense far greater
than Iago could or would understand, are the producers of his
plot. That is why the mood of the audience subsides quickly
from the laughter roused by the word "asses" into a sort of
simmering, amused, confused horror at the end. For us this
villain is a dual person. In himself he is a small, smart, bi-
zarre fellow. But now we realize that after twenty-eight years

[59] Hence the commas in F1 after "Hell" and "Night."

(313) of petty but assiduous selfishness and hypocrisy he is ripe for enormous evil. At the first we saw him futilely hating Othello "as I do hell-pains" (I. i. 155). Now he has come to hate, worse than hell-pains, and efficiently, the mysterious power that has brought about Othello's strange marriage: love, with all its beauty, at once "daily" and heavenly. "Heaven is my judge" (I. i. 59), the villain exclaimed at the outset with profound dramatic irony. And now he appeals to the "Hell" which, along with "Heaven," he thinks he does not believe in. But the normal audience does; and it perceives that this small man has gradually slidden, in the end plunged suddenly, into the service of the big powers of hell. So he and his plot are, precisely, "monstrous," at once absurd and horrible. To love hate and hate love is both hellish and foolish. Hell has given little Iago the role of a big villain but cannot make him a *heavy* villain; for heaven, working through his conscience, has turned him into an extraordinary buffoon.

Patience . . . Grim as Hell

(a) *unknown fate*   II. i. 1—214

T HE storm that muttered while Iago was
ending his soliloquy (on the stage of Shakespeare's imagination)
bursts out now in sudden, full fury, responding demoniacally
to the villain's last two lines. His phrase "this monstrous
birth" applies also to this very "monstrous" (13) tempest. The
"Hell and Night" invoked by him are displaying their powers
here in the realm of nature. The "world's light" (I. iii. 410),
which is presently to be affronted by Iago's dark deviltry, is
now entirely dimmed "at sea." "Nothing at all" can be
discerned there by an onlooker standing on "the cape" (1 f.)
and peering out; as we, from the vantage ground of the first
act, are peering now into "unknown fate" (195). The "flood"
is "high wrought," worked up against "heaven" (2 f.), by
some mysterious force, unnamed in the opening lines of this
scene. Naturally that force is the "wind" but it is a wild,
demonic "blast" (5 f.). On the land, where it is opposed by
the works of man, it "hath spoke aloud," screaming among
and shaking the very "battlements" (6) despite their mighty
stones and "mortise" (9). If it has "ruffianed so" (7) at sea
making "mountains melt" on ships, no mere "ribs of oak,"
shaped and joined by human hands, could hold together, seemingly. We are made to feel that Othello, though he is not at
first mentioned, is in great danger on his sea voyage—and his
life voyage.

And now, standing in imagination "upon the foaming
shore" (11),[1] we view those mountainous waves close up:

[1] The "banning shore" of Q1 may have been Shakespeare's first choice: the

> The chidden[2] billow seems to pelt the clouds,
> The wind-shaked surge, with high and monstrous mane,
> Seems to cast water on the burning Bear,
> And quench the guards of th'ever-fixed Pole:
> I never did like molestation view
> On the enchafed flood.

That passage is at once powerful, particularly in its great second verse, and grotesque; like Iago's soliloquy above; like the "monstrous" spirit, horrific, absurd even while potently evil, which he has come to embody, and which now seems to be riding the storm. This storm's air of naughty buffoonery prepares for the large exhibition of the same that Iago will presently give (101 ff.) in the presence of Desdemona—she untouched and pure above it, like the "ever-fixed" North Star.[3]   In the close of the quoted passage that star burns quietly, among the celestial bodies guarding it, far from the tempest. The triple occurrence of the word "seems" (understood before "quench") is significant.   The pelting "billow" underneath the low-flying clouds is infinitely beneath the heavens. Its "molestation" of the stars, as the exaggerated images and heaping movement of the lines suggest, is merely a melodramatic and fantastical seeming.

Here then is a compressed, intense preview of the "high wrought flood" (2) of evil that will rise in the ensuing acts, and of its final outcome.   It will be "pernicious" (V. ii. 155, 317); but it will not "quench" (15, V. ii. 8), except seemingly and transiently, the light of celestial love.

---

shore like the "battlements," above, and unlike the ships, can withstand the storm, "banning" the evil spirit of it.   But of course that spirit is not really banned: it will step ashore presently in the person of Iago. And the word "foaming," like "ruffianed," above, is expressive of that spirit.   Perhaps reminiscent of this line is Browning's "foam white as the bitten lip of hate" (*Paracelsus* V. 659).

[2] This word, unlike the conventional "chiding" of Q1, carries on the implication that the sea is here provoked and driven—in the last line,"enchafed"—by supernatural evil power.

[3] See the second quatrain of Shakespeare's Sonnet 116.   In his time the "fixed" stars were still generally believed to be immutable; hence they were extremely vivid symbols of all that is eternal.

Auspicious is "a noble ship of Venice"[4] that now glides into the harbor, a symbol of civility over against the background of the "desperate tempest" and the "grievous wrack and sufferance" of the fleet of the hostile barbarous Turks (17-25). But human civility, lovely when safe and fortunate, is a frail thing, always in danger from the dark powers. So is Cassio. On landing, we are told by Montano, he speaks of "comfort" but "looks sadly, / And prays the Moor be safe; for they were parted / With foul and violent tempest." Montano adds, "Pray heavens he be . . . . " And Cassio when he comes on the stage supplicates the "heavens" (44) on the Moor's behalf, "For I have lost him on a dangerous sea." In the close of this act he will indeed have "lost" Othello: the two will be parted by "foul and violent" means.

Now, however, the "hopes" (50, 55) of the sanguine Cassio rise quickly above his fear, producing the very airy mood in which he launches into high-flown laudations of the wife of his adored general. He praises him in praising her. Othello has crowned his great achievements in achieving this paragon (61 f.). She is now "our great captain's captain," says Cassio with gay chivalry (74). But a serious diplomatic purpose underlies this and everything else he says in the present episode.

Montano, the peacetime governor of Cyprus, is to be superseded by Othello, whom, however, he generously commends (29 f.). Cassio seizes upon and strives to increase that esteem. Tactfully in his opening words (43 f.) he praises Montano and his associates, "the valiant of this warlike isle," while thanking them for "so" approving—with an insight that does them credit, such is the implication—"the Moor," still more experienced and capable than they, whom, however, Cassio refrains from entitling "Governor" (55) except once and casually. Thus we see here in action an important trait of Othello's second in command which Iago could not or would not discern (I. i. 22-33), his ability as diplomat. The lieutenant's

---

[4] The quiet, stately glide of this phrase is completed below by "the ship is here put in" (25). Contrast the imagery and movement of "what ribs of oak" etc., above (8).

chief effort is to render the new ruler of Cyprus doubly attractive by reason of his wife. All know Othello's military
greatness; his human greatness, so Cassio suggests, appears
through his love of Desdemona. Her unexpected early arrival (76 f.) is employed by Cassio to prepare a hearty acclam-
ation for her husband on the part of the islanders:

> . . . . Great Jove, Othello guard,
> And swell his sail with thine own powerful breath,
> That he may bless this bay with his tall ship,
> Make love's quick pants in Desdemona's arms,   80
> Give renewed fire to our extincted spirits,
> And bring all Cyprus comfort.

All the world loves a lover: nothing could more warmly humanize the great general in the eyes of Cyprus than those "quick
pants" in his wife's arms (actually to be witnessed by "all" as
soon as he enters, below). And all "spirits," whether "extincted" or not, shall share the light and "comfort," the vital force,
of the "renewed fire" of a great love.[5] Cassio's enthusiasm,
sincere while tactical, is very infectious. It brings the islanders
to their "knees" (84) on Desdemona's arrival, which his oratory converts into a state entrance preparatory for Othello's:

> Oh behold,
> The riches of the ship is come on shore. . . .

This ship has brought to Cyprus a great wealth of beauty; but
close in the background, Cassio hopes, is the "tall ship" bringing the "powerful" person of Othello himself (78 f.), his
power ushered by and partaking of that beauty. Homage to
the "lady" (85) is preliminary to the complete homage to be
given to her new lord who is, far more importantly, the new
lord of "this warlike isle" (43).

---

[5] The final word "comfort" has its original, etymologic connotation of
strength; and "extincted" is an elaborate echo of "quench," above (15).
Cassio's diplomatic art ignores now the "comfort" which all have experienced in "the Turkish loss" (31 f.). He wants them all to feel "extincted"
by "the great contention of sea and skies" (92) that has so greatly endan-
gered their new governor; whose safe arrival will consequently seem all the
more providential, the work of "Great Jove" or, in other words, "the grace
of Heaven" (85).

All very fine!   But the audience in the theater is aware
that the sense of dark fate aroused by the storm continues to
run like an undercurrent through Cassio's lofty speeches without his cognizance.   The previous scene showed us that Othello
has small insight into Desdemona's character; and now we see
that the same is true of his best friend: in this matter Cassio
is totally incapable of aiding his beloved commander.   His
view of this girl, like Othello's, is unconsciously patronizing.
But also it is entirely impersonal.   Significantly his first speech
about her cites "the quirks of blazoning pens" (63), the verbal
subtleties, devoid of personal feeling, which poets had long
employed in describing and proclaiming feminine beauty as
symbol of the divine.   Cassio tries to outdo those "pens" with
his tongue.   And certainly he coins a striking phrase in declaring that Desdemona is supreme "in th'essential vesture of
creation" (64), that beauty derived from the divine essence
itself with which God has clothed his loveliest creatures.   The
idea is continued in the next speech: the "high seas" etc., as
"having sense of beauty," set aside their "mortal natures, letting go safely by / The divine Desdemona."   This is unwittingly prophetic.   In the final scene of the play the "divine
Desdemona" will triumph over "mortal [death-doing] natures"
—by reason, however, of that "divine" self-sacrificing love in
her of which Cassio despite his religiosity has no inkling.   He,
like Roderigo, watched and heard her in the Senate scene without illumination.   The present scene shows that the true and
poetic gentleman Cassio has no more insight than the vain
and selfish gentleman Roderigo into the "essential" (64) nature of this girl's love for the Moor.   However, his prayerful
wish for her is sincere enough; it will be answered in ways beyond his understanding:

> Hail to thee, lady: and the grace of Heaven,
> Before, behind thee, and on every hand
> Enwheel thee round.

Something of that "grace" appears in her now.   Her opening words are as wisely simple and charitable as those she

uttered at her first entrance (I. iii. 180 ff.). There she brought her father firmly to the point by silencing without rebuking his melodramatic imperiousness. Here she responds similarly to the showy and pietistic chivalrousness of her husband's friend. A slight though gracious inclination of her head is her sole acknowledgment of the homage of the kneeling gentlemen. Then she answers the lieutenant's forty rich words of greeting in these five: "I thank you, valiant Cassio" (87). Valiant! The epithet "gentle," at the least, would conventionally be called for by the extraordinary courtliness of his welcome to her. Her adjective accepts him as a brave and loyal officer while politely declining all his poetry. Then comes the important point: "What tidings can you tell me of my lord?" His reply (89 f.) has a pregnant simplicity induced by hers, even while it tries to comfort her. "Oh, but I *fear*"— she says very slowly with gradually increasing weight of stress.[6] Her wordless fear is infinitely deeper than that expressed above by Cassio and others in many words.

But she represses that fear, together with the painful suspense aroused by the sighting of another "sail" (93, 121), to express very touchingly, in looks more than words, her defensive affection for her new attendant Emilia (who in the end will give her life to clear her mistress's name and expose her husband Iago). "Alas, she has no speech" (103), says Desdemona, who in private, so the suggestion is, has tried in vain to draw a relieving confession from this unhappy woman. By nature Emilia is voluble enough, as Iago hints (101-103) and as we shall see later; but at present she is dumbly confronting an impasse. She cannot enter yet the fresh world of charity opened to her by her mistress, her love of whom, however, is rendering her inertly dissatisfied with the world of sheer cynicism she inhabits with her husband. Of his positive wickedness she knows nothing: the present episode intimates, what is shown later, that the accomplished hypocrite has on that point succeeded in deceiving completely even his own wife.

[6] Properly, therefore, F1 prints those four words as one line. Q1 follows them with a dash.

Moreover, though she fears her husband, she shares his coarseness of nature and admires his sort of wit. She encourages his diatribe against women (110 ff.) with her single, jocular protest (117) and then, in sharp contrast with Desdemona, imbibes all the rest in an amused silence which elicits from her mistress the light-toned serious warning, "Do not learn of him, Emilia, though he be thy husband" (163). But she *does* learn from him. Near the very end of the play, again in Desdemona's presence, she will in her own words give vent to the Iagoan sex-cynicism (IV. iii. 61 ff.). She repudiates it in one case only, that of her mistress. And at present she summons up enough courage and independence to deny mildly her husband's insinuation that she has let him see that "in her heart" she is critical of her lady (106-108). "You have little cause to say so," she rejoins quietly, so quietly that he fails to discern here a preliminary sign of her eventual revolt from him.

He is blinded to that by his large self-esteem and by his need of reinforcing it in the presence of Desdemona. He is "nothing, if not critical" (120); but her very being is a vital criticism of *him*, the gentle-mightiest that he has ever encountered.[7] She renders him profoundly uneasy and desperately anxious to hide that uneasiness from himself. Her sudden casual and arch challenging of him to "praise" her (118) puts him off his balance for a minute. His "invention" truly "labours" (126-129) as we have not seen it do hitherto. His funny double-metaphored description of that process covers his disquiet; but also it throws into painful relief the dulness of his ensuing sentences upon womankind, glaringly contrasting with his brilliant sayings to Roderigo in the preceding and, later, in the present scene. That fellow is Iago's chosen zany; whereas Desdemona is the last interlocutor he would wish: this girlish angel makes him feel and speak dully. But she, so unclever herself, commends his art while condemning his matter: "Oh heavy ignorance, that praises[8] the worst best"

[7] No doubt Shakespeare intends a *double-entendre* in "nothing": Iago is of no account unless he can discredit all that Desdemona means.

[8] From Q1. F1 reads "thou praisest"; but her aim is to censure his ignorance rather than him.

(145). Unintentionally she has uttered a terse critique of his whole view of life: he has gained a massive ignorance of true humanity along with the "gained knowledge" (I. iii. 390) of which he is so vain. In reprimanding the buffoon she unawares hurts, beyond his pardon, the very serious self-conceit of the villain. Her passing remark upon his "paradoxes to make fools laugh i' th' alehouse" (139) is parodied with studied "malice" (148) in his summation of the purposes in life of an entirely good woman: "To suckle fools and chronicle small beer" (161).[9]

Thus Iago assures himself that Desdemona is an exemplar and potential breeder of the world's fools. Surely her fitting mate is this other sweet fool, Cassio. This gentleman caps the climax of the dialogue with a patronizing comment that makes Iago wince: "He speaks home, madam; you may relish him more in the soldier than in the scholar" (166 f.). Here, in Iago's view, the effeminate scholar-lieutenant (I. i. 20 ff.) is smugly exulting, even more definitely than above (97-100), in his superiority of "breeding" and "courtesy" over his brainy and capable but unsuccessful rival. At once, therefore, the matter of the lieutenancy recurs to the villain's mind with new force. The cool aim "to get his place" (I. iii. 399) becomes now a hot desire to "strip you out of your lieutenantry" (173). But Iago's far deeper yearning, as will be shown fully in scene iii below, is to "strip" Cassio "out of" all his "courtship" (courtliness) and "courtesy" (172, 177).

Here the lieutenant displays those graces to an extraordinary degree because of keen pity, shared by all the company except Iago, for his commander's lady. She has not really succeeded in beguiling her fear and suspense (123 f.) by amusing herself with Iago. In the upshot his sort of fun deepens her depression; so she turns from him to Cassio appealingly (162-165): her forebodings in regard to her husband, now desperate though still bravely withheld from her lips, ap-

---

[9] She presses congenital imbeciles to her breast with one hand while the other carefully keeps the accounts of petty cash expended for *another* weak fluid which they will later learn to imbibe in company with their parent.

pear in her face. Therefore the lieutenant takes her hand and in a low tone—for Iago, a sensual "whisper" (169)—comforts and gently adjures her, employing all the courtly gestures of the time to sustain her in her role of first "lady" (85) of Cyprus, a role demanding courageous composure before Montano and the others who are to be, in effect, the new governor's court. The girl maintains her self-command well, to the admiration of all, particularly Cassio, as his regardful motions show. She, grateful for his support, presses his hand with a simple warmth—a gesture which even the foolish Roderigo, here present in his disguise (I. iii. 346), perceives to be pure courtesy (259-261).

Superfoolish, then, as well as superwicked is Iago's present monologue (168 ff.). In fact it is unique among his main speeches, standing out in special contrast to his preceding soliloquy at the end of the first act. There and elsewhere his remarks have some thread of human sense and humor. Here they have absolutely none. We smile, if indeed we do so, entirely *at* him, not in the least *with* him. The smile which he himself tries to muster is a sheer, gross grimace—a gargoyle hanging over figures with "free and open" (I. iii. 405) faces. The fact is that if Cassio and Desdemona were even a tittle less innocuous his bitterness towards them would be far less extreme; a conscious effort on their part to snub him, during the dialogue above, would have afforded his malice a rational foothold. But now it has none. Their innocence towards him was prologue to their present entire innocence towards each other. All the circumstances invite the two to experience a touch, at the least, of the "carnal sting," which, unlike the intellectual Iago, they would not be able to "cool," or entirely dissemble, by the exercise of "will" and "reason" (I. iii. 330 ff.). But the peering villain cannot find that least touch: his mind forces him to perceive in the two a purity which confutes his sort of "reason" and, indeed, appals him. Hence his heart overflows with venom. His hatred of them, previously rather cool, becomes now the equal of his burning hate of Othello and

thus provides him with complete driving power for his plot.
And his imagination revels in making them seem as sensual
as he yearns they should be. Thus his malice in this soliloquy
is at once diabolical and fantastic. Stroke by stroke, as he
watches the two innocents, he builds up about them a thick
vapor of "clyster-pipes"—till suddenly that dirty fog is pierced
by the clear "trumpet" of "The Moor" (178-180).

OTHELLO	O, my fair warrior—	
DESDEMONA	My dear Othello—[10]	
OTHELLO	It gives me wonder great as my content	185
	To see you here before me.	
	Oh my soul's joy:	
	If after every tempest, come such calms,	
	May the winds blow, till they have wakened death!	

His initial line with its striking image is spoken resonantly,
with outstretched arms. She, in his arms, clasping him con-
vulsively, with a "world of sighs" (I. iii. 159), has for a moment no words; then just three, low, slow, and intense, re-
giving him her unspeakable world of love.[11] For her he is
simply, profoundly "dear." For him she is "fair," wonderfully so but not profoundly, not in her "very quality." His
inmost being is symbolized for her by his name (I. iii. 252 f.):
it comes at once to her lips here; but hers does not come to his.
Shakespeare knows that we know that when our affection is
deeply real we instinctively, on the occasion of such a reunion,
exclaim the loved one's name.[12] "O, my Desdemona"[13]—thus,

[10] The spacing of these three words is mine; so are the dashes after "warrior" and "Othello." In both F1 and Q1 these two short speeches are aligned
at the left. But the modern editor has generally indented the second so as
to make it the completion of a pentameter verse. Surely, however, it is meant
to have the same oral time as the first; "dear," lingeringly uttered, is dis-
syllabic. (Together the two lines constitute, if anything, a hexameter or perhaps an octameter.) Othello's ensuing verses are arranged, above, as in F1.
[11] Of course she gives him also "a world of kisses" in response to his.
That phrase is pertinent here as not above; see Act I, note 31.
[12] In the Balcony scene Romeo, at first sight of Juliet, utters her name;
she exclaims his in her opening verse and twice re-enters speaking it to him
(II. ii. 3, 33, 142, 159).
[13] This phrase, like his actual one, would agree rhythmically with her
reply. As it is, the rhythmic harmony emphasizes the spiritual difference
between the two.

we feel, Othello would normally begin, postponing his "warrior" metaphor. This in itself is handsome and appropriate, well deserved by her. But coming first it reminds us instantly of the military profession which he has loved so much longer than her and with far more intimate knowledge and understanding. Moreover, it echoes, uneasily for us, perhaps also for her, the chivalrous poetic vein with which she was greeted above by Cassio. The lieutenant saw her external beauty and he has just been commending her courage: Othello sees both those traits in his "fair warrior." But here and in what ensues we are again made to feel that he knows little more than Cassio about her "very quality."

Of course he may learn; we hope he will: he is gentle, pure, true; and her love can teach him. But the present episode shows us that *the very nature of his love for her obstructs his perception of the nature of her love for him.* So far his love, unlike hers, is mainly emotional; that was clear in the first act. But there his emotions regarding her were restrained by the imminence of war and by the presence of his masters, the duke and senate, when he told his love story. Now, however, it is peacetime and he himself is master: his heart can speak freely and fully. He pours forth superb love poetry, so superb that it conceals from himself entirely, and at first perhaps from us, the deficiency of his love. When the episode ends we realize that he has shown us all the depths of his love—and that those depths are shallows, lucent and lovely shallows.

The self-centeredness of his love, palliated by circumstances in Act I, is here completely evident and very ominous. He himself senses the omen but not its cause. Almost oblivious of his wife's feelings, he is obsessed by his own, his "soul's"[14] great "wonder" and "content" and "joy." In common experience such "calms," such rapt moods of self-centered delight, bring on a sense of danger: the full tide of "soul" has a vague undertow of "death."[15] He proceeds:

[14] For Shakespeare the word "soul" is morally and spiritually very ambiguous: it may denote specious powers along with beneficent ones. The "soul" may be hiddenly selfish. In the dozen lines of the present speech the first personal pronoun singular occurs six times.
[15] Notably in the poetry of Shelley.

And let the labouring bark climb hills of seas,
Olympus-high, and duck again as low   190
As hell's from heaven. If it were now to die
'Twere now to be most happy. For I fear,[16]
My soul hath her content so absolute,
That not another comfort like to this
Succeeds in unknown fate.   195

The first three verses recall the fantastic storm with its suggestion of something "monstrous" assailing high "heaven"
(3, 13-15); a something now named by Othello "hell"—the
power invoked in the close of the first act by Iago to animate
his plot against Othello. The grotesque extremeness of the
imagery conveys the speaker's overwrought, apprehensive emotion.[17] This subsides like a wave into the intense deadly-happy
lines that follow, while he grips the girl to him in a way that
accentuates for her the "fear" conjured up by his words.

She frees herself and stands back a little with hands on his
arms and eyes looking up full into his. She speaks slowly and
simply, with an intensity opposite in kind to his:

The Heavens forbid   195
But that our loves[18]
And comforts should increase
Even as our days do grow!

Those "Heavens" have the steadfastness of "the guards of th'
ever-fixed Pole" (15). So has her love; and his too may become high and steadfast if only it will entirely unite with hers.
He has spoken only of his own "content" and "comfort": her
phrase "*our* loves and comforts" reproves lovingly the self-
love in his love of her. But mainly she tries to supplant his
sealike mood with a homely vision of daily growth in love.

[16] Contrast her "I fear," above (91), so simple, actual, and altruistic.
[17] Like Macbeth's farfetched image, "tears shall drown the wind" (I.
vii. 25).
[18] This and the next line appear as one verse in Q1. But the modern
belief that the printers of the folio did not hesitate to break a verse in two
when it was too long for their comparatively narrow columns, does not apply
here. This verse is slightly shorter than, for example, line 188 above, "May
the winds blow," etc. Incidentally Othello's swelling "winds" are conspicuously absent from the "Heavens" of Desdemona's two short, plain lines.

Thus the passage is sequel of her desperate resolve to "go with him" (I. iii. 260) far abroad so as to win all his love by sharing all his life, by making all *his* days "*our* days": her hope is for steady "increase" of the love they have in common "as our days do grow."

He does not see her dedication; he does not partake of her vision and faith. But now looking intently into her uplifted face he glimpses, in the passage quoted below, "sweet Powers," supernal harmonies, transcending the "discords" sensed by his prophetic soul. But he will not speak explicitly of his premonitions though her anxious exclamation has invited him to do so. The cause of those premonitions is the extreme difference, elaborately shown in Act I, between him and her, between their ways of life and, far more deeply, between their ways of love. The earthly happiness of these two persons demands an extreme frankness between them in regard to their extreme differences. Obviously she is entirely ready for such frankness; he, entirely not: his pride and self-centeredness stand in the way. In the Senate scene when she was forced to reveal, unintentionally, the superiority of her love to his, Othello's response was a patronizing obliviousness (I. iii. 249-275), considerably due, however, to his then situation. But now, when that situation has been left far behind, his response is essentially the same, though strikingly emotionalized. Glimpsing her high love he is swayed by it momentarily. He has a fervent "Amen" for the *feel* of her prayer, but not for its meaning. She would like to face their future frankly; but he does not concur. He dismisses that doubtful future in favor of a present harmony, lovely and blinding:

> Amen to that, sweet Powers![19]
> I cannot speak enough of this content,
> It stops me here: it is too much of joy.

[19] These two words are parenthesized in F1 for emphasis in direct address. Q1 reads, "Amen to that sweet power," as though the "power" were in Desdemona; which indeed it is. I have reproduced the folio's capitalization of her word "Heavens" (195) and of Othello's respondent "Powers": both speakers are solemnly invoking the Divine Being—in contrast with Othello's "Fate" (195).

> And this, and this, the greatest discords be   200
> That e'er our hearts shall make.

Catching her to his breast again, kissing her repeatedly, he catches up too her word "our," his first use of the plural pronoun. For the moment he experiences "our hearts," instead of "my soul" (187, 193), under the influence of her stress upon "our loves." As for her thought of "our" growing "days," he submerges his sense of potential growing "discords" under the present overflowing "joy" and "content," omitting from those two words his previous "my" (185 f.): here he identifies his joy with hers.

But unlike hers his joy, as his words confess, is "too much"; it is ominously intemperate. In reaction from his dark fear regarding "unknown fate" his mood is now swinging to the other extreme: his delight is becoming fond, even doting. All the while she maintains an expressive silence: her happiness, quietly intense, is lit with hope but tempered by concern for the shifting play of his feelings. He notes her concern, in the end of the following passage, but takes it lightly:

> Come, let us to the castle.—
> News, friends, our wars are done:
> The Turks are drowned.   205
> How does my old acquaintance of this Isle?—
> Honey, you shall be well desired in Cyprus,
> I have found great love amongst them. Oh, my sweet,
> I prattle out of fashion, and I dote
> In mine own comforts. . . .   210

So finally the "comforts" are not "our" (196 f., 201) but "mine own." He can "dote" in them fully because, as he exclaims genially to his fellow warriors, "our wars are done."[20] And his "fair warrior" has become what he at the first designed (I. iii. 236-240) and she so much dreaded, "a moth of peace"

---

[20] The double fact that this line (204) repeats almost verbatim a line (20) by a previous speaker, and that the new governor has not mentioned the "wars" till now, reinforces our sense of the softness of his present mood. His doting word "honey" (207) prepares for "sweet" (208), which in turn recalls his use of "sweet" above (197).

(I. iii. 257), the lovely pastime of a great soldier's leisure, his uncongenial, very "soft" (I. iii. 82 ff.) leisure. She could have far better won his intimate fellowship if she had shared his "flinty and steel couch of war" (I. iii. 231), companioning him in the state's "serious and great business" (I. iii. 268). Those circumstances would have brought the essential strength of her character quickly into overt action; and they would have rendered him self-oblivious and mentally alert, ready to know the depth of her love. As it is, his best powers are relaxed: the "calm" (187) that he has welcomed with such dubious emotion is far more fateful than the receded storm of battle.

And so we see here definitely a fact that was intimated from first to last of Act I. Desdemona is the "fair warrior" in a sense far beyond Othello's meaning. Her love of him is like his love of war: whole-souled, steady, calm; determined to win; indeed too absorbed, as will appear later, in her peaceful battle to win *him*. On the other hand his love of her, underneath its poetic charm and intensity, is, so far, like his experience of peacetime life: self-concerned, restive, comparatively imperceptive and superficial, devoid of "dearest action" (I. iii. 85).

As the two leave the stage we have the same feeling, but now far more pronounced, that we had upon their previous exit. There the Moor's proud waiving of Brabantio's evil insinuation was attributable, more or less, to "the time" (I. iii. 293-301). But here the time is all his own; and high "Powers" have suggested to his "soul" that there is a fateful difference in the nature of his and Desdemona's "loves" (193-197) which he ought to ponder. He waives that intuition, however, before it can take tangible shape, not because he is naïve but because he is self-centered. And his final speech, of which the first part was quoted above, makes us feel that off stage he will not ponder the matter nor advert to it when alone with his wife, as in the case of her father's wicked parting thrust. Instead he will lavish upon her all his loving emotion, true, pure, tender, romantic, and doting. He has ample leisure now for that: also for other matters; which here, as previously (I. iii. 300),

are suggestively alluded to along with his marital joy.   He
remarks with unconscious irony that amongst his friends in
Cyprus he has "found great love": the greatness of hers he
has not yet discovered.   And the thought of "mine own comforts" is succeeded, with unintentional humor, by the recollection of "my coffers" (211) needing to be disembarked.
His prosaic final words, "Come, Desdemona,[21] / Once more,
well met at Cyprus," are extremely anticlimactic to his opening
salutation to her.   His poetic ecstasy, in subsiding, has been succeeded, not by deepened insight into love, but by a peacetime
confluence of sentiment and prose.   For us the upshot is a
"wonder" very different from Othello's initial feeling (185):
we wonder what his next current of emotion will be.   In this
island of "unknown fate" Desdemona is very far from "well
met."   Her husband's consonance with her is deeply, hiddenly
dissonant.

Iago, like Othello, has no understanding of the fundamental
quality of that disharmony.   But whereas we feel that Othello
may learn, the present scene as a whole, particularly the ensuing episode, makes absolutely clear that Iago will not.   What
happens in the sequel is that, in playing upon the superficial
differences between the two lovers, he accidentally vibrates the
basal discord of which he is totally ignorant.   The shallowness
of his insight, along with his coarse cruelty, is indicated by his
leering aside (202-204) while the lovers kiss: "Oh you are
well tuned now; but I'll set down the pegs that make this
music, as honest as I am."[22]   Mistakenly he deems the two are
"well tuned" now: he is entirely insensible to the underlying
divergency in the nature of their loves which the dramatist has
made us perceive.   His metaphor is accurate: he can and will
loosen the "pegs"; he can interrupt "this music."   But he does
not understand the score.   He knows neither the tragic discords

---

[21] These two words gently remind us, as on the previous occasion (I. iii.
299), that he is her lord and master as well as Iago's, to whom he has just
been giving a command.

[22] Obviously the prose form of this speech in F1 is right.   Q1's verse
form weakens the dramatic contrast between Iago's mood and that of the
lovers.

that can arise in love nor its high harmonies, its "sweet" and great "Powers" (197). Caught between them in the end of the play, he is destroyed by his proud, clever obtuseness: he has no real feeling for the potent strings and instruments with which he evilly meddles. In the rest of this scene he prepares with superficial expertness to "set down the pegs"—oblivious of "unknown fate."

(b) *egregiously an ass*   II. i. 215-321

Notably he is oblivious of certain signs that even Roderigo, the instrument he seems to have entirely mastered, has strings which the villain can loosen but not break. The fact, the dramatic fact, is that Iago has been rendered desperate by his experiences in the first part of the scene, by the "music," the harmonies, of his three superiors together with their casual, unconsciously patronizing treatment of him. The friendly encounter of Cassio and Desdemona, so obviously pure and not in the least ruffled by the ensign's salacious diatribe against women, was followed hard upon by the loving reunion, flawless in Iago's shallow view, of Desdemona and Othello. Here the Moor's joy, that "delight" which from the start Iago has yearned to "poison" (I. i. 68), seemed completely fulfilled. And Othello capped the climax by letting his happiness overflow casually upon Iago, terming him "good" along with the "good" shipmaster, to whom, however, the ensign, as Othello politely suggests, must show "much respect" (210-214), at which point (I think) Iago exhibits to the audience a comic, vicious grimace. The result is that the villain in the present dialogue has two purposes: to set Roderigo against Cassio; and, far more significantly, to utter freely his accumulated venom against his superiors. And this venomous mood, more than his feeling that he can now fully domineer over the fellow he has "brought from Venice" (270), causes him to insult Roderigo gratuitously at the outset: "if thou be'st valiant (as, they say, base men being in love have then a nobility in their natures more than is native to them) list me . . . . "

Imprudently Iago has made a concession to his ultimate
enemy, namely "love." The concession registers immediately
with the "base" Roderigo. His faint "nobility" bestirs itself
far more than in the preceding scene. There he had merely
three words of protest (I. iii. 338) against Iago's identification
of love with lust. Here in three "valiant" lines (222, 254,
261)—incidentally his inspired term "blessed" for the girl's
"condition" (disposition) recalls Cassio's invocation of "the
grace of heaven" (85) for her—he utterly rejects the villain's
claim that Desdemona's friendly attitude to Cassio is "love"
(221) in the Iagoan sense, i.e. "lechery" and "lust" (262 f.).
So that finally Iago gives up tacitly his effort to convince his
companion on that point: "Pish! But, sir, be you ruled by me"
(269). Dismissing the subject of Desdemona he concentrates
on the case of Cassio. And Roderigo's doubtful "well" (278)
indicates a willingness to believe that there is in him the "hidden loose affection" (246) that he "cannot believe" to be "in
her" (254). In any case the courtly lieutenant is obviously an
"impediment" (287), now, in the way of Roderigo's approach
to Desdemona. And the silly gentleman's yearning to out-
weigh his heavy sense of nullity (I. iii. 306) by a ruffling naughtiness of conduct in soldierly disguise, that yearning so cleverly
fostered by Iago in Act I, is vividly appealed to by the project
of so playing upon a weakness of the highly superior Cassio as
to cause his displacement from the lieutenancy,[23] an event essential to "our prosperity" (288), as Iago concludes with fine art,
insisting on the flattering fact that his dupe's and his own interests are entirely "conjunctive" (I. iii. 375). Thus Roderigo's
vanity (like Othello's pride, later) triumphs over true instincts
aroused by Desdemona's presence and mien.

Her demeanor in the first part of this scene has roused
into fullest activity the most devilish instincts of Iago. In this
"fair warrior" he now senses, more or less subconsciously, an

---

[23] In the first part of this scene a good actor of the part will evince by
the looks and gestures of the silent Roderigo his admiration and envy of
Cassio's great courtliness. Compare Sir Andrew Aguecheek in *Twelfth Night*
III. i. 95-102 and his subsequent challenge to Cesario; Sir Andrew is a comic
prototype of the pathetically evil Roderigo.

impregnable embodiment of his enemy, true love. At the first she was for him a negligible thing, a soft and passive "white ewe" (I. i. 89) or a rich "land carack" that Othello had "boarded" (I. ii. 50) and would mayhap lose by law. But her extremely positive part in the Senate scene forced him to pay embarrassed heed to her: she evinced strange power. Her effect upon Roderigo annoyed the villain excessively, challenging his view of love as merely "a lust of the blood" (I. iii. 339). Her passion for Othello, at once "violent" and "supersubtle," could not "long continue"; she "must change": so Iago must imagine (I. iii. 348-364). But in the present scene, after a close-up, catlike watching of her, he has not been able to detect the slightest sign of change. On the contrary her final speech was intense with the conviction that her love for the Moor would "increase" (196). So now, alone with Roderigo, the villain gives her and her love a brilliantly vicious tongue-lashing, trying to make himself, far more than his listener, believe all he says.

His beginning (224 ff.) is very astute. Again, as above (I. iii. 350), he seizes upon and twists her own word "violence" —applied by her to the outward aspect of her marriage; by him to the essential nature of her love, in contravention of the whole meaning of her great speech on that subject (I. iii. 249-260). That inward and deep meaning Iago cannot, dare not, consider. He hurries away from the thought of it into a vivid parody of Othello's eloquent monologue before the Senate (I. iii. 128 ff.)—"bragging and telling her fantastical lies; and will she love him still for prating? Let not the[24] discreet heart think so." The word "prating" intimates, veraciously enough, that the Moor's words of love in the present scene (184 ff.) have a rich poetic flavor as they did in the Senate scene. And "the discreet heart," obviously Iago's, vicariously Roderigo's, must be certain that the Moor cannot continue to charm the girl's ear. Consequently her "eye" will revolt and seek a lovelier person. So, more strongly, will her "blood,"

---

[24] This word is from Q1. Instead of "the," F1 has "thy."

her passion, reinforced by her "delicate [i. e. fastidious] tenderness." In short she will be impelled by "nature" (238) itself. This vague, elastic entity is the goal of Iago's progressive argument. His naturalistic reasoning is carefully logical; establishing, as he phrases it with satanic pedantry, "a most pregnant and unforced position." This being so, Desdemona's "second choice" will surely be the entirely alluring and available Cassio: "and the woman hath found him already" (253). In this smiting conclusion Iago shifts abruptly from the future to the perfect tense, from "will find" above (236) to "hath found" here.[25] His *imagination* has now found, what it could not find previously (168-180), that the evil he yearns for in prospect is already actual.

Hence when Roderigo exclaims "I cannot believe," etc., the villain is thoroughly angered (256 ff.). He rightly sees the religious word "blessed" as the most telling symbol of what he most hates. He attacks the word with new, hot vigor, steeping it in "very nature" (238). Shakespeare has shown us that, whatever Desdemona's faults, she can "consecrate" her "soul" to Othello (I. iii. 255) because her disposition is *blessed*. Iago declares on the contrary, "If she had been blessed, she would never have loved the Moor." He coins a luscious double-stemmed beatitude: "Blessed fig's end . . . Blessed pudding!" And now his angry heat inspires a "foul" (263) vision of Desdemona and Cassio with "breaths embraced" anticipating "th' incorporate conclusion."

Never, here or elsewhere, does Iago dare acknowledge his deep, consuming hatred of Desdemona: to do so would be to confront the fact that she whose love and purity he cannot help sensing as impregnable is one whose very being condemns all of his. He relieves himself, in the course of the present scene, by ridiculing her goodness one moment and denying it the next. The former method, however, has proved to be very unsatisfactory: it brings him too close to her embarrassing reality (145-165); and he as a verbal artist must have felt there was truth

---

[25] A scholar may find that Iago is not guilty here of a logical *non sequitur*; but the point is not very relevant.

in her judgment of his "most lame and impotent conclusion."
His present "incorporate conclusion," cited above, is better. Far
more satisfying than the effort to make light of her goodness
is the vivid smirching of it in his imagination. This, therefore,
is the method he will in future favor. But it has the disadvan-
tage of requiring a would-be rationalist to lean heavily on fancies. The best way of all, he finds, is to outflank the girl's
goodness, so to speak, by assailing her associates, who so much
admire it while far from fully sharing it: these others are in
various ways vulnerable. And throughout the play it will be
found that the presence or even the thought of Desdemona inspires Iago always with new venom against one or other of her
associates.

For example, his animadversions upon her above (224 ff.),
so measured and factitious, are followed (241 ff.) by a hot and
bitter outbreak against her admiring friend Cassio, so much
more easily assailable. His too elaborate chivalry may be regarded with a little forcing as "the mere form of civil and humane seeming" disguising a "most hidden loose affection." For
Cassio is a "subtle knave"; as Desdemona previously was a
"supersubtle Venetian" (I. iii. 364). The repeated adjective
"subtle" has a certain plausibility; but knavery[26] is a quality
that not even Iago can attribute to that "gentle lady" (119)
though he awards her "folly" and a "green mind" (252 f.).
So he relieves himself by four times terming Cassio a "knave":
at first merely a "very voluble" one; soon, "slipper and subtle"; then downright "devilish"; but, in the finale, "pestilent
complete"[27]—a swift flash of the envy which the villain feels
also for Desdemona but which in her case he tries, studiously
and restlessly, to avoid or hide.

His heavily increased embarrassment regarding her accounts
for the grotesquerie of the soliloquy that ends this scene. "That

[26] The word "knave" is a happy one here for Iago's purposes. In its common old meaning, a male servant, it denotes Cassio's subservience to Desdemona; but also in its present context it connotes the sensual knavery of which
the villain wishes to believe him guilty.
[27] This term would suggest to the Elizabethan audience that so-called
Complete Gentleman, the ideal figure of that time.

Cassio loves[28] her, I do well believe it"(295); that is, he can
make himself conceive it. But "that she loves him"—this is
merely "apt and of great credit," a plausible "position" as he
termed it above (241). By all the rules of "nature" (238),
that is of love-lust, she ought to do so; but unfortunately, from
the standpoint of "Hell" (I. iii. 409), she plainly does not.
Iago cannot "well believe" she does, any more than the provoking Roderigo could "believe" it (254). So now he makes
a blinking pause[29]—then abruptly changes the subject:

> The Moor (howbeit that I endure him not)
> Is of a constant, loving, noble nature,
> And I dare think he'll prove to Desdemona
> A most dear husband. Now, I do love her too,   300
> Not out of absolute lust, though peraventure
> I stand accomptant for as great a sin,
> But partly led to diet my revenge. . . .

The sneering praise he gives to the Moor belongs still more
to the Moor's wife; but Iago does not "dare think" it of her,
even sneeringly, when alone with himself: the recollection of
her awes him. So he utterly dismisses the thought of her
strange, unaccountable, constant love of the Moor. But the
fact that his plot against her husband must be directed centrally
against *her* is considerably dispiriting. Therefore he tries to
inspirit himself with the sudden ridiculous fancy that he, "too,"
is one of her lovers. If he, the sexually cold, self-centered
rationalist, could have just a touch of "lust" for her, that very
human "sin" would enable him to feel that he "too" shares
the humanity which he secretly envies in the Moor, in Cassio,
and even in Roderigo. But quickly and confusedly his mind
drops that wild fancy—it never recurs to him—and seizes upon
his real, warm motive of "revenge": this enables his "cause"
to be really "hearted" (I. iii. 373 f.).
    And now he proceeds to "diet" his "revenge" with his

---

[28] Important here is the fact that "love" in Shakespeare's time denoted
also friendship, as in line 317 below. The ambiguity aids Iago's self-deception.
[29] Therefore F1's period, instead of Q1's semicolon, after "credit" is right.
We might substitute a dash.

former fancy (I. iii. 392-396), here blatantly developed (304 ff.), that the Moor had formerly seduced Emilia; thereupon playing for a moment with the vague and swiftly "failing" notion of being "evened with him, wife for wife."[30] Then, having warmed himself with a make-believe sexual jealousy of the Moor, he concentrates in the rest of the speech upon the design of arousing in the Moor a "strong" baseless "jealousy" (the first occurrence of this word) regarding Cassio. The villain will "abuse [falsely accuse] him to the Moor in the right garb" (in the most effective manner). Thus Iago, when alone, but in the very heat of his evil mood, is mentally forced to discard his comforting effort to believe "that Cassio loves her" (295); and in the same breath he comforts his conscience by asserting, "For I fear Cassio with my night-cap too" (316). Here the audience laughs aloud. That sudden impossible picture of the fastidious lieutenant, a forced picture derivative from the speaker's similar slander of Othello above, is the villain's summary effort to ridicule the "courtesy" (100) he deeply envies (251 ff.). But he pulls upon himself a quick load of ridicule, which, however, he immediately evades by deriding Othello with new force and cruelty:

> Make the Moor thank me, love me, and reward me,
> For making him egregiously an ass,
> And practising upon his peace and quiet
> Even to madness.—'Tis here: but yet confused;   320
> Knavery's plain face is never seen till used.

That "love me," sardonically echoing the words "loves her . . . ," "loves him . . . ," "loving . . . ," "love her," above (295-300), is the brilliantly wicked acme of all his censures, from the first (I. i. 45 ff.) until now, upon human affection and good will. But if its cleverness makes us smile, our amusement is stopped by the progressive cruelty of the passage culminating in the

[30] Iago's vagueness here is remarkably suggestive. Logically, but against all reason, he would mean that he hopes to seduce Desdemona himself. In reality he is just hoaxing himself for a fleeting pleasurable instant, as when he spoke of his "lust" above. Compare his vague previous clause, "will do [i.e., act] as if for surety" (I. iii. 396).

word "madness." And the villain's conscience pricks him; and so in closing he plumes up his evil will, as at the end of the preceding scene, by conceiving himself as a channel of impersonal evil, assigning now to himself the "knavery" (321) he tried to read into Cassio above (241 ff.).

The upshot, however, of Iago's total part in the present scene is that he appears, far more than before, as thoroughly grotesque as he is evil. This would-be superman is really subnormal. To normal minds his sidesteppings and self-deludings are fantastically absurd, particularly in his attitude to Desdemona. This logical thinker when he gives the lead to his fantasies can be "as tenderly led by the nose / As asses are" (I. iii. 407 f.). Othello's romantic "soul" (193) may well be susceptible to "madness." Iago's little "soul" (307), immensely conceited, makes him, what he would love to make but cannot make Othello, "egregiously an ass."

(c) *Reputation, Reputation, Reputation*   II. ii—II. iii. 341

II. ii

As hidden "knavery" retires, a herald enters reading to the assembling people of Cyprus a genial proclamation from Othello. It recalls the tone of his last speech above (II. i. 204 ff.), and it signalizes him, over against Iago, as compatible with everyday mankind: with the "every man" (4) who loves on occasion to "dance" or "make bonfires" and, above all, to have "full liberty of feasting"(10). But that "liberty" is strictly though gently limited to a period of six hours (11 f.); and "each man" is to go in for that particular kind of "sports and revels" to which his "addition[31] [his social rank] leads him" (6 f.)—a tactful way of insisting upon good order. And the very formality of the proclamation as a whole reminds us that "our noble and valiant general" (1), however gracious and genial, is now supreme ruler of "the isle of Cyprus" (12 f.).

---

[31] For this word Q1 has "mind" and later quartos have "addiction." But the "addition" of the folio texts intimates that each person may pursue the pastime he has a mind to only if it is suitable for his social position or office. This principle is presently violated by Cassio.

He must be obeyed implicitly. Incidentally we are reminded of the great reputation of this "worthy Governour" (II. i. 30), a point that will later be of much importance in the plot of the play.

[II. iii. 1-341] [32]

At present, however, owing to Iago's scheme for "tonight" (II. i. 271-283, 311-314), the audience is concerned about the reputation of Michael Cassio. His commander's words to him continue and intensify the friendly but strict tone of the proclamation above:

> OTHELLO Good Michael, look you to the guard tonight.
> Let's teach ourselves that honourable stop,
> Not to outsport discretion.
>
> CASSIO Iago hath direction what to do.
> But notwithstanding with my personal eye
> Will I look to't.
>
> OTHELLO Iago is most honest:
> Michael, good night. Tomorrow with your earliest,
> Let me have speech with you.—Come, my dear love;
> The purchase made, the fruits are to ensue;
> That profit's yet to come 'tween me and you.—
> Good night.

For the first time Desdemona is "my dear love"; but his ensuing pretty allusion to the consummation of their sacred "rites" (I. iii. 258) is remarkably conventional in imagery and tone. For us it is disquieting. It connects unpleasantly with his word "outsport" above (3), which in turn recalls the phrase "my disports" (I. iii. 272) in his speech to the Senate upon the present subject.[33] To be sure he is now, as then, very

---

[32] The scene-head is a mid-eighteenth-century insertion. In the original performances "Othello's Herald," as F1 terms him, would doubtless declaim the proclamation from the rear upper-stage, representing a balcony of the "castle" (II. i. 204), to a crowd below, which would retire respectfully upon the entrance of Othello himself. The Herald's words herald the first speech of Othello, as noted in my text. See Ronald Watkins's remarkable book *On Producing Shakespeare* (1950).

[33] But contrast Iago's use of "sport," below (17). The difference is the difference between a soldier-gentleman and a soldier-boor, both of them outspoken on the subject of sexual relations. (Elizabethan frankness is beside the point here.)

much concerned to set vocational duty above personal pleasure; the "celebration of his nuptial" (II. ii. 8)[34] is deliberately subordinated in his proclamation above and in his colloquy with his lieutenant here.

This is Othello's first night as military governor of Cyprus; yet he must depute his command to his new lieutenant "tonight" (1). He is obviously very anxious; the suggestion is that he is not entirely unacquainted with Cassio's potential weaknesses. But he will not affront the young man by direct reference to them. With fine gentility and sound tactic he aligns himself with his subordinate: we must *both* "teach ourselves that honorable stop, / Not to outsport discretion," a dictum as choice as his remark below to his wife is banal. And Cassio's somewhat facile response is countered with the intimation that the "most honest" Iago, however excellent in his limited way, is not a gentleman-officer nor the general's friend and second in command like "Michael," who, incurring full responsibility, must report to the governor at the "earliest" possible hour in the morning. The iterated words "good" and "night" (1, 7, 11) underline the commander's quietly strict adjuration to Cassio to be his best on this happy but crucial occasion.

Above (II. i. 184 ff.) we have Othello's first very crucial speech to his wife; here, to his lieutenant. In both cases he evinces premonitions; otherwise what a smiting contrast! In his *vocation* he has a superb "discretion" (3), a human insight, tact, and wariness, that so far he has not at all attained in his *avocation*, love.[35] His attitude to Desdemona is naïf: not so his view of Cassio. This officer's ensuing fall does not impugn his general's choice of him and reliance upon him. In a fateful hour the lieutenant disobeys not merely the orders given him above but his own best self. Yet his best traits have been so

---

[34] This brief passage in the proclamation is diplomatic and humane rather than egoistic. All the world loves a lover; and Othello knows (II. i. 207), as Cassio knew (II. i. 61 ff.), that his marriage will heighten his prestige as governor.

[35] In Shakespeare's works, unlike those of many modern interpreters of him, discretion (or prudence) in love is regarded as a prime virtue.

fully displayed to us in the opening of this act that we assume, and commend, Othello's tacit perception of them at the beginning (I. i. 16 f.), and we find his present trust in his lieutenant entirely reasonable and judicious.

Nor does Iago's plot for tonight seem at the first likely to be successful. The egregious asininity of his soliloquy, above, is recalled by his opening dialogue here with Cassio concerning Desdemona. Against all reason he tries hard to make the lieutenant show some sign of sensual regard for her, and is utterly baffled. Cassio listens to the fellow with the same indulgent, casual smile as when this "profane . . . soldier" (II. i. 165-167) previously displayed his natural coarseness. With fine tact the lieutenant refrains from giving the least sign either of arrogance towards his underofficer or of condonation of his nasty words about "a most exquisite lady" (18) who, Cassio ends, "is indeed perfection" (28). Certainly, we may again reflect, Othello is fortunate in his choice of second in command. And Iago's obtuseness here vis-à-vis true gentility—a wilful blindness due to his envious arrogance and not characteristic of the average practical man even when coarser than he—seems to preclude success in swaying the gentleman who confronts him. His scheme for "tainting his discipline" (II. i. 275) seems now very impractical.

But in the slight pause that follows Cassio's final word "perfection" Iago darts at him a glance of renewed deadly hatred. And we realize that he has been successful in one respect: that is in the process, now familiar to us, of warming up his villainous mood. And his slow "well" (29) marks a very dramatic transition from his inane vagaries of fancy in the first half of this act to his effectual tactics in the remaining half. In military operations (as Othello must know) Iago would be a poor strategist and an excellent tactician: the same is true of his operations in the field of wickedness. His insight into human nature is shallow and confused, often fantastically so, and his long-range plans have fatal flaws. But under specific and favorable conditions his small, acute mind, when thoroughly heated with jealous hate, works with brilliant effectiveness.

Here, while devoid of Othello's instinctive comprehension
of Cassio's whole personality, the villain shows diabolical cunning in playing upon those weaknesses which are the reverse
aspects of that young man's virtues and which the present occasion, precisely, serves to accentuate. Cassio is joyous tonight in
the thought of the "happiness" (29) of his beloved general's
union with Desdemona. This night certainly calls for drafts
"to the health of" him whom Iago now terms "black Othello"
(33). That adjective, a flash of pitchy hell-fire, blends porten-
tously with the darkness of the night as at the first (I. i. 88).
The villain knows it will help by antithesis to inflame Cassio's
loyal emotions regarding his white-souled general. And the
"Cyprus gallants" (31), "our friends" (38), are those whom
Cassio is extremely anxious to have richly "approve the Moor"
(II. i. 44). Diplomacy and "courtesy" (36), the courtesy so apt
in his case to be supersensitive and overelaborate, join in impel-
ling him to carouse with the gentlemen of Cyprus on this "night
of revels" (45): Iago's climactic word is the strongest one used
in Othello's proclamation (II. ii. 6).

But Shakespeare, still more astute than Iago, makes perfectly clear that Cassio, not his tempter, is in the main responsible for the ensuing disaster. The lieutenant has already im-
bibed "one cup" (40) on his own motion: obviously all the
motives so smartly touched by his present interlocutor were at
work in him beforehand. The cup was "craftily qualified"
(41), secretly diluted with water by him, secretly because of
his diplomatic and courtly anxiety to avoid any possible of-
fense to the Cyprus gallants. Thereupon he decided that, to
make an "honourable stop" (2), he must escape their company
for the rest of the evening: he "must to the watch" an hour
before the limit set for the revels (12-14, II. ii. 12). And his
tone is still firm when he politely declines Iago's invitation:
"Not tonight . . . " (34). "Tonight"—the word is a bright-and-
dark refrain running through the whole episode—is the one
night when he is in danger of overdrinking; but, unfortunately,
it is also the very night demanding a special display of friend-

ship for the "gallants" whom "Othello" (31-33) has to rule.
And now Cassio's "one cup" begins to operate, with twofold
effect. Dropping the dignified reticence he has hitherto maintained towards his inferior he pours out an unwary confession
to him (40 ff.). Then he consents to "call" the gallants "in,"
naturally and properly enough unwilling, as Iago knows, that
his inferior should be their chief host; but unwisely, as he confesses (49), breaking his initial resolve to avoid further company tonight.

However, his resolve against further drinking still holds
when he leaves the stage. Iago faces the not too easy task of
fastening another "cup upon him" (50). But that task is obviated by the lieutenant himself. Like Othello later (III. iii.
288, 330 ff.) Cassio is off stage, free from the villain's personal
pressure, when he yields to his definitive temptation. It comes
from within, from his temperament and present mood; and its
chief external agency is not Iago but Cassio's fellow gallants:
Iago can claim to have "flustered" *them*, not his lieutenant,
"with flowing cups . . . " (60). " 'Fore God," exclaims Cassio on
re-entering, "they have given me a rouse already" (66). The
gallants have innocently, as Montano insists (68 f.), occasioned
his drinking of that "little . . . pint" which has flustered the
lieutenant. His overgeniality, entirely against his judgment
and initial resolution, has led him to accept the one "more"
cup (44) that determines his fate.

And in the ensuing drinking scene Cassio takes the lead.
He gives the cues; Iago follows them up expertly. The episode is a tragicomic parody of the normal relations between
lieutenant and ancient: Cassio unfolds the strategy of his own
ruin; Iago works out the tactics. The villain chimes with
Cassio's drunken mood as it passes from joviality (66 ff.) to
gradually rising gravity (88) and finally to self-assertiveness
(113).

Iago's first song is a masterpiece of metallic hilarity. Catching up Montano's word "soldier" (69) it marches quickstep
with the initial mood of the assembled gallants; even while
its sharp note expresses, for us, the proud contempt (57-61)

the singer feels for them all: the iterated "clink" is in tune
with the malicious glints of his eyes:

> And let me the cannikin clink, clink;
> And let me the cannikin clink.
> A soldier's a man: oh, man's life's but a span;
> Why then let a soldier drink.

In the third line[36] the tune softens and lingers upon a sentiment a soldier may harbor for just a fleeting moment to quicken
his zest to "drink." The second song, however, is all for sentiment, sentiment and nonsense, in sequel to Cassio's drunkenly
solemn toast to "the health of our general" (88). "King
Stephen," like the general, is "a wight of high renown" and
very exacting; the rest of us, like the "tailor," are "but of low
degree" and must be content with our humble place. Cassio's
delicious, vague comment, "I hold him to be unworthy of his
place that does those things," is a dim judgment upon his own
present conduct. Hence his ensuing mood of drunken, self-
concerned religiosity. He needs to be "saved"; he hopes to
be so: "no offence to the general, nor any man of quality, I hope
to be saved" (104-111).

> IAGO   And so do I too, lieutenant.

That slight, well-timed rub, the first the villain has ventured
upon, stimulates Cassio's final and fateful vein, defensive self-
assertiveness (112-123). "'Tis pride," says truly the otherwise nonsensical ballad above (98), "that pulls the country
down." Here it pulls down the normally modest Cassio. But
first it pulls him *up*: getting to his feet, declaring "The lieutenant is to be saved before the ancient," he determines to act
the lieutenant's part as well as he now can, in obedience to his
general's orders (1-3). He stops the drinking and politely
directs the others to "look to our business," the watch. And
certainly he can "stand well enough" and "speak well enough,"

---

[36] A single line in the original texts and regarded as such by subsequent
editors until Capell (1768) broke it in two. Notice that this verse, while
dropping the "clink," repeats the "an"-sound of the first two lines, avoiding thus a real breach of tone and mood.

though not perfectly. Refusing to admit his drunkenness he will overcome it by action. So far so good. But in departing he lets his pride issue a final and impolite command that the others cannot possibly obey: "You must not think, then, that I am drunk."

All might yet be well, however, if his pride were not exacerbated in the sequel by Montano and Roderigo, both influenced by Iago but responsible, like Cassio, for what they do. Montano wrongly allows himself to be overswayed by Iago in private conference. The villain, after feeling him out and finding him receptive (126 ff.), produces the blatant falsehood of Cassio's habitual drunkenness (134-136). Far too readily Montano assumes that Othello's judgment or "good nature" may be at fault regarding his "second" in command.[37] But this being the case, the right procedure is to bring the matter to the general's attention, as Montano himself twice intimates (137, 146). The wrong procedure would be to take direct and strong action against Cassio; and Iago gambles, successfully, on the probability that the former governor will do just that. Meanwhile off stage the "sick fool Roderigo," intoxicated with wine and confused "desires" (love-lust we may term them) regarding Desdemona (53-56, II. i. 285), affronts the lieutenant extremely: a common soldier pretends to "teach" the head of the guard his "duty" (151)! Roderigo richly deserves his beating.[38] No doubt Cassio should desist at Montano's request (154 f.); but on the other hand Montano should confine himself to a verbal protest. He badly oversteps the limits when he boldly, and at that in the presence of two underlings, seizes and keeps strong hold of the lieutenant's arm (155). Both now utter in their rage unpardonable things. Cassio will "knock . . . o'er the mazzard" the first gentleman of Cyprus. And Montano, roughly shaken off, exclaims still more roughly

[37] Shakespeare lets us imagine that Montano, the former governor, thus compensates himself subconsciously for his necessary yet sincere submission to the new "worthy governor" (II. i. 30).

[38] Which he was fool enough not to anticipate. Iago had said that Cassio "haply may strike at you" (II. i. 280): actually Roderigo is, as he later complains, "exceedingly well cudgelled" (373).

to Othello's second in command, "Come, come: you're drunk."
That climactic, fatal word!   Montano had refrained from
uttering it above when Cassio was staggering (117-123). But
now he speaks it with wrathful rudeness when the lieutenant
has considerably regained sobriety by means of action and
"wrath" (298). "Drunk?"³⁹ he cries, and proceeds to justify
his question with his sword: he is not too drunk to fence well.
Fighting more skilfully than his opponent, he presently succeeds in wounding him severely (197) though far from mortally.   Montano, enraged and excited, fancies for the moment
that his injury is fatal and tries desperately to respond in kind:
" 'Zounds, I bleed still, I am hurt, to the death—he dies!"
(165).⁴⁰   Cassio, in turn, defends himself and reattacks.   The
fight is equally balanced, and both fighters are equally deaf to
appeals, when Othello enters exclaiming, "What is the matter
here? . . . Hold, for your lives" (164-166).

On the surface Othello is here the strict commander; close
beneath the surface, the doting (II. i. 209) lover who has just
consummated his marriage (8-10).   In this double role he
plays into the hands of Iago and is separated tragically from
his best friend and supporter, Cassio.

In the glow of his love for his wife his first reaction to the
brawl is extremely mild.   When his command to "hold," iterated by his ancient, has made the two fighters reluctantly pause,
he appeals to their Christianity.   Shall "we" (170), all who
have at heart the Christian cause against the "Turks," supply
for "ourselves" the warfare which "Heaven," by means of the

---

³⁹ The question mark of Q₁ and F₁ has been generally changed to an
exclamation point by modern editors, who, along with many an actor of
the part, have regarded Cassio here as drunker than Shakespeare intended.
The claim that Montano is wounded because he tries merely to "defend" (203)
himself is confuted by the immediate context and negates the whole dramatic
design.   Shakespeare intends Cassio to be mainly but not too obviously, not
melodramatically, guilty.

⁴⁰ For the text and for interpretations differing from mine, see the *Furness
Variorum* edition, pages 137 ff., and Richard Flatter's *Shakespeare's Producing
Hand*, pages 58 ff.   I have substituted a dash for the colon after "death"
in Q₁, which omits, I think by printer's error, the ensuing "he dies" but is
otherwise superior to F₁ in its version of this line.   Q₂'s stage direction *"he
faints"* is an editor's bad mistake.

tempest, "hath forbid the Ottomites? / For Christian shame, put by this barbarous brawl." Here, however, the two begin to renew it. Instantly their general steps between them with lifted sword, loudly proclaiming death to whichever "stirs next to carve for his own rage" (i.e. instead of reserving "rage" for the "barbarous," non-Christian Turks). But quickly Othello softens his tone again. After dispatching a soldier to "silence that dreadful bell" (175, 162) he inquires with gentle urgency, "What is the matter, masters?" And when they fail to reply he says in the same tone, turning to his ancient, these significant words:

> Honest Iago, that looks[41] dead with grieving,
> Speak: who began this? On thy love, I charge thee!

Iago's "love"! In the beginning he was for his commander merely a "man" of "honesty and trust" (I. iii. 285); but Othello's "too much of joy" in rejoining Desdemona made him into "good Iago" (II. i. 199, 210); and now the Moor's connubial rapture, overflowing into new affection for all, endows the fellow with "love," with warm friendship for all, particularly for Othello. Iago responds instantly and effectually: " . . . friends all, but now, even now . . . like bride and groom." He enters fully into the mood of the "groom" Othello: unlike Cassio and Montano, he himself, he intimates, would be incapable of quarreling when their general was engaged in love's embrace.[42] Moreover his affectionateness renders him unwilling to "know" (179) or at any rate to "speak" (184) the "beginning" of this untimely and unnatural (182-184) quarrel, so utterly different from the "action glorious" (186) of true war; to which Othello had alluded above (170-172) and Othello's enthusiasm for which, so the villain hints, is entirely shared by the congenial Iago (cf. I. i. 28-30).

Thus Iago's "flag and sign of love" dissembling his "hate"

---

[41] Changed by Hanmer (1744) to "look'st." But "looks" implies that Othello is, while he turns to Iago, still including Cassio and Montano in his address, calling their attention reprovingly to Iago's deep concern.

[42] Iago's versatility is shown by the contrast between his present and his preceding (13-29) mode of referring to that embrace.

(I. i. 155-158, II. i. 317) is stationed in the territory of Othello's very soul. And this fateful maneuver is due mainly to Othello, not Iago: the general sets the strategy which the ancient fulfils in clever tactics. The villain's histrionic hypocrisy is indeed consummate but its success is due to the romantic heart of the hero. That initial success, however, is far from being conclusive. Othello's mind is that of a very just and competent commander; and as he proceeds to investigate the situation with patient urgency we have hope that at any moment he may catch a glimpse—one glimpse would suffice—of Iago's real motives.

Such a glimpse would be afforded him if Cassio and Montano would speak out frankly upon an incident that Iago has carefully avoided mentioning, the drinking episode and the ancient's part in it. But the pride of the two superior officers, abetted by their limited intelligence, keeps them silent on that score; they follow Iago's lead. "Michael" (188), simply and movingly appealed to by his commander and friend, has now the opportunity of a lifetime, if he only knew it. He sees how deeply disturbed the general is by the mystery of the strange brawl. For Othello's sake if not for his own he should here be entirely outspoken. To be sure, as he later informs Iago (285 ff.), he has forgotten the origin of the quarrel, but that fact throws into relief his vivid memory of his antecedent drunkenness (278-317); and this, if confessed to Othello, would have brought on an illuminating inquiry into the drinking episode. But Cassio will not confess; weakly and ominously he echoes Iago's assertion, "I cannot speak" (184, 188). As for "worthy Montano" (189), adjured by the new governor with finest tact and courtesy, he is at least as blameworthy as Cassio. He speaks eight evasive lines to Cassio's one. His concern for his extremely "civil . . . reputation" (190, 194) is sufficiently voluble[43] despite his too much proclaimed wound (165, 197). His smug "self-charity" disclaiming anything "said or done

[43] We may recall Juliet's comic critique of her nurse: "How art thou out of breath when thou hast breath / To say to me that thou art out of breath?" (II. v. 31 f.).

amiss this night" (201 f.), oblivious of certain questionable words and deeds of his above, is peculiarly irritating to us of the audience.

So we sympathize with Othello's sudden anger; for him Montano's smooth speech is the consummation of what appears to be a conspiracy of silence. Yet the rage of his opening lines is dismaying. But notice, first, how it is gradually subdued as the great speech advances towards the loftier attitude of the close.

> Now by Heaven,
> My blood begins my safer guides to rule,   205
> And passion, having my best judgement collied,
> Assays to lead the way. 'Zounds, if I stir,
> Or do but lift this arm, the best of you
> Shall sink in my rebuke. Give me to know
> How this foul rout began, who set it on;   210
> And he that is approved in this offence,
> Though he had twinned with me, both at a birth,
> Shall loose me.—What, in a town of war,
> Yet wild, the people's hearts brim-full of fear,
> To manage private and domestic quarrel?   215
> In night, and on the court and guard of safety?
> 'Tis monstrous.—Iago, who began't?

The general's language becomes nobly simple (213-216) when he strives to make his officers see the ignobility of their attitude. They, preoccupied with their "private" feelings, are shockingly insensible to the fact that their brawl, so "barbarous" (172) for Christian soldiers, is furthermore "foul" (210), indeed "monstrous" (217), on plain human grounds and, incidentally, from the standpoint of politico-military common sense. Note that those four succinct lines are in significant contrast with Othello's elaborate verses to Desdemona above (II. i. 185 ff.) rendering his own "private and domestic" feelings. In that crisis the lover's self-centered "soul" had to soar "Olympus-high" in windlike "joy" and then "duck again" to a "fear" of "unknown fate." But in the present crisis the known danger of "fear" in "the people's hearts," a danger envisioned by Othello at the start (175 f.), obviates all "private" considerations in the mind of the realistic soldier-governor. Every syllable in those brief, plain, but thoroughly moving lines goes to its mark and stays there, shaped and driven by a great man's public-spirited indignation.

All the more striking, then, is the flash of *personal* rage in the opening of this speech: "Now by Heaven," the heaven he had so religiously cited above (171). " 'Zounds, if I stir," i.e. by God's wounds if I take hot action. In the first scene in which he appeared Othello was roused by great provocation to a moment of loud and stern command which was nevertheless dispassionate: he maintained his serenity completely (I. ii. 81-91). For there his underlings obeyed him. Here they have disobeyed his injunction (as will Desdemona on a later crucial occasion) to speak to the point with utter frankness; they have disobeyed despite all his hitherto patience. So now he swings from one extreme to the other; as he did upon his reunion with his wife, but here with angry violence (later to be turned upon her too). Here, for the first time in the play, while Iago gloats silently, his "blood begins . . . to rule" his reason and controlling will. Accordingly his emotion is notably self-centered—the first-person pronoun is reiterated (205-213) as in his reunion speeches to Desdemona (II. i. 184-209)—until he manages to submerge his clamant "me" in selfless concern for his "town of war" (213).

He regains his better self. But not before we have glimpsed the fact that this man in a wrathful, suspicious mood could fling "loose" (213) from himself a person far more closely "twinned" (212) with him by nature and love than Cassio, namely Desdemona. Moreover, although he gets control of his present "passion" its working persists, under the surface, until the close of the episode. It has "collied" (blackened as with soot) his "best judgement" (206); and this is the faculty required for penetrating Iago's hard hypocrisy.

That faculty would have made the careful commander question, at least, some of the supposed facts adduced in his ancient's ensuing long speech instead of swallowing it whole. The villain begins solemnly:

> I had rather have this tongue cut from my mouth
> Than it should do offence to Michael Cassio.

This whopper, from the "mouth" of one whom the general knows to have ardently desired and expected Cassio's position (I. i. 8 ff.), does not strike him as even a slight exaggeration. Nor will he ask his ancient just what had happened before the point at which the fellow casually begins his story, "Montano and myself being in speech . . . " (225, 126 ff.). Here Iago again omits, as above (179 ff.), all mention of the antecedent drinking bout, supported by the shamefaced reticence of his two companions. Subtly he exaggerates Cassio's assault of Roderigo, and passes over the important fact of Montano's laying hold of the lieutenant (154 f.): "this gentleman / Steps in to Cassio and entreats his pause" (229). Properly that statement should be investigated by the general in the serene and just manner in which he probed a questionable utterance of Brabantio (I. ii. 85-91). But Othello's mood now is not just and serene. Notably his outbreak of impatient wrath, above, obviated a cool investigation of Montano's insinuation regarding Cassio's "violence" (204): ironically enough, the general's own rage took the place of an effort on his part to comprehend the extraordinary rage of his very gentle lieutenant. And now, although Othello has regained outward calm, the inward aftermath of his wrathful outbreak keeps him from questioning his plausible ancient. Did Montano really do nothing in the least "amiss" (201)? What happened before Cassio pursued the "crying fellow" (226, 230)? What were all three officers of the watch doing earlier? Did they perchance "outsport discretion" (3)? We of the audience, knowing the answers, are sharply aware that the great general would normally ask those questions. Othello's "best judgement," however, is still "collied" by smoldering "passion."

Iago artfully fans that fire by appealing to Othello's most disinterested feeling, his deep concern for the "fright" of the "town" (232, 213 f.). Previously the villain had hinted his special sympathy with his commander's love of "glorious" (186) war over against personal brawls. And now he suggests that he, unlike his two companions, was quick to anticipate the danger of the people's alarm—of that possible "mutiny" (158) which actually he himself had hoped for. Othello hearkens with silent, warm interest. Iago, as true "soldier" (220), is winning from his general the approval which Cassio has for the present lost. But he must not proceed too fast. At any moment the commander, rearousing his reason, may take into account his ancient's desire for the lieutenancy. So the villain concludes his speech with a wily, bold display of affectionate disinterestedness, citing an absolutely true and crucial point:

> Yet surely Cassio, I believe, received
> From him that fled some strange indignity
> Which patience could not pass.

"Some strange indignity"! For a moment we hold our breath: surely that vague phrase will challenge Othello's love of simple clarity. No doubt his military strictness can accept no excuse for his chief officer's conduct. But that conduct, so very "strange" in a person of Cassio's "patience,"[44] must indeed have been occasioned by "some" exceedingly "strange," possibly deliberate, provocation, which the general should now investigate patiently, summoning all the soldiers of the guard and trying to identify "him that fled." He should do this before his inevitable, if so it be, discharge of Cassio from the lieutenancy. We know that such a procedure is demanded by merciful justice, especially in view of Cassio's great devotion to his master.

But here Othello (later his bearing to his wife will be the same) is not thinking of his friend's love of him: he is preoccupied with his own love of his friend and his friend's rebuff

---

[44] Compare Iago's implicit admission here of Cassio's *habitual* "patience" with his statement to Roderigo above (II. i. 279), "he's rash and very sudden in choler." If there is truth in that statement, and if Othello may be supposed to know it, the mystery still remains: why did Cassio's *usual* patience yield to his *unusual* "choler" on the very occasion that, above all others, required of him an "honourable stop" (2)?

of it. Thus he fails to employ in his own case the Christian ethic he urged upon the two fighters above. That ethic, ignored by their hot "rage" (173), is more effectually ignored by his quietly, deeply burning anger. Certainly the fixed silence of "Michael" (188) in his proud shame is provoking; but far more culpable is the proud response in kind of his superior. Othello, hurt by the "strange indignity" done to his love by Cassio, is heedless of the "strange indignity" done by another to Cassio; and he is deaf to the hypocritic tone of Iago's plea. The following terse lines are calm in manner but fired with the speaker's underlying sense of his own "honesty and love," so deeply offended by his friend, and so tragicomically attributed now to the villain:

> I know, Iago,
> Thy honesty and love doth mince this matter,
> Making it light to Cassio.—Cassio, I love thee,
> But nevermore be officer of mine.

Unconsciously hypocritical, that "nevermore" following hard upon "love," and equally emphatic in tone, is definitely cruel. Soon (III. iii. 55 ff.) that bitter word will be tacitly retracted by Othello—but not by fate. That final line states, as the sequel will show, a fateful, fixed fact; very sad for Cassio, dreadfully tragic for Othello; and due far less to Iago's art than to Othello's "blood" and "passion" darkening his "best judgement," i.e. his reason and charity.

His emotionalism is emphasized in the closing lines of this episode with keen dramatic irony. Suddenly Desdemona enters, gazing upon the scene with wondering dismay. And Othello, losing again his calm air, concludes his speech to Cassio with sudden loud anger:

> Look if my gentle love be not raised up:
> I'll make thee an example!

The word "love" echoes ironically the "love" twice uttered in the preceding lines, quoted above. The speaker's heart, so severe to his friend, is extremely soft to his wife. In the

Senate scene he ridiculed elaborately the possibility that
"Cupid" might dull his professional intelligence (I. iii. 267-
275). That very thing has now occurred. The general will
"make . . . an example" of his chief officer for causing, supposedly, a riot that has broken the postnuptial slumbers of the
general's wife!

We smile but do not laugh:[45] Othello's dictum, not Othello,
is absurd. And the more we sense its absurdity the more we
perceive the confused emotional violence that produced it.
That dictum is a final flash illumining the inward turmoil,
gradually increasing throughout the episode and now at its
height, which Othello would fain conceal. He dissembles it
to Desdemona. Instantly he controls himself when she, advancing and perturbed by the tone and mystery of his harsh
declaration to their friend Cassio, exclaims, "What is the matter, dear?" He soothes her fondly, and unfrankly, with "All's
well, sweeting: / Come away to bed."[46] That "sweeting," in
contrast with her plain "dear" (cf. II. i. 185 and context), is
the soft acme of all his doting epithets for her: it sugars over
the acid fact that within him "all" is very far from "well."
He maintains his mild tone throughout the remainder of this
his final speech in the second act. All the more pointed, therefore, is his studious ignoring of the fallen Cassio, except for a
bitter glance at him in alluding to "those whom this vile brawl
distracted" (256). Othello himself, deep inside, is one of
those—the chief one, the most "distracted."

Cassio, like Othello but far more obviously, is given to
emotional extremes. His mood, all air at the opening of this
act, sinks now to heavy gloom. The last straw was the depart-

---

[45] We ought to laugh, however, when the actor yields to the Romantic
and academic notion that Othello, sadly sweet here, instead of wrathful, does
merely a painful military duty in making his lieutenant an example—a notion
agreeing with a falsehood uttered by Iago below (275 ff.).

[46] The quartos and the majority of modern editors omit her "dear" and
add "now" to his "well," thus smoothing the rhythm and injuring the drama.
Incidentally her "What is" and his "All's" were changed in many later texts
to "What's" and "All is." But properly she, in her great concern for his
state of mind, which she perceives to be deeply agitated, makes her "is" distinct and not unemphatic; whereas he slurs that verb, as in the proverbial
"All's well that ends well," in emphasizing "well."

ing commander's refusal to his former lieutenant of even a healing glance while, in cruel contrast, declaring to Montano, "Sir, for your hurts, / Myself will be your surgeon" (253). So now Cassio conceives himself as "hurt . . . past all surgery" (259 f.). Iago's ironic exclamation "Marry, heaven forbid!" is ours too, though we add sympathy. We see that Cassio's ensuing prose poem of ecstatic despair is the counterpart of his ecstatic verses in praise of his general's lady, rising to a note of rhetorical religious hope (II. i. 77-87). But now hard personal experience has put a simple intensity into his words and rhythms, and the climax conveys a realistic, worldly hopelessness. Comparison is facilitated if we arrange the lines into free verse:

> Reputation, Reputation, Reputation!
> Oh, I have lost my Reputation.
> I have lost the immortal part of myself,
> and what remains is bestial.
> My Reputation, Iago, my Reputation!

That fourth and final "my," stressed slightly but certainly by its metrical position,[47] follows sinisterly upon the resonant "Iago" uttered by the hapless speaker with piercing appeal. Cassio's self-concern here, like Othello's above, plays directly into the hands of Iago's consummate selfishness. Certainly the villain continues to put on an extremely clever show of plain "honesty and love" (247);[48] and we of the audience are well aware of our advantage over Cassio and Othello of having seen the fellow when he was off guard. Yet we see it is very abnormal that neither of them, in the whole course of the present scene, experiences even the faintest glimmer of doubt regarding their ancient's purposes; and we know that in everyday life an egoistic mood makes everyone abnormal, especially persons whose disposition is normally excellent; for that mood gains strength in proportion as it succeeds in overcoming excellence.

---

[47] This line like the first and third is very slow, almost hexametric.

[48] Coleridge's naïf comment upon that line is: "Honesty and love! Ay, and who but the reader of the play could think otherwise?" (*Notes on Othello*).

It opens them to the promptings of the devil—of that entire
and hypocritic selfishness which whispers within even while
it speaks from the mouth of some neighboring "honest Iago."

Thus the present episode accentuates the main motif of the
preceding one. There Othello's distinguished strength of character was able to control his emotional intensity: he succeeded
considerably, though very far from perfectly, in subordinating
the man in him to the commander-governor. Only against
his will did he reveal to us the deep personal resentment underneath his official condemnation of his silent lieutenant. But
now the slighter Cassio, reacting extremely from his hitherto
silence, pours forth his feelings to his ancient; too preoccupied
with his own shame and "hurt" to reflect how deeply his silence
must have hurt his beloved general, or how specious and dangerous are Iago's suggestions. Thus Cassio's behavior here
is a sort of revealing parody of Othello's above: he gives full
vent to the self-concern that is blinding both of them to the
villain's machinations.

Obviously Cassio should go to his general and confess his
drunkenness. That course is demanded by simple honesty and
right devotion to Othello. His first consideration should be
those two virtues and, incidentally, a clear reputation for them:
such concern belongs to what he calls in the passage quoted
above "the immortal part of myself." But his chief concern
actually is for his very mortal self. The reputation he be-
mourns so lyrically is, at least in the main, mundane repute.
And Iago, seizing upon that fact, flatters at once his own real-
ism and his companion's sentiment by satirically decrying "reputation." This, Cassio must think, is again the crude, blunt
"soldier" whom he as "scholar" could smile at for his ridicule
of chastity (II. i. 166 f.):[49] this "honest man" (266) could not
honestly sympathize with a gentleman's lofty regard for reputation. Cassio's gestures silently repudiate his companion's
view. All the more, then, is his mind fixed upon his "reputa-

---

[49] And of whom Cassio in a moment of vinous religious frankness, now
no doubt forgotten, declared, "the lieutenant is to be saved before the ancient"
(114).

tion" instead of the honorable course, confession to Othello, which an honest *gentleman* should pursue. Accordingly Iago now dares to flaunt his own disinterestedness by hinting at that very course; telling a truth, as he did above (244-246), which he is confident will not appeal to his hearer's present state of mind. "Sue to him again"—i.e. as you presumably did when you instead of me became his lieutenant—"and he's yours" (276 f.).

That result, we know, would in all probability come about if only Cassio in his suing would make a clean breast to him whom he terms "so good a commander" (278). But truth is obscured by his vanity. This he proceeds to indulge unconsciously by heaping opprobrium upon himself. Intemperately exaggerating his own intemperance he solaces himself for his faults by his sense of perceiving them fully; also by shifting much of the blame to the "invisible spirit of wine," that "devil" (282-284), that "enemy" who can "steal away" the "brains" of "men" (291 f.). In semisoliloquy he adverts incessantly to that "devil" (297 f., 312), heedless of the leer on the face of the hostile devil beside him. We of the audience, keeping a sharp eye on that face, note that Cassio scarcely glances at it, never once looks *into* it. He eyes only his own emotions.

Nor has he even a fraction of an ear for the villain's tones. Iago queries with an eagerness which he cannot all conceal, "What was he that you followed with your sword? What had he done to you?" (285 f.). Cassio replies with gloomy abstraction, "I know not." "Is't possible?" exclaims the villain with incredulous, unwary delight at the extraordinary success of the shakiest feature of his plot. But his note of exultation, like his insinuating tone to Othello and satisfied mien in the upshot (241-251), is entirely missed by his hearer. The lieutenant here, like the general above, is entirely preoccupied with his own painful feelings though, unlike him, very obviously and vociferously. "I remember a mass of things, but nothing distinctly . . . . " Cassio begins with low voice; but it rises more and more as his emotion becomes ecstatic (289-312). And we see that his remorse for his drunken oblivion is, though genuine, not nearly so great as his mounting dismay at the thought of confessing that oblivion to his general. In the end he feels overwhelmingly that he cannot face that prospect. He vociferates, "I will ask him for my place again, he shall tell me I am a drunkard" (306 f.)—

A "drunkard"! This word, uttered by Cassio suddenly and for the first time, is certainly the last that "shall" (must) be uttered by Othello whatever else he *will* say or do. He, knowing his friend is not an habitual overdrinker,[50] would not, even in extreme displeasure, insult him with that opprobrious epithet unless entirely transported by rage; and we have just seen him master his rage despite great provocation. His eventual "mood" (274) in the preceding episode was one of controlled anger due to his lieutenant's persistent silence. If this silence were presently broken that mood would be assuaged; but now Cassio's own mood is in the way. Normally he would realize, as do we and Iago (301, 318 f.), that his spree's badness is mitigated by its uniqueness; but instead its badness seems to him, in his sentimental self-concern, dreadfully and hopelessly unique. And his prolonged brooding on the fact that he, of all men, has been *once* "so drunken" (280) incubates the false vision of himself as sheerly a "drunkard" in Othello's eyes in case he pleads to him confessionally: "had I as many mouths as Hydra," he proceeds rhetorically, "such an answer would stop them all" (307-309). And so his single human mouth shall remain closed to his very human commander and friend! Though even if "such an answer" from Othello were conceivable it is nevertheless Cassio's plain duty to go to him presently

[50] Those who like to think Iago is telling the truth when he declares to Montano that Cassio, without Othello's awareness, is an habitual drunkard (126-149) should note that the villain had previously relegated Montano himself to a "flock of drunkards" (61) and that the circumstantiality of his present averment is designed to dispose Montano to check Cassio determinedly. Still wilder is the supposition that Cassio has a mighty flair for drink of which his commander is tacitly aware: this is never hinted anywhere in the play. The whole plot demands the fact that Cassio, knowing himself allergic to alcohol and therefore generally careful (34-44), is oversroyed on this extraordinary occasion by his own sentimentality, the very trait which now keeps him from confessing to Othello.

and confess his drunkenness. But we see that he is tacitly determined now not to face that duty, much less perform it, if he
can possibly avoid doing so.

Iago, inwardly exulting, proceeds to show him how. But
first the villain's jubilance throws him off guard for a moment.
Previously his adjurations to Cassio were, on the surface, flattering (266 ff., 301) but here he is openly presumptuous:
"Come, come! good wine is a good familiar creature if it be
well used: exclaim no more against it" (313-315). Can so sensi-
tive a young gentleman, so anxious to elude a reproof from
his general, put up with such a bald rebuke, from his subordinate, of his fine self-comforting oratory? Instantly, to be sure,
Iago proceeds to soften his quick bold tone into a slow whine;
expressing however an exultant and extremely palpable sneer:
"And good lieutenant, I think, you think, I love you."[51] But
Cassio, deaf to the antecedent rebuke, is here deaf and blind to
the villain's sneering leer. His self-love easily swallows the
"love" of the fellow whom he now for the first time sirs: "I
have well approved it,[52] sir—I drunk!" Drunk with his own
"I" (he repeats with unconscious irony the twofold "I" of
Iago's line) he overlooks the blatant ego of his interlocutor,
ignores it disastrously.

And now he listens dumbly to his companion's long speech
proposing that he privately seek the aid of the "general's wife"
(320-331). Ordinarily this project would strike Cassio as utterly preposterous: unfine, imprudent, cowardly, dishonest; natural enough on the lips of so crude a fellow as Iago *especially*
if really actuated by "love" (316) of his hearer; but impossible
for a gentleman-soldier *especially* if animated by a sincere and
strong desire for a sound reputation. Normally Cassio would
interrupt the ancient's speech and decline the project. But the

[51] No punctuation can be perfectly satisfactory for this subtle line, printed
as follows in F1: "And good Lieutenant, I thinke, you thinke I love you."
Incidentally Cassio's reply, quoted above, is given in that text thus: "I have
well approved it, Sir. I drunke?" Q1 and Q2 change the period after
"sir" (which they do not capitalize) to comma and dash.

[52] That is, examined and tested it; the very thing that Cassio, like Othello,
needed to do in the present scene and has not done.

fact is that he is hearkening, as he has done all along, far more to his own self than to Iago: subconsciously the very questionable project is his own. He will not put it into words; but he is relieved and glad when Iago does so.

At the outset the ancient declared that "there are *more*[53] ways to recover the general again," i.e. "ways" not requiring Cassio to "repute" himself a "loser" of repute, of "reputation" in the superficial sense (271-273). That was Cassio's own secret hope. And now, having made himself believe that his general, if honestly confessed to, "shall" (306) reject his plea insultingly he hearkens readily when Iago, nicely echoing that "shall," declares "what you shall do . . . Confess yourself freely to her" (319-324), freely and therefore secretly. This suggestion is uttered casually by the clever villain in the middle of his long speech: he and we know that his listener will not miss the point. This sort of confession, instead of the right sort, is the "way" that has been more and more desired by Cassio's soul. And the dishonesty of that way is submerged by Iago's elaborate exposition of what his companion well knows, the kindness of the general's wife and her influence upon her husband. Accordingly when Iago has completed his speech Cassio, having completed his own inner argument, can remark casually, "You advise me well" (332). In reality he has so "well," and so badly, advised himself as to ignore the viciousness of the project.

But the casual and abstracted tone of that brief reply is misinterpreted by Iago: it intimates, he fancies, a doubt of his motives. So he warmly protests his advice was given "in the sincerity of love and honest kindness." For a normal ear he protests too much. But Cassio, continuing his unconcern regarding the other, replies, "I think it freely"; then voices his determination in a tone of steadily rising self-concern: "I will beseech [of course in confessional secrecy] the virtuous Desdemona to undertake for me—I am desperate of my fortunes

---

[53] The vital word "more," preserved by the folios and Rowe (1709), is omitted by the quartos and by most subsequent editors.

if they check me."[54] Thus the plain truth leaps out at last: "desperate of my fortunes" (337); careless now of "the immortal part of myself . . . my reputation" (263-265), i.e. virtuous reputation. Certainly Desdemona as he says is "virtuous"; and earlier he fervently hoped she would be encompassed by the "grace of heaven" (II. i. 85). But now this gentleman has not the faintest misgiving that embarrassment for her, let alone danger, may be the result of his graceless and unvirtuous design. In his case, as so often in actual life, emotional chivalry yields to "desperate" self-concern.

Cassio is no more the "honest [i.e. virtuous] fool" (359) that Iago presently terms him, behind his back, than Othello is a "noble . . . ass" (II. i. 298, I. iii. 408). The villain revels in his ability to manipulate his two superiors; but in fact he deceives them far less than they deceive themselves. Their self-concealed pride, not his concealed deviltry, is the main cause of the rupture of their friendship. Both of them are possessed of normal human perceptiveness; otherwise they would not have *for us* such a full human appeal. But in the present crisis their perceptions of each other, as well as of Iago, are tragically dimmed by their pride. Othello's pride is chiefly responsible. Superior in character and station, he holds the initiative. But his haughty wrath keeps him from facing and patiently investigating the mystery of his friend's obnoxious silence, a silence that becomes the more fixed because of that very wrath. His fault, however, is fully complemented by his friend's. Cassio's vain self-blame and reputational sophistry prevent him from taking the sole course that could appease Othello, frank personal confession. So far from being an "honest fool" Cassio is a virtuous and intelligent gentleman who, subtly fooled by vanity and pride, becomes for the nonce dishonest.

[54] The quartos and the majority of modern editors add the word "here," improving the logic seemingly (not really, I think) but weakening the repeated, climactic "me" that conveys his self-concern.

(d) *turn her virtue into pitch* [II. iii. 342-394]

Supreme, however, is the self-deception of Iago. Elaborately here he hides from himself, while displaying to us, that the chief object of his hate is Desdemona.

In the Senate scene he was abashed by her apparently pure devotion to the Moor: it contradicted uniquely his principle of self-love (I. iii. 302 ff.). Presently he conceived a comforting theory: "It cannot be long that Desdemona should continue her love to the Moor" (I. iii. 348 f.). Thereupon he began transmuting that thin theory into a thick hope, a hope at once misty and ardent, a burning fog. Into it he poured every reason he could muster, every circumstance he could snatch at and distort, befogging himself hotly along with Roderigo (I. iii. 350 ff., II. i. 220 ff.). But when lacking the stimulus of that dupe's presence, Iago could not keep his hope from looking very meager. And in Desdemona's presence it fades utterly away. Attending closely to her every word, look, and gesture in the Storm scene, when everything conspired to render her emotionally tense and off guard, he could find nothing with which to impugn her in his inmost self. In soliloquy, he could attribute sensuality to Cassio (II. i. 168 ff.) and to Othello (I. iii. 392-396) and, climactically, to both of them (II. i. 304-316), but never to her: the mounting, grotesque ardency with which he unearths it in them is self-compensation for his failure to discover it in her. Ultimately his big hopeless hope is reduced to a misty disappearing flicker. He assures himself that " 'tis apt and of great credit," i.e. natural and very believable, that she "loves" Cassio though Iago cannot "well believe" it (II. i. 295 f.); and never again, in the sequel, does he try to make himself do so. But presently (it is one of Shakespeare's keenest strokes of humor) the fellow, unable any longer to imagine her as unfaithful to her husband, gives himself the odd yet "apt" satisfaction of imagining her as very sensual in her embraces of that husband (II. iii. 17-27)! Here, incidentally, he tacitly relinquishes his adulterous suspicions of Cassio also—he never recurs to them—while deepening his soul's bitterness towards him, towards Othello, and above all towards Desdemona.

And so in the course of this play we must picture Iago as always abashed and uneasy, whether speaking or silent, in her presence; also in her absence whenever her gracious mien recurs to his mind. Under her his very genius is rebuked, far more than Macbeth's under Banquo (*Macbeth* III. i. 55 f.). But unlike that naïve hero-villain Iago will not confess to himself this humiliating situation, nor his deep, increasing, festering hatred of her. His hate of Othello, in dramatic contrast, he repeatedly avows to us and elaborately rationalizes, while, however, concealing from himself its fundamental ground. No more than in the case of Desdemona will he *directly* admit that what he really and enviously abhors in Othello, as in Cassio, is the beauty of goodness. But those two gentlemen, as the villain has helped to demonstrate in the present scene, are vulnerable because of pride. She, not so—because of a quality which she alone has and which nullifies pride, namely blessedness. Iago has averred sneeringly that Othello's nature is magnanimous: "free and open," "constant, loving, noble" (I. ii. 405, II. i. 298). But the villain has had to perceive that Desdemona, while possessed of all those traits, has also something more, something suffusing and sublimating all those; as even the foolish Roderigo could see: "she's full of most blessed condition." This fact, instantly repelled by Iago with a vehemence betraying his anxiety to obscure it from himself (II. i. 254-260), is admitted by him perforce in baiting Cassio: "she is of so free, so kind, so apt, so blessed a disposition" (326 f.). And this fact, as the sequel shows, is for his soul nothing less than appalling.

Generally human affection is more or less tainted with selfishness, in one way or another; and all along we have seen Iago noting and hoarding every species of that taint. The "duteous" type of servitor whom he cited at the first was implicitly self-approving in his "doting on his own obsequious bondage" to his master (I. i. 45 f.). More obviously self-indulgent is Othello's present doting on his wife (320-324, 250-258, II. i. 207-209) and of course, by reason of his greatness, far more significant. Indeed Iago's studies of egoism have been increasingly consequential; so have been his efforts to encourage it. In the opening scene he easily evoked the proud and angry selfishness of Brabantio's parental affection. Roderigo's sexual love, chivalrous and egoistic, required more careful handling. Those two cases, however, were thrown far into the shade by the pure friendship of Othello and Cassio; and its element of self-concern, revealed in a crisis with the aid of their ancient's subtlest efforts, has yielded definitive testimony to the omnipresence of egoism. Thus Iago has been able to confirm, more and more, his belief that human affection, never entirely disinterested, is utterly unreal apart from that basal self-love which men are too cowardly or weak or stupid to acknowledge and cultivate carefully. They do not constantly keep "their hearts attending on themselves" (I. i. 51). "I never found a man that knew how to love himself" (I. iii. 315 f.). Iago alone has the real know-how; but all, however blindly and uneffectually, are *centrally* moved by self-love.

Except Desdemona. She is *centrally* humble; and this is the trait that the villain finds awfully baffling. For clearly she is not cowardly or weak-willed; quite the contrary. He is compelled to admire her will power and her influence over her husband (320-325, 348-354), two things upon which he has all along plumed *himself*. And so he is secretly afraid of her. If her humble strength, her blessedness, is really real, then his own proud strength, his very "soul" (I. i. 54), is really unreal.

But what if he can demonstrate that her unselfishness serves mainly to educe the selfishness of others? Thus her goodness, seemingly so real in itself, shall appear unreal by reason of its effects. We can see him gradually forming that notion, at first very vaguely. In the opening of this act, confronted with her face to face for the first time, and uniquely nonplussed, he ponders the possibility—he will not yet face the fact—that her goodness is unassailable because of her firm humility (II. i.

149 ff.). She seems "never proud"; accordingly "never loud"
or gaudy, averse from "revenge" no matter how much provoked, never sexually "frail," strong in her moral "wisdom"—
in short, he ends impatiently, destined to "suckle fools." But
that, palpably, is a "most lame and impotent conclusion." A
far more able and potent one is attained by Iago in the close
of the act. Whether or not her body may give birth to "fools,"
her spirit, that "blessed disposition" of hers, can certainly pro-
duce and nourish them. For here Iago, having finally aban-
doned the least hope that her own virtue can in any way be
weakened, has in compensation discovered the fact that her
benevolence is apt to abound imprudently (327-329). And
so, through his manipulation, her humble affectionateness shall
bring out and nurture, more and more, the self-love in Cassio
and, above all, in Othello (359 ff.).

Such is his conclusive project. But it is too grossly unhuman
to be envisaged nakedly even by Iago. His submerged conscience has twinges; and his pride will not confess that he has
been forced to regard as his deadliest enemy this "gentle lady"
so anxious for the welfare of others; so much concerned, at
once naïvely and acutely, for his own moral welfare (II. i. 119,
139 ff.). Consequently he now protects himself against the
thought of her, as he protected himself against her presence in
the opening of the act, by playing the buffoon. But now he does
so far more intensively and artfully. Addressing the world in
general, including the theater audience, and taking for his cue
Cassio's parting words, "honest Iago" (341), he begins very
slowly, leering in all directions, with jerky, comic gestures;
trying to whiten the black "advice" he has just given to Cassio:

> And what's he then,
> That says I play the villain?
> When this advice is free I give, and honest,
> Probal to thinking, and indeed the course
> To win the Moor again.

> For 'tis most easy   345
> Th' inclining Desdemona to subdue
> In any honest suit. . . .

Those last lines may recall to us the Moor's initial picture of
her: "These things to hear, / Would Desdemona seriously incline" (I. iii. 145 f.). Iago intimates that, like "the Moor" and
like us, like the world in general, he himself can harbor a sentiment for Desdemona, of whom he had remarked to us, above,
"Now, I do love her too" (II. i. 300). Under the cloak of
his buffoonery the villain is seriously trying to humanize himself in our eyes and, more importantly, in his own. He, a
man of the world, can have like the world a feeling for all
that is "free" and "honest" (342). He is not subhuman: he
would not "change" his "humanity with a baboon" (I. iii. 318).

But, in the present crisis, he would change it with "devils":
suddenly in the midst of his speech he invokes the "Divinity
of hell" (356 f.).[55] His effort to make himself feel human,
in the first half of the speech, was inwardly unsatisfying: he
will now feel *super*human—as clever as "hell." He can easily
"put on" the world's moral sentiments and with equal ease
repudiate them as unreal in comparison with what the world
pleases to call "sins" (357). Thus he bolsters his pride, at
the same time relieving his conscience, as at the end of Act I, by
viewing his evil scheme objectively, i.e. as inspired by the
self-love everywhere at work in the world and conventionally
attributed to "hell." But his deeper intents are masked
throughout by his humorous manner. With the zest of a
comic actor he swiftly sketches the triangular drama of Cassio
plying Desdemona while she "pleads strongly to the Moor,"
and while Iago pours "this pestilence" into the Moor's ear
"That she repeals him for her body's lust." And this final
touch to the picture—the virtuous "fool" Cassio lusted for
grossly by the pure, refined, and devoted wife—is indeed ab-

[55] This abrupt change is in line with the opportunism shown in Iago's
previous soliloquies. To fancy he had planned the change deliberately, when
he began his speech, is to elevate *his* art and intellect at the expense of
Shakespeare's.

surd enough to make us laugh. But quickly the laugh dies as the villain chants his dire coda, hiding his awed hate of her with utmost buffoonery of tone and gesture:

> So will I turn her virtue into pitch,
> And out of her own goodness make the net,[56]
> That shall en-mash them all.

That passage is a hellishly beautiful equivoke. Her white and unturnable "virtue" can be virtually turned into "pitch"; an ensnaring net can be made "out of" the very stuff of her "goodness." Thus her humble benignity shall no longer seem to the villain essentially and dismayingly real. It shall be shown to have the "virtue," the essential potence, for reducing the interrelations of "them all," herself included, to a black, tangled muddle, a pitchy "mash."

"I," declares the conceited villain, will bring all this about; but we know that by himself he cannot. The powers of evil can, however—if they can sway Othello along with Iago. This small fellow does not believe in those powers: " 'tis in ourselves that we are thus or thus" (I. iii. 322). But we have seen them working in his self and, more subtly and ominously, in selves better than his; working, we now feel, to make a "net" of love and hate that can indeed entangle "all"—including Iago. Unwittingly he has displayed their large strategy and strength.

Hence there is deep dramatic irony in Iago's melodramatic references to those dark powers at the end of Act I and, climactically, in the close of Act II. Here the earlier "Hell and night" (I. iii. 409) are resolved into the far more definitive and portentous "Divinity of hell," i.e. the supernatural science, hypocrisy, and power of "devils" (356 f.). And Iago's initial and vague "monstrous birth" (I. iii. 410) has now become a very definite monster, one of the "blackest" possible "sins" (357): the resolve to turn Desdemona's goodness into "pitch."

[56] The comma, absent in Q1, indicates that "pitch" along with "net" is subject to the verb "en-mash" ("enmesh" in Q1). The sound of "mash" in close proximity to "net" inevitably suggests a mesh while its denotation relates it to the softness of pitch.

Certainly that hellish "Divinity," for Iago merely an instrument of self-relieving buffoonery, has succeeded in making an
instrument of him. Unconsciously he frames his citation of
the "Divinity of hell" with allusions, equally casual, to the
Christian sacraments, "baptism," "the mass," "seals and symbols of redeemed sin" (349 f., 384), never elsewhere mentioned
by him. Here his own person is in our eyes, not his, a hellish
sacrament: this little naturalist is an embodiment of supernatural evil. This worldling devoted to self-centered "will" and
"reason" (I. iii. 330-335) becomes now, beyond his reason and
will, *religiously* wicked.

Accordingly, at the end of his soliloquy, his buffoon mien
gives place to a new look of hellish *patience*. This look settles
and deepens while he hearkens to the loud complaints of the
suddenly and comically inrushing Roderigo, here much dis-
illusioned and newly rebellious in mood.[57] On previous occasions Iago has responded with quick sharpness to his dupe's
exceptions (I. i. 4 ff., I. iii. 305 ff., II. i. 223 ff.). Here, after letting him speak his fill, he says with querying deprecation, slowly
lifting his hands in company with his rising tone: "How poor
are they that have not Patience?"[58] A religious consideration!
The audience perceives that the villain is employing one of the
leading Christian virtues[59] in the service of evil. His patience
of "wit" is more preternatural than "witchcraft" (378 f.): it
is the very devil's deliberation. We feel that particularly when
he remarks yawningly of the dawning light, old symbol of religious hope: "By the mass, 'tis morning; / Pleasure and action
make the hours seem short" (384 f.). Here is the bored zest
of hell. The impatient Roderigo retires speechless, overawed

[57] Roderigo's seriocomical prose speech, leading over from the buffoon
villainy of Iago's preceding verses to the hypocritic moralism of his succeeding ones, is a nice example of Shakespeare's art of tonal and dramatic transition.

[58] The question mark (F1, Q1, Q2) has been generally replaced in
modern texts with an exclamation point. As to F1's capitalization of "Patience": Q2 suggestively retains the capital, apparently for emphasis, while dropping it in all other cases where it is used in Iago's present speech in F1, e.g.,
"Wit" and "Witchcraft." Incidentally, "Patience" is here trisyllabic.

[59] See the sequence of Faith, Hope, Patience, Charity, etc., in *The Faerie
Queene* I. x.

by his companion's tone. Then Iago, stifling his yawns, tells himself briefly and coldly "two things" that "are to be done"; and ends by abjuring "coldness and delay." He dare not pause in his course now; he dare not consider its outcome. His smothered conscience infects him with a chilling ennui which can be countered only by incessant, steady, villainous action. The whole speech tells us what Iago does not know: he has devoted himself religiously to the patience that is infernal.

(e) *Cassio . . . guilty-like*   III. i—III. iii. 154

III. i.

Cassio enters saying to his musicians, "Masters, play here . . . and bid *Good morrow, general.*" The powers of evil could be baffled, we know, by a restoration of harmony "here" in this new "morrow" between Cassio and Othello. That fact is symbolized by the serenading music, sweet enough despite the clown's disparagement of it. Its fine strains and his raw jokes[1] give us sentimental-humorous relief immediately before the drama's central crisis. At the same time this episode (1-32) prepares for that crisis. For we see that Cassio will persist in avoiding plain speech with the "general" unless, perchance, the general will take the initiative: Cassio's music seems a dumb appeal to him to do so. But Othello does not appear; and his vicarious dismissal of the music by means of his clownish servant intimates what appears plainly in this scene later: he does not yet "greatly care" (18) to try to elicit the confession which "Michael" had so offensively refused to make at the proper time (II. iii. 188 f.).

Consequently Cassio proceeds with his fateful project of appealing secretly to "the general's wife" (27), whom he has hitherto refrained from mentioning in this scene though rightly his serenade would have been offered to her as much as to her husband.[2] Indeed every detail of his procedure betrays his

---

[1] His jest upon "wind-instruments" (6 ff.) parodies the sex motif of this drama.

[2] In accordance with the old custom of saluting a couple with music on the morning after their union.

hidden awareness of the dishonesty of his project. To Iago
he speaks uneasily of procuring "some access . . . to virtuous
Desdemona" (37 f.), here as above (II. iii. 336) so terming
her to ease his sense of his own unvirtuousness, and omitting
mention of the unpleasant fact that the "access" must be private.
Excessively grateful is he when the villain, also omitting the
word "private," promises "to draw the Moor / Out of the way,
that your converse and business / May be more free." Cassio,
oblivious as ever of the other's diabolical looks, declares warmly: "I humbly thank you for't. I never knew / A Florentine
more kind, and honest." Thus Iago has rivaled Cassio's closest
friends in his famous native city (I. i. 20)! Cassio is "humbly"
thankful for a friend so "kind" and "honest" (the devil, we
know, is often such a friend) as to help him conceal from himself the fact that his present project is unkind and dishonest.
Cassio, thus abetted by Iago, presently beseeches Iago's wife
(53 ff.):

> If you think fit, or that it may be done,
> Give me advantage of some brief discourse
> With Desdemon alone.

"Alone"! That final word, emphasized by the intimate and
rhyming "Desdemon," comes to his lips frankly at long last;
but now it is saturated with his awareness that such an interview, no matter how "brief," "may be" brought about only
by questionable means and is really not at all "fit."

But that unfit interview, now assured by the complaisance
of Emilia (56 ff.), would have been forestalled if Othello had
sought a private talk with Cassio; and this, we know, is what
Othello should have done and still should do. It is demanded
by his professed Christianity and friendship, by his abiding
"love" of Cassio the man in spite of the lieutenant's fall (II.
iii. 172, 248, 349 f.). In the opening of the preceding scene
the general enjoined his "Michael": "tomorrow with your
earliest / Let me have speech with you" (II. iii. 8 f.). That
friendly conference, obviated by Cassio's weakness, ought to be
brought about by Othello's magnanimity.

Hence the meaningfulness of the talk reported by Emilia between "the general and his wife" concerning Cassio (46 ff.). Desdemona speaks "stoutly" on behalf of him. Othello, tacitly rescinding his angry and cruel "nevermore" (II. iii. 249), promises to consider the reappointment of Cassio. But his cool, politic, and evasive manner stands in strong contrast with the love which he again "protests" (50) for his friend, a contrast felt by Cassio along with us. It is true that "wholesome wisdom" (49), as Othello avers, is a valid ground for postponing indefinitely the former lieutenant's reappointment; but the suffering thus involved for his friend should not be regarded so callously by Othello. Friendship and charity together with his nobility of nature demand that he should immediately "take . . . occasion" (52) for a private interview in which Cassio would be induced to "speak" his "bosom freely" (58). But Othello will not do so. His pride, deeply hurt by his best friend, withholds himself from that friend, all the more cruelly because he has fully subdued the anger that blazed up in the crisis of the preceding scene. His temper has cooled down into a hard, serenely proud aloofness. And this is accentuated by his wife's strong advocacy of Cassio even while he himself is curbing his own strong "likings," i.e. inclinations, towards his friend: significantly he tells her that he "needs no other suitor" (51).

III. ii.

And so it is with great relief, we must feel, that he turns now to his other love and older friend, his military profession. At the same time this brief scene, properly to be regarded as the concluding episode of scene i, establishes a main impression that the dramatist has been building up in us: the chief onus, in this crucial act, is to rest upon Othello. Absent from the stage in the preceding scene, he was incessantly and cumulatively referred to.[3] And now he takes the center of the stage commandingly. Iago's scheming "to draw the Moor apart," "out of the way" (II. iii. 391, III. i. 39 f.), proves to have been

---

[3] Notice how those references, sparse at first (III. i. 2, 12), come thick and fast towards the close (III. i. 46 ff.).

supererogatory. The Moor, the military governor and "lord"
(4) of Cyprus, has drawn himself away from his wife and from
the thought of Cassio to write "letters" to the Venetian "Senate" (1 f.), his "approved good masters" (I. iii. 77), and to
inspect the island's "works" (3). Iago, for the time being, is
dismissed: with a slow, rueful "well," comic to us, the fellow
contemplates the packet handed him by his master and then
departs reluctantly, a letter carrier. And notice that the succinct decisiveness of Othello's present speeches is the opposite
of his manner a few minutes ago in talking of Cassio (III. i.
46-53). So that "this fortification" (5) on which the supreme
commander is now so intent seems an external defense against
an urgent internal problem. We of the audience "wait upon"
his "Lordship" (6) for a human, instead of a merely military
procedure, regarding his late lieutenant who is now his exigent
friend.

III. iii. 1—154

In Cassio's confession to Desdemona, made meanwhile off
stage for dramatic economy, he has unbosomed himself, we may
assume, in regard to his shameful drunkenness, a subject now
dropped, however, as having no importance in the coming
crisis. Of main importance is the girl's perception that her
"lord," despite his protests above to the contrary, is not at
present really friendly in spirit to Cassio, who, on the other
hand, does as ever "love my lord" (6-11). She avoids any
semblance of censuring her husband behind his back. But clearly she knows that his "strangeness" to Cassio is far from being
completely motived, as he has claimed, by "wholesome wisdom" (III. i. 49): he is, in fact, standing "further off / Than
in a politic distance" (12 f.). He is contravening, though she
will not say so, the canons of friendship. But as to herself: "If
I do vow a friendship, I'll perform it / To the last article"
(21 f.).

And so she now, like the others, evinces pride, though surely in its most innocent and humane form; but fateful because
it precludes that which she now extremely needs, uttermost

prudence. That conjuncture was foreseen by Iago only in a dim, distorted way, his insight into pride, in himself and others, not being acute. His definitive thought regarding her was that her "blessed disposition" or "goodness" (II. iii. 326 f.), though excessive and silly, also unreal (he would fain believe) in comparison with self-love, was in itself impregnable. We, on the contrary, know that her goodness, while real and strong, has all along had in it a vein of self-will that could easily render it vulnerable; and that the least touch of pride is especially dangerous in a "blessed disposition."[4] In the first act Desdemona was humbly and boldly prudent, as in her speech to her father regarding her husband (I. iii. 180-189). But her present speech to Cassio regarding her husband is boldly imprudent (19 ff.). To be sure its tone is half light: she is trying hard to cheer Cassio because his despairing grief impugns, for her, the goodness of his "general" (18), her own beloved lord. But clearly she is carried away by her sense of new power over her husband consequent upon the consummation of their marriage: "His bed shall seem a school, his board a shrift" (24). And her solemn pledge to regain Cassio's "place" (20) for him, the first—and worst—interference on her part in her lord's affairs, is ominously overweening. And for us the omen is intensified by the silent entrance of Othello and Iago, in the background, just when she has ended her speech with the assertion that she "shall rather die" than desert Cassio's "cause."

Cassio himself is disconcerted by the extremeness of her tone. His conscience, all along uneasy, is "now" so "very ill at ease" (32) that he insists on departing when Othello appears, despite her quick injunction to him to "stay" and her slow, reluctant "well" in permitting him to go. She, unlike him, had not contemplated the least element of secrecy in connection with their interview. So now for a silent moment (34-40) she is very much abashed, glancing after the disappearing Cassio, whispering a little with Emilia, and watching uneasily her approaching lord.[5]

[4] Witness the story of the once blessed Lucifer and his angels, a story the point of which would be lost on Iago.

[5] To conceive her mien as innocently serene during that silent moment is to injure the drama badly.

Thus the total scene confronting Othello is from his stand-point the very worst possible. The last place the dismissed lieutenant should be is here; the last thing he should do is to slink from here when discovered by his commander. Othello's friend, strangely silent to *him*, has secretly sought his wife, who a short while ago was speaking "stoutly" (III. i. 47) for him; and who, instead of hastening to greet her husband now, is visibly discomposed. He is deeply, silently shocked. "Hah?[6] I like not that," the watchful Iago exclaims for him (34). Othello hears the words clearly, as he shows later (109 f.), but responds with startled vagueness, his gaze fixed upon the scene before him: "What dost thou say?"—as though heark-ening in a bad dream to his own thoughts voiced at his ear by another person—*if indeed it be another?* Iago's diabolic answer, "Nothing, my lord; or if—I know not what," implies that he has said really nothing—unless "my lord" knows "what." Othello's demeanor has shown him, and us, that he has been heavily struck by great suspicion of Cassio and Des-demona both.

But now Othello, gripping himself, banishes all *conscious* suspicion of "my wife": she of course may be innocent in in-tention though "Cassio" not (37). Moreover he sees, and Iago sees he sees, that the one absolutely damning fact against Cas-sio is his stealing "away so guilty-like" (39). Othello would fain believe, against the evidence of his senses, that the depart-ing figure was not his friend: "I do believe 'twas he"; the tone is incredulous, dreamlike.

Desdemona sharply challenges his daze: "How now, my lord?" Normally she would have inquired "What is the mat-ter?" and have listened with silent sympathy to whatever he had to say, as above (II. iii. 251-258). She must see that his mien is more darkened now than it was upon another crucial meeting with her when, after letting him tell his mind, she gave him quiet love and comfort in her arms (II. i. 196). But this time, after her moment of hesitation, she takes a strong

[6] The question mark, omitted in the quartos, introduces the interrogative tone used in the ensuing speeches, especially Othello's.

and wrong course, blinded by her new and proud sense of power over her husband. She should have at once confessed to him that she, like him, is disconcerted by Cassio's sudden departure; but she decides, very mistakenly in this case, that taking the offensive is the best defense. She covers her own discomposure and increases Othello's by pleading vehemently for a "suitor" whom, as he told her previously, he alone would deal with (42, III. i. 51). Her assertion that this suitor—she boldly terms the ex-officer "your lieutenant"—"languishes in your displeasure" and "truly loves you" augments her husband's daze. Why should a suitor who is properly *his,* as her "your" and "you" have emphasized, seek his wife privately instead of himself and then slink away? "Who is't you mean? . . . Went he hence now?" But she, intent on her own purpose, overrides his dubious mood. She intensifies her plea: "My lord" becomes "Good my lord" and finally "Good love": "I prithee, call him back"; "Good love, call him back" (41-54).

And that, indeed, is precisely what Othello ought to do, whether or not he continues to postpone his decision regarding the lieutenancy. Here the fate of all concerned is placed definitively in his hands. A personal interview in which he would cross-question Cassio with friendly, searching firmness has been needed all along: now it is needed desperately. It could banish Othello's new suspicions; but these, unfortunately, have deepened his pride's hidden wound. All that is best in him requires him to summon his friend at once; but his pride refuses to do so. "Not now, sweet Desdemon," he says after a moment of uncharacteristic hesitation—"some other time."

But those words, naturally, challenge her to try to make him "name the time" (62), pressing close to him with warm and patently sincere endearments. These he welcomes gratefully: they enable him to keep at bay his dark suspicion of her; but her increasingly insistent advocacy of Cassio has a contrary working. And so Othello's state of soul becomes two opposite tides meeting; concealed from her, however, by his proud self-control. She demands, "When shall he come" (67)? No an-

swer.   She urges, "Tell me, Othello"[7]—wondering that he
should "stand so mam'ring."[8]   She assumes he is hesitating
crucially between the demands of friendship and military discipline.   And so she proceeds, lucklessly, to recall to him the
picture of "Michael Cassio" as an old and intimate friend of
them both; but she does so with gently mocking playfulness
to relieve his stiff tension.   He stops her, however, in mid-
course.[9]   He has managed to listen patiently to her talk of
Cassio's humble grief (52 f.) and sincere penitence for a very
slight (in her view) "fault" (63-67).   But he cannot bear the
memory, no matter how playfully recalled, of his smooth
friend's intimate part in his courtship of Desdemona (70 ff.).
"Prithee no more," he exclaims sharply; but at once softens
his tone: "Let him come when he will"—any time except now—
"I will deny thee nothing."

Nonplused she draws back from him, looking into his eyes:
she has an extremely dim and passing glimpse of the truth.
"Why, this is not a boon. . . . "   Not for her own sake is she advocating Cassio but for her husband's: she is entreating him to
do a "profit" to his own self.   That is the simple truth; but unfortunately she proceeds to blunt its edge.   She cannot resist declaring, with renewed playfulness, that she may later proffer "a
suit" verily designed to test his "love" for her, a weighty suit,
"difficult" to frame and "fearful to be granted."   Othello, the
reverse of playful in mood, doting but more and more doubtful,
is well aware that she could "touch" his "love" in a way that
would indeed be "fearful" (80-83).   Suddenly, therefore, he
craves to be away from her "a little" (85).   And she promptly,
unquestioningly, obeys his strange mood; for now she feels that

[7] Here F1 has a period, Q1 and Q2 a colon.   An expectant pause is demanded of the actor by the context and the rhythm.
[8] Q1 has "muttering," a much narrower but suggestive term.   See "mam-
mering" and its cognates in the Oxford English Dictionary and also in older
lexicons.   It denotes a deeply perplexed, quivering hesitation accompanied
generally by muttering or stammering.   Obviously Othello is silent here, but
his visage works and his lips move expressively.
[9] The dash inserted by Q2 after her "I could do much" is obviously called
for.   She means that having done "much" (73) she is ready to do "much"
more (74)—when he checks her.

she has been overweening. And so, in moving off after a quick
"farewell," she turns to humble herself before him utterly.
Reversing her initial tone (41-43) she says with simple, pathetic
devotion (88 f.): "be as your fancies teach you: / Whate'er
you be, I am obedient."

Othello, struck to the heart, banishes for a moment the
rising blackness within him. Raptly gazing after her he exclaims with great intensity:

> Excellent wretch![10] Perdition catch my soul
> But I do love thee: and when I love thee not,
> Chaos is come again.

Her plain last words were full of selfless sympathy. His lovely
lines are full of sympathy for self, like his lyric greeting to her
yesterday but with far darker omen. Then, "my soul" feared
"unknown fate" and sensed coming "discords" (II. i. 184-200);
now, "my soul" shrinks from "perdition" and "chaos." And
his soul entirely fails to enter upon the way of reason and salvation. Instead of pondering her love of him, from the beginning until now, a love in the main unselfish and meek, he
envisages solely his own love of her, not in the least apprehending, but revealing to us, how mainly emotional and infirm
it is. For his own sake, not hers, he is desperately determined
not to confront his black suspicions of her.

Therefore he would fain banish also his far more plausible
jealousy of Cassio. But, as Iago along with us has perceived,
he is deeply shaken by his recollection of "Michael Cassio" as
go-between in his wooing (70-74, 94-100), the close friend who
is now "so guilty-like" (39) using "my wife" (110) as go-
between in the matter of the lieutenancy. Cassio's present conduct is obviously not "honest" (103),[11] not straight and candid,
not befitting and comely, despite the fact that his past conduct
has always been all of that—or *seemed* to be (124-127). There's
the rub! Othello struggles against the feeling, so "horrible"
(115) to him, that his best friend has all along deceived him.

[10] An expression of extreme yet superior pity and fondness.
[11] See in the *Oxford English Dictionary* the various meanings of this word,
formerly so comprehensive in its denotation and connotations.

Cassio, underneath his loyal and chivalrous surface, may be dishonest, not only crooked but, as Iago finally intimates, "foul" (137), unchaste. The word is Iago's but it expresses Othello's feeling that Cassio has "wronged" him (143) by making love, successfully or not, to Desdemona. In the same breath Othello, for the first time and in our view dreadfully, calls himself Iago's "friend" (142).[12]

Dreadfully, for in this episode Iago becomes the alter ego of Othello's worst self. He is a fiendish "friend" who "echoes" (106) the other's monstrous emotion and suggests insistently that this emotion must become conscious thought (96, 107, etc.). And so it must, unless dispelled. It could have been and still (75) could be dispelled by a private, honest conference with Cassio. But we see that such a conference, all along so repugnant to Othello's pride, is now being utterly obviated by the rising intensity[13] of his jealous emotion. And this, at the same time, prevents him from justly scrutinizing Iago as we of the audience are doing. Iago acts cleverly; but much more must Cassio, if false at heart, have done the like! And the more Othello is shocked by his conviction of his *old* friend's speciousness the more wary, we know, he ought to be of his *new* companion's display of "love" and "honesty" (118, 153). Cassio's slinking away, above, was certainly "guiltylike"; but more so is Iago's present slinking demeanor; and here his commander, as never before, gazes searchingly into his face.[14] Othello sees that the fellow has, "shut up" in his "brain," "some horrible conceit" (113-115). This, we know, is the hell-inspired design of turning Desdemona's "virtue into pitch." And we know that Othello should perceive, at the least, that the ancient's very conscious and furtive mien cannot

---

[12] The new intimacy is emphasized by Othello's warm "thou" and "thy." Iago responds with "you" (144-154) omitting, however, his customary "my lord," which he resumes presently (155) but employs more sparsely in the future than formerly.

[13] Denoted effectively by his "By heaven" (106) in Q1, ruinously displaced by the weak "Alas" of F1; see Note on the Text. Incidentally we of the audience, unlike Othello, feel that Iago echoes him "by hell"!

[14] Just the opposite was Othello's nonchalant bearing towards him at the start (I. ii. 1-28).

be accounted for entirely by a supposed reluctance to impugn Cassio's honesty. But Othello thus accounts for it because Othello thus wills: his own will, here and throughout the sequel, betrays him to the devil in disguise, a disguise far from impenetrable. Proudly unwilling to cross-examine his old friend Cassio, and yet unable to endure the formless looming of his jealous feelings, he must project those feelings into definite "thoughts," with the aid of his new "friend" Iago (142-144). He believes that his own feelings are his present alter ego's "thoughts": he is dreadfully forming his own meaning when he demands fervidly, "What dost thou mean" (154)?

(f) *Good name*   III. iii. 155—390

Othello means, as the devil knows, to preserve at all costs his "good name," "my estimation" (I. iii. 275), i.e. good repute. Previously Iago had expressed his own prosaic, cynical view of "reputation" (II. iii. 266-272). Now, suddenly and startlingly, as though rapt, he emits lofty poetry in praise of the same, a passage seemingly beyond his natural powers, but immediately prepared for by the potent verses wherein he proposed to imitate the "devils" in arraying "blackest sins" with "heavenly shows" (II. iii. 356-359). The present passage is a heavenly show that makes us shiver. It is hellish ventriloquism: Iago's voice is uttering the "soul" (90, 156) of Othello.

Shakespeare and we, also Iago in his satanic negative way, know that reputation should *not* be "the immediate jewel" of any soul; but that it constantly tends to become such in highly stationed persons, even those of noble nature like Othello, especially in moments of crisis. In the beginning Othello put reputation in its proper secondary place (I. ii. 17 ff.), below love and duty, and kept it there throughout Act I, though naturally concerned for it. But now his "name" is pre-empting the forefront of his thoughts because his pride, normally controlled and right, is becoming more and more passionate and wrong. Yet even in blaming him we sympathize with him keenly. For Cassio, now entirely concerned for his own re-

putation instead of the fair fame of "the Moor" (II. i. 43 ff.),
is blindly acting the part of one "that filches from" Othello
his "good name" (159); and thus is instigating in the great
man a sin that will in *him* be far deeper-going, the sin of cherishing reputation as "the immortal part" of oneself (II. iii.
263), "the immediate jewel" of the soul.

And now Othello's soul is so passionately self-concerned
that he can no longer repress his suspicion of Desdemona.
Hitherto only Cassio's "honesty" has been in question. But if
"*men* should be what they seem" (128) yet are not, the same is
true of *women*. The tempter at his ear, and in his heart, says
loudly:

> Good name in Man, & woman (dear my Lord),
> Is the immediate Jewell of their Souls. . . .[15]

Ostensibly this means merely that Desdemona's repute will
suffer from Cassio's advances. But to Othello it means that
she has secretly accepted those advances: she, more than Cassio,
is stealing (157), filching (159), her lord's good name, robbing
him of a great "Jewell," making him "poor indeed." Accordingly his previous ejaculation regarding Iago, "By heaven, he
echoes me" (106), has now the violent, flaming sequel, "By
heaven, I'll know thy thought" (162).[16] But he is perfectly certain he knows it already: it is his own. So he scarcely heeds the
triumphing villain's three ensuing speeches. Normally he
would resent very forcefully the fellow's word "cuckold"
(167). But it is merely a low echo of the thing his soul is
saying loudly now to itself. Othello's long-drawn-out, shud-
dering "Ha?" (165) questions his own soul; and the answer
is deep "misery" (171). The subconscious "monster" (107)

---

[15] The capitalization and punctuation of these two lines in F1 have, together with the word "their," the effect of insinuating that the "woman" is
necessarily, even *if* subordinately, involved.

[16] The "thought" of Q1, instead of the "thoughts" of F1, seems to me
correct here. Othello's and Iago's "thinkings," "thoughts," and "meditations"
(131 f., 136, 141, 154) are now resolved into one "horrible conceit" or
"thought" (115 f.) which Othello has tried to suppress, his wife's unfaith-
fulness.

in his own "heart" (163)[17] has become a fully formed
"thought"; and this, inbreeding with his emotion, has produced the "monster" that now "feeds on" him, as Iago and
we see—the all-consuming passion of "jealousy" (165-167).

But Othello, rousing and turning sharply upon his companion, rejects with proud scorn "thy inference" (183) that
"I'ld make a life of jealousy" (177). This, we know, is precisely what Iago himself does: his loveless life is a "vicious"
process of spying "into abuses"; for him "jealousy" is a constant state of mind (145-148), not a passion of the soul. His
only passionate emotion is hate. Ignorant of love, he, unlike
Othello and us, has no *inward* sense of the extreme, burning
resentment produced by love gone wrong. He can help feed
the flame: he perceives acutely the symptoms, but he knows
not the essence, of the *passion* of jealousy. Hence he is genuinely surprised when Othello declares with passionate intensity that "on the proof, there is no more but this: / Away at
once with love, or jealousy" (191 f.). Never once had the
villain, even in his most malignant visions, anticipated in his
general such a "madness" of "jealousy" (II. i. 310, 320) as
would make him put his love and wife absolutely "away."
The villain is astonished—and hellishly "glad" (193), Desdemona being his central aversion.

Meanwhile Othello has unwittingly biased the "proof" by
protesting that it does not make him jealous

> To say my wife is fair, feeds well, loves company,
> Is free of speech, sings, plays, and dances well: 185
> Where virtue is, these are more virtuous.
> Nor from my own weak merits, will I draw
> The smallest fear, or doubt of her revolt,
> For she had eyes, and chose me. . . .

"To say . . . ." But Iago has not said nor even hinted at what
follows: not a soul suggested it, except Othello's soul. All
along he has allowed himself subconsciously to know the "fear"
—the word echoes his yesterday's "fear" (II. i. 192)—that

[17] When Iago declares that "You cannot" know the thought of "my heart,"
Othello, turning away from him, looks into his own.

her bearing and temperament, so very different from his, would occasion "her revolt." Sadly enough his very modesty regarding his "own" social "merits" (187) is feeding his jealousy. An unpoetic poet, a gentleman charmingly unaware of his great and distinctive charm, deprecating his own basic reserve and plain simplicity (I. iii. 81 ff.), he is fascinated yet hiddenly shocked by his wife's freedom and buoyancy. Nevertheless if he were not now befogged by jealousy he would reflect, as we do, that she was so very "free of speech" (185) in her pleading for Cassio, as for herself in the Senate scene, just because of her strong devotion to Othello; and that her present social exuberance, so different from her maiden retiredness (I. iii. 94 ff., 145 ff.), is the overflow of her wifely love and joy.

Tragically revealing is his curt, axiomatic reference above to "virtue" (186), his first use of this word in relation to Desdemona. He avers that, *supposing* she has it, whatsoever she does is "virtuous." But she has never been and is not for him, what she is for Cassio and all of us, "the virtuous Desdemona" (II. iii. 336, III. i. 37). Iago, dreading and hating it, is certain of "her virtue" (II. iii. 366). Othello, in ironic contrast, observes impersonally, "Where virtue is . . . . " He says, "She had eyes, and chose me"; but *she* said, "I saw Othello's visage in his mind": her love pierces to "his very quality" (I. iii. 252), his essential virtue. *His love has "eyes" for all her qualities except her essential virtue.* This he would normally have learned to perceive soon; but now his jealousy has made his blindness passionate. And so the very warmth of her love is bound to suggest more and more that it is not confined to him: all her charms will testify against her virtue.

Indeed, not yet really knowing her as a person, Othello is impelled now to think of her as a type, a lovely, lively, unmoral feminine type. Therefore he is not wrathful, as he would properly be even if convinced his wife has sinned with "Cassio" (197), when Iago, affronting all the facts of her individual life, dares to class her coarsely with Venetian wives addicted to hidden "pranks" (202).[18] "Dost thou say so?" cries Othello, instead of his initial "What dost thou think?" (105). His thinkings have become identical with Iago's pretended thinkings; he will assure him, below, with a dreadful depth of suggestion for us, "I am bound to thee for ever" (213). So Othello's soul is not surprised, much less enraged, by his companion's present thought: he is startled and dismayed by the fact that the other can "say" so plainly the thought forming in his own mind. Later he will say it with utmost plainness himself: his wife belongs to the type called "whore" (359).

But at once Iago is emboldened to make Othello confront two facts very incriminating in the case of a woman of that "disposition" (201): his wife's deception of her father (206 ff.) and the outward unnaturalness of her marriage (227 ff.). These things, which deeply disturbed Othello in the first act, while Iago watched with silent gloating, were thereupon dismissed from his mind, dismissed—as the villain has just hinted while Othello, though averse to flattery, acquiesces silently— because of his "free and noble nature" (199). But we know this is only a partial truth. Othello's pride, imperfectly noble, overrode those two facts instead of justly considering them, and thus stamped them into his subconscious mind. Hence his "soul's" sense that "unknown fate" threatened great "discords" and eventual "chaos" (92, II. i. 195, 200). And now the "foul and violent tempest" with its "hills of seas" (II. i. 34, 189) that rose between him and his wife is succeeded by a rising storm in his own soul; he can "discern . . . Nothing at all" (II. i. 1 f.) of her real self. He sees her in the dim, lurid light of her supposed type. And the heaving depths within him yield up those deeds of hers that seem to him so damnably characteristic of that type.

Iago elaborates upon the theme, "She did deceive her father" (206-211), while Othello tells himself silently, "She

[18] Compare his "foul pranks," above (II. i. 144). Iago, as ever, can say with an air of strong conviction what his soul would love to believe: he excels in make-believe.

has deceived . . . thee" (I. iii. 294). He becomes more and
more deeply moved, the more so because of his efforts to maintain a surface calm (214-224). His better mind tries for an
instant to regain control: "I do not *think* but *Desdemona's*
honest"—his first use of her name in the present episode. His
reason tells him, faintly, to think of her as the individual person that she is, the one whose love of him made her break so
violently with her "world" (I. iii. 251), with her father and
her social class. But the dark tide within him sweeps that
thought away. Her personal nature, the "Desdemona" actual
and "honest," is submerged in a "nature" as impersonal as the
spirit of the "enchafed flood" (II. i. 17): he proceeds, "And
yet how *nature* erring from itself" (227)[19]—

"Ay, there's the point," exclaims his alter ego. This is
the point which, when plausibly and vividly expressed by Brabantio, shook and silenced Othello in the Senate scene. Her
marriage, externally viewed, was "against all rules of nature"
(I. iii. 101), directly counter to that "Whereto we see in all
things, nature tends" (231), as Iago now puts the matter; he
continues:

> Foh, one may smell in such, a will most rank,
> Foul disproportions, thoughts unnatural—

Abruptly the villain checks himself and asks "pardon," scared
by the dreadful look in his companion's face. And here if ever,
we know, Othello should smite the fellow's mouth. But Iago
avers he is speaking, not "distinctly" (definitely and distinctively) of "her" (235), but of her "clime, complexion [tempera-
ment], and degree" (230), i.e. her type, which is exactly what
Othello himself is doing. Silently he is shaping the gross notion
touched by Iago which, no longer really believed by the villain,
has become now Othello's own: the notion that this woman's
"love to the Moor" was a "violent," unnatural, transient "lust"
for his "body" (I. iii. 336, 348-360). The "thoughts unnatural,"

---

[19] The whole context shows that Othello does *not* mean (pallidly and
academically): Desdemona may have an "honest" (chaste) "nature," i.e.,
personal character, which may, perhaps, have gone astray.

in Iago's lines quoted above, would be natural in the type of
woman produced by, in Othello's phrase, "nature erring from
itself."

How horridly that idea has mastered his imagination, restrained in the presence of the exceedingly "honest," observant,
prosaic "creature" Iago (242 f., 258-260), is shown by his ensuing soliloquy. Passionately he cries out, "If I do prove her
haggard"[20]—a wild falcon, a thing of "nature erring"—she
must be cast off to "prey at fortune," to swoop upon whatever
quarry her "will most rank" (232) shall choose, ripping away
"my dear heart-strings" (261). Self-pity, here, sinks his voice
(and our pity exceeds his): he envisages the external charms
which "chamberers," such as Cassio, have and he himself lacks;
the sort of charms to which, we know, Desdemona has from the
first (I. ii. 68) been impregnable. For him, however, she is
now not "Desdemona": in the following lines "Shee" (emphatic
for "she") is the pronoun for a type, "these delicate creatures."
The first words are whispered; the rest is rising horror:

> Shee's gone. I am abused, and my relief
> Must be to loathe her. Oh curse of marriage!
> That we can call these delicate creatures ours,
> And not their appetites: I had rather be a toad,   270
> And live upon the vapour of a dungeon,
> Than keep a corner in the thing I love
> For others' uses . . . .

Here he is absolutely convinced of her guilt. The reasonable
doubt that his mind had endeavored, more and more weakly,
to maintain has been swept away by his imagination. The "if"
and "haply" of his preceding clauses are verily "gone."[21]
His whole self-centered soul is unconditionally certain that "I
am abused." And the certainty produces instantly a proud,
terrible loathing. Unless he rejects utterly "the thing I love,"

---

[20] This word is alliteratively opposed to the preceding "human" (260).

[21] Hence the crucial importance of the full stop after "gone." The
quartos give a comma, retained or changed to a semicolon by certain modern
editors; but the sense demands a period. Note that Othello's and Iago's fourfold "if" above (239, 248, 250, 260) was softened down to "haply" (263)
in preparation for its present disappearance.

every "corner" of it, his *own* "appetite"[22] must be worse than promiscuous; must be worse than that of the least delicate of "creatures," a dungeoned "toad," imbibing nothing but vaporized rottenness. For us his delusion is the "vapour" of his own very horrid "dungeon" of jealousy.

But the conclusion of his soliloquy is far more ominous than anything he has hitherto said. "Yet 'tis the plague to Greatones . . . . " He regains his surface calm by regarding himself, like her, as a type, one to which her sort, those "delicate creatures" with their "appetites," are bound to be unfaithful. Thus he relieves his pride and, in the same breath, hardens his delusion. That which has happened to him is "destiny unshunnable, like death" (275). That "plague" (273)—the term recalls the poisonous "vapour" above (271)—he terms finally the "forked plague," the horns of a "cuckold" (167), "fated to us" from birth (276 f.). This notion, so *coldly* wild and coarse, absolutely at variance with his innate noble-mindedness, makes us see how solid has become the prison of his black obsession—just before Desdemona re-enters the scene:

> . . . . Look where she comes:[23]
> If she be false, Heaven mocked itself:
> I'll not believe't.

He is astounded, fascinated, by the contrast between what "she" is in her living, moving presence and the "thing" (272) that "Shee" (267) has become in his mind. For a fleeting moment he has an inkling of the truth: "I am to blame" (282). The underlying meaning of those muttered words throws us into great suspense. He may do what he plainly ought: confess to her the gist of what he has just been saying to himself. That

---

[22] The question mark after "appetites" in F1 indicates inexpressible disgust, but it breaks the train of imagery: the colon of Q1 and Q2 is therefore preferable.

[23] The quarto reading, "*Desdemona* comes," is surely out of context. She is not now the "Desdemona" from whom he parted (87) and whom he tried abortively, a few minutes ago, to regain (225). The quarto prefers sonority and metrical smoothness in these lines (277-279) to dramatic abruption. Hence its version of the second line: "If she be false, O then heaven mocks itself."

is demanded by his better self, his "free and open nature" (I.iii. 405), a ray of which shone out in the lines quoted above, responding to his wife's free, open, and lovely mien. She could now do much to clear his "chaos" (92) if only he would tell her frankly why he is "not well" (283). But quickly he turns away from her. Lifting his hand to his head, as he did a moment ago when brooding alone upon "this forked plague," he avers stonily, "I have a pain upon my forehead here."

The comic touch there, for us, serves to accentuate, and is at once submerged by, our sense of the dreadful fixity of his tragic obsession. Very tragic is his deception here of his wife. Previously he had been reserved and even unfrank to her; but now, giving the audience a weird shiver, Othello employs something very like the devilish,[24] grotesque, Iagoan dissimulation. Of course he feels that she is dissimulating to him. Previously he withdrew himself as gently as possible from her warm endearments (80-87). Now when these are intensified by her sympathy with his supposed illness he finds them absolutely intolerable: abruptly he puts away her hands and her "napkin" (287). "Heaven mocked itself" indeed when it created this lovely "thing" (272) animated by an "unnatural" (233) yearning for him among her other "appetites" (270). His momentary and merely emotional belief in her while she was approaching invited her caresses. So in swift revulsion he rejects the caresses and the belief: "she" is nauseatingly "false"; that feeling is violent in him. But all the more hellish, therefore, is his dissembling. Humanly he would here be provoked to utter some wrathful word betraying to her his suspicion of her and Cassio. But pride prevents: he proudly maintains his "government" (256).

Thus the present episode lays bare the essential tragedy that has been growing steadily since the opening of the play. There a hateful villain, apparently the direct opposite of Othello, represented him as "loving his own pride and purposes" (I. i. 12).[25] Presently we were shown that his "purposes"

[24] The devil, like the cukold, has horns that he prefers to conceal.
[25] In retrospect this passage is very outstanding because it is Iago's sole explicit reference to his commander's pride.

were good, his "pride," and therewith his self-control, in the main noble. But increasingly we were made to feel that those two traits, so excellent in his politico-military profession where they were entirely subordinate to his sense of public duty, were dubious in the realm of love, wherein his "purposes," in striking contrast with his wife's, were very much self-centered. We saw his proud composure becoming more and more dangerous because it waived the conscious and frank attention demanded by the potential sources of discord with his wife. And now we see that his pride, in the service of jealous love, has become utterly blinding, while his virtuous habit of self-control is converted into a vice. Thus he is no longer Iago's opposite. Iagoan egoism and hypocrisy, latent in all men, are now active in Othello. The hero of the play has come to share the villain's deceptiveness. His jealousy could be cured if openly vented.[26] His rage is not, in itself, inevitably tragic: his dissimulation is. The essence of the tragedy, to be shown increasingly from now until the end, is Othello's proud, jealous *control*, both patient and violent, of the violence of his jealousy.

Hence the intensely symbolic quality of the episode of the handkerchief. We easily conceive that if Othello's jealousy were simple and open he would notice that the "napkin" with which she tries to bind his head is the very precious one he gave her, and would fling it far from him with revealing anger and disgust. But his difficult dissembling, his inward conflict, prevents his viewing it: he does not even *see* the handkerchief. With eyes averted he merely feels it; and he feels it to be "too little"—like her love for him. At the same time her all-absorbing love, which had caused her to "reserve" the handkerchief "evermore about her / To kiss and talk to" (295 f.), renders her entirely oblivious of it in her concern for his supposed illness. Thus we are made to perceive more sharply than ever her fond imprudence. Her heedlessness now of the "token" which he "conjured her she should ever keep"

---

[26] As in the case of Leontes in *The Winter's Tale*. He tells his innocent wife to her face that she has committed adultery with Polixenes (II. i. 60 ff.), the Cassio of that play. His jealous obsession, open and curable, is tragicomic; so is the play as a whole.

(293 f.) emblemizes her blindness to the possibility of jealousy in him. We know that her feminine intuition, generally so excellent, should discern in his present demeanor a "pain" (284) far deeper than physical; and indeed her words intimate (285-287) that she is aware his headache is more or less due to "fancies" (88). But her love, which at the first caused her to ignore the Moor's complexion, refuses now to divine the least dark tinge in her husband's "fancies." She is so sure, unhumbly sure, of seeing his "visage in his mind" (I. iii. 253) that she will not, in the present crisis, see his mind in his visage. Thus her white fault supplements his black sin. She is pre-occupied with her ideal of his inner goodness; he, with his image of her specious badness; and that image is fatefully intensified by her demeanor. Her obtuseness to the morbid agony of soul which he cannot all conceal, seems to him feigned by her to conceal her awareness of its cause. She, i.e. the type of woman he thinks she is, regards her own foulness lightly. Therefore she can treat his pangs with light, kind sympathy, confident that she can easily caress them away. And so the unnoted falling of the handkerchief beside them signifies their loss of a rare bond of love that required utmost humble heed and care: discreet in her; in him unselfishly frank, "free and open."

Thereupon the bad bond between Iago and his wife comes to the fore. Emilia's affection for Desdemona, though warm and increasing—a fact to which Iago is characteristically blind—is still sheerly sentimental, not in the least dutiful. It is easily overtopped by her fear of her hard, suspicious mate and her will to "please" and conciliate him (299 ff.). Her good impulse to give him merely a copy of the handkerchief (296 f.) is thin and momentary, like Othello's kindly impulse regarding his wife, above (278 f.). Emphatically we are told that all along she has been quite willing to "steal" or "filch it" for him (292 f., 309, 315). And when he snatches it from her hand her pity for her mistress is external and coarse: "Poor lady, she'll run mad." Emilia is substituting sympathy for conscience; and we are sure she will obey, in the immediate

future, Iago's harsh injunction of silence regarding the theft
(316-320).

The outcome, however, of the villain's design of secretly
getting the handkerchief into Cassio's hands is still more dubious to us than it is to him. "This," he says, tossing it in the
"air," and then pocketing it, "may do something" (322, 324).
It *may*, we know, clear the air by eliciting from Othello an open,
passionate avowal to Cassio and Desdemona of his suspicions
of them. This is what ought to happen; and the possibility of
it, however slight, remains open till the end. But it is rendered
extremely unlikely by the ensuing terrible climax of the present
scene.

Othello's last words to Desdemona above were curt, formal,
and desperately effortful: "Come, I'll go in with you" (288).[27]
So speaking he moves off quickly with face still averted; while
she follows closely, saying with blind, deep pathos, and with
full-flowing rhythm in contrast to his stabbing sentence, "I am
very sorry that you are not well." We are left to imagine their
"dinner" with "the generous islanders" (280): Desdemona,
"well desired" by them (II. i. 207) and loving their "company"
(184) because of their high esteem of her husband, but keeping a warmly anxious eye on him; Othello, loving and loathing
(268) her graces, dissimulating his jealousy with more and
more difficulty, thereby intensifying the dungeoned toad
"poison" now at work in his very "blood" (270 f., 325, 328).
So that eventually his hidden obsession burns deep within,
fiercely and fumingly, "like the mines of sulphur" (329). His
reason is stupefied by the confined fumes of his hellish[28] passion,
which therefore rages all the more in his imagination. He re-
enters alone, somnambulantly; like one who, having lost the
"medicine" of "sweet sleep" (332), is walking in the vapors of
a diseased daydream. The thing he has kept himself from

[27] In F1, and there alone, this line is immediately followed by *"Exit."*
The later folios have *"Exeunt"*; the quartos, *"Ex. Oth. and Desd."* after
line 290. He rudely departs ahead of her, I think, despite his words "with
you."

[28] Sulphur and brimstone being redolent for Shakespeare's audience—
somewhat less for us—of the fires of hell.

saying to his wife, in her presence, bursts out now in his cry
to his nightmare image of her: "Ha, ha, false to *mee?*"

The twofold expletive is a doubled echo of the "Ha?"
(165) he uttered when his false image of her first became explicit. And the mournful "Shee's gone" above (267) has now
a sulphurous sequel, "false to *mee?*" The pathos of her false-
ness to her *own* self and "Heaven" (278)—not a jot of that
better emotion remains in him now. All his soul is concen-
trated upon his own "much abused" (336) self, his balefully
proud "mee." And so for a moment he can actually harbor
the flagrant wish that he had remained ignorant of her unfaith-
fulness: "it harmed not *me*" (339).

> I found not Cassio's kisses on her lips . . . .
> I had been happy if the general camp,   345
> Pioners and all, had tasted her sweet body,
> So I had nothing known . . . .

The nameless female he is speaking of becomes here a mere
"sweet body" in his morbid fancy, which ranges down all the
way from "Cassio's kisses" to the gross touches of the dirt-
digging "pioners."

But instantly he recovers, evoking a better vision of the
"general camp" (345). Raising his sunk head, looking off into
the distance and back through all his soldier years, he sees "the
plumed troop" under the "royal banner," listens to "the neigh-
ing steed and the shrill trump," sees and hears all the "Pride,
pomp, and circumstance of glorious Warre" (349-354). At
the same time he looks through the gleaming surface into the
real "quality" (353) or business of war, symbolized by the
cannon, the "mortal engines" whose "dread clamours" may
partake the meaning of the "immortal" heaven's thunders
(355 f.). War at its best exemplifies the divine justice. So
the noble-spirited soldier has a "tranquil mind," contentment
with his lot, and "ambition" transfigured into "virtue" (348-
350) by devotion, courage, magnanimity: such virtues are felt
in the imagery and in the very march and lift of the glorious
verses. And we think of the "very quality" of Othello him-

self, "his honours and his valiant parts" (I. iii. 252-254). He, however, is uttering no self-praise. For the moment he drops the first-person pronoun so clamorous in his previous, and succeeding, speeches. He is rapt by a noble vision of the profession to which he belongs—or *did* belong: the pageant has the intensity of something sadly, vividly beautiful seen for a moment in the midst of a bad dream.[29] The initial "farewell," iterated (348-351), then submersed, keeps on throbbing beneath the ensuing verses. And at the end it suddenly rearises (357) to dismiss "for ever" (347) all the risen glory, in the andante of this great line:

> Farewell—Othello's occupation's gone.[30]

Those final words, anticipating the finale of the play, are for us a plangent though prepared surprise. "Is't possible, my lord?" we exclaim with Iago. Act I from first to last showed that the Moor's professional devotion was not in the least impinged upon by his marriage. Thereafter we saw his love for his wife swiftly growing in quantity though not in quality, in profuse romantic emotion, not in real depth. Its selfish quality engendered his secret jealousy, which, in turn, has terribly augmented that. *His kind of jealousy has intensified his kind of love.* And now we realize fully that the self-centered intenseness of his love has rendered him incapable of giving it up without wrecking his very life. "Chaos" (92) has indeed displaced the "tranquil mind" and "virtue" that he possessed in his profession: inevitably "Othello's occupation's gone."

His chaotic agony together with the visional "stirring" of his better "spirit" (352) in the great war speech makes him turn fiercely for a minute—a breathless minute for us—upon the "villain" (359 ff.). Seizing the fellow, and, for the first time, looking very critically into his eyes, he has a true intuition: "If thou dost slander her and torture me . . ." (368). But Iago,

---

[29] Like Prospero's greater vision in *The Tempest* IV. i. 145 ff.

[30] His sudden and unprecedented reference to "Othello" in the third person, capping the impersonality of the whole passage, has a piercing primitive appeal: he is now simply a name. His individual being is "gone"—like his wife (267).

genuinely startled and scared, can enact the part of a simple, honest "friend" (380, 142) more convincingly than ever, assisted by his master's "waked wrath" (363). However, Othello's passion defeats his wakened intuition in a far more tragic way: it keeps him from perceiving that Iago might be both upright and mistaken. This thought presses upon us of the audience as we listen to the villain's very intense and plausible asseverations. Suppose his unique appeal to "Grace" and "Heaven" (373) were genuine; suppose that in this "monstrous world," where "honesty" is a "vice" and "not safe," he, nevertheless, is "direct and honest." All the more, then, his simple, constant, zealous "love" (380) of his "noble lord" (367) would make him "spy into abuses" and imagine, in persons close to his master, "faults that are not" (147 f.), even at the risk of incurring, as now he has eventually done, his lord's great wrath. Accordingly now, if ever, Othello should suspect his ancient's accuracy, should reflect that the fellow's loyalty, here so blatant, has prejudiced all along his "observance" (151) of *others'* loyalty. Othello's roused intuition, the more it inclines to trust the fellow's emotion, should all the more distrust his discernment. And that, precisely, seems about to occur when Iago, apparently overcome by his hurt feelings, begins to move away. Mastering his own passion Othello says quietly and frankly:

> Nay stay: thou shouldst be honest . . . .
> By the world,
> I think my wife be honest, and think she is not:
> I think that thou art just, and think thou art not—   385

A touch of the humility he so deeply needs! Doubtful of Iago he is also doubtful, far more promisingly, of his own thinkings. His intuition tells him that he and his ancient, particularly now when both have been evincing violent feelings, are untrustworthy witnesses. And we know that there are two others whom he has not yet fairly examined, Desdemona and Cassio. Properly he would now fulfil his promise to interview Cassio (75), then straightway go to Desdemona

alone (87), all the while maintaining his present effort to
"think" dispassionately and humbly.[31]   But that effort, though
real, is weak and confused.   His climactic word "just," above
(385), substituted for the previous "honest" (381), may mean
either honest or accurate, but the heat of Othello's underlying
emotion has melted the two meanings into one.   He fails to
"think" that Iago may be both honest and mistaken; that inchoate thought is swept away by his resurging passion.   His
moment of rational doubt, instead of resulting in rational inquiry, rouses in him a blind rage against his doubtful situation:
his touch of saving humility is consumed by flaming egoism.[32]
He shouts out:

> I'll have some proof!   My name that was as fresh
> As Dian's visage, is now begrimed and black
> As mine own face.   If there be cords, or knives,
> Poison, or fire, or suffocating streams,
> I'll not endure it.   Would I were satisfied!   390

"My name"[33]—"my estimation" (I. iii. 275), renown in
"glorious war" (354), eminence in the "serious and great business" of Venice (I. iii. 268), the great and good "name" that
is his soul's "immediate jewel" (155 f.)—once as clear and
radiant as the "visage" of the goddess of chastity, is now
imaged by his "own face," a face "begrimed" with the sweat

[31] The reality of the effort is stressed by the fourfold "think" in the
passage quoted above; contrast his previous single "think" (225).   Ominous,
on the other hand, is the conditional "be" of the third line followed by the
positive "is."   Compare and contrast the present "be honest" with the "be
false" which he predicated of her above (278).

[32] The main point is *not* that Othello's nature is exceptionally averse to
suspense but that passionate pride, in every man, is the foe of suspensive
reason.

[33] The "her name" of Q2, etc. (the whole speech is omitted in Q1) is
intended, of course, to connect with "my wife" above (384).   Then, however, he was speaking quietly and trying to think objectively.   But now his
egoistic passion, as in the previous and preparatory episode (154 ff.), submerges the thought of *her* repute (155) in favor of "*my* good name" (159).
"By heaven, I'll know thy thought" (162) anticipates the present raging
cry, "I'll have some proof."   And his previous obsession with the image of
himself as "cuckold" (167, 276) prepares for his present preoccupation with
his *own* blackened "name."

of his real agony and the soot of his imagined shame.[34] "My name": the phrase parallels Cassio's "my reputation" (II. iii. 265); the lieutenant's lament was dramatic preparation for his commander's. But the thin though fateful vanity of Cassio's concern for his repute is terribly overtopped by the passionate pride of Othello's solicitude for his "name." Cassio was selfishly heedless of endangering the good name of "the virtuous Desdemona" (III. i. 37): Othello's rage has lost her, and is almost ready to destroy her. His phrase "Dian's visage" is redolent of the purity and beauty of "Heaven" that he formerly saw reflected in the face of "Desdemona" (277 f.). But her name now is gone, and her real "visage" is supplanted in his soul by the face of his "own" writhing dishonor, the "it" that he will not "endure." Almost he has identified his "wife" (384) with his own agony: he is striving subconsciously to make the identity complete. "If there be cords . . . . " He yearns to strangle or stab, or poison or burn, or suffocate "it," the black infamy—now well-nigh one with his image of his wife—that is suffocating him. He must destroy the thing which is destroying him, which is spoiling his "occupation" (357) and degrading the very essence of him, "my name."

(g) *wide revenge*   III. iii. 391-479

But first he must destroy the recurrent notion, created by his love, and climactically urgent a moment ago, that his wife may be not "false" but "honest" (225, 278, 384). "I'll have some proof! . . . Would I were satisfied!" (386, 390). That loud, vague phrase "some proof" is in ironic contrast with the clear and calm word "just" in the preceding verse. His wish for just and rational "probation" (365) is devoured by the terrible craving to be "satisfied." He is "eaten up" by a "passion" (391) that must be, if anything, all in all. The "proof"

---

[34] Above, his dark complexion became as "black" (263) in his own morbid fancy as in Iago's malicious caricature (I. i. 88, II. iii. 33); and his present extreme term "begrimed and black" recalls Brabantio's "sooty" (I. ii. 70). For the Elizabethan audience a lost soul was black; for all of us, blackness symbolizes evil passion.

he must and "will" (393) have is "some" further experience[35] *in his imagination* which, nullifying his love's promptings on behalf of his wife, will identify her absolutely with his misery and concentrate his whole soul upon the destruction of both.

Iago aids him by suggesting three lying tableaux, extremely vivid and subtly cumulative: "her" in the act of adultery, Cassio's dream of that act, and the handkerchief in the possession of Cassio. But Othello's ensuing determination for revenge had really been made already by his inmost soul in the "my name" soliloquy[36] quoted above. And Iago's first two pictures simply externalize a horrid thing at work in Othello's own imagination. He has fancied "Cassio's kisses on her lips" (341) and imaged "her sweet body" (346) as that of a "whore" (359). So now when he groans out "Death, and damnation—oh!," sinking his head and covering his face with his hands, his soul's eyes see "that prospect" which they had already envisioned, see it as convincingly as if it had appeared to his "mortal eyes" (395-400), while Iago proceeds, uninterrupted, with his "salt" and "gross" words (404). Then Othello, lifting his head, makes a very faint attempt at mental recovery: "Give me a living reason she's disloyal" (409). The word "living" is ambiguous; and "reason" is as sharply ironic for us as for Iago. We know that Othello's soul desires, not a real "reason," but imaginational "satisfaction" (390, 393 f., 401, 408). And Iago proceeds to give him "the ocular proof," i.e. to "make" him vividly "see" (360, 364) what he has already made himself believe: that the smooth and fluent Cassio while possessing "Sweet Desdemona"—the villain uses piercingly the long unuttered lovely name—abets her fully in being "wary" to "hide our loves" (419 f.). For both their sakes she must continue

---

[35] In Shakespeare's time "proof" could mean "experience." Othello, after toning down "ocular proof" (360) into "some proof" (386), drops the word altogether.

[36] In that passage Othello becomes oblivious of Iago's presence and has to be roused by him at the close (391), as in the case of preceding monologues (165, 228, 334, 358). And during the remainder of this scene a number of Othello's lines are semisoliloquy. Thus his responsibility is emphasized: Iago is merely a helper.

to seem, as "cursed fate" demands, to belong entirely "to the Moor" (426).

Thus the more intent the two supposed lovers are upon indulging their lust, the more intent they must be upon concealing it. This idea is the apex of Othello's delusion, the definitive feature of the monster in his soul. At the first it was a shapeless thing "in unknown fate" (II. i. 195). It took on dim but real form when Cassio, in sequel to his evasiveness in the Brawl scene (II. iii. 188 ff.), slunk away "from my wife" (37) at Othello's approach. And her ensuing frankness and warmth conjoined with his gnawing notion of the unnaturalness of her passion for her husband (227, 263 ff.), has come increasingly to seem to him *her* way of concealment. She and Cassio are both extremely "wary" but in opposite and complementary ways. She, sensuous and amoral, busily affectionate to her husband, covers over genially the guilt she does not deeply feel. Cassio, acutely conscious of sin but anxious to regain the lieutenancy, is circumspect and sly; "loose of soul" (416), however, in a dream inspired by his guilty conscience.

No wonder, then, that the fictitious "dream" denotes for Othello "a foregone conclusion" (428): *it is really his own dream!* And Iago is now, more than ever, an embodiment of the evil spirit working in Othello's own soul. This has indeed produced a "monstrous birth" (I. iii. 410). The "monster" fictitious in Iago's "thought" (107) is real in his master's imagination. Othello's agonized cry "O monstrous! monstrous!" (427)—the antithesis of Iago's hypocritic cry "Oh monstrous world!" above (377)—is addressed to a thing that is for him utterly real and living. That thing is not merely an adultery: it is an adulterous prodigy. The very sweetness of that "sweet creature," Desdemona (419, 422)—all the intimate, lovely kindness, more or less sincere, which she has shown and will continue to show to her lawful husband—expresses, even while it hides, the "unnatural" sensuality of her "nature" (227, 233), of her "sweet body" (346) and "sweet soul" (V. ii. 50). Such is the monstrosity; nigh incredible; but his own eyes, from the first very myopic regarding her and now entirely swayed by the devil of jealousy, have given him in watching her "the ocular proof" (360). His cry of monstrous horror is followed by a cry of demonic rage: "I'll tear her all to pieces" (431).

But his rage is at once restrained, deepened, and widened by the thought of the symbolic handkerchief, vivid with its strawberry pattern, so often—not just "sometimes" as the villain puts it artfully—seen by him in his "wife's hand" (434 f.). He will not speak to his coarse companion of its great preciousness. He says with restrained intensity, with simple dignity and, for us, piercing pathos, "I gave her such a one: 'twas my first gift." Iago, pretending ignorance of that fact (308, 437), is really unaware, is incapable of apprehending, how much this "trifle" (322) signifies. When he avers that in all probability this is the handkerchief he saw "Cassio wipe his beard with," he is startled by the terrific reaction of his listener.

"If it be that"—Othello is choked, as never before, by surging emotion. The actual handkerchief fades out (it is not further alluded to in this scene) while his imagination seizes upon all its vital, and deadly, meaning. The "that" signifies his costly love, entirely given to his wife, lightly regarded by her and disdained by her paramour. His proud, blind rage sweeps away the "if," his own and Iago's (439 f.). His soul, already sure of "Cassio's kisses on her lips" (341, 422 f.), can "see 'tis true" (444), see with vivid finality, when he pictures the "slave," his onetime best friend, wiping his mouth with "that," that which is unspeakably precious:

> Oh that the slave had forty thousand lives:
> One is too poor, too weak for my revenge . . .
> All my fond love thus do I blow to heaven—'Tis gone.   445
> Arise, black vengeance, from the hollow hell!
> Yield up, O love, thy crown and hearted throne
> To tyrannous hate . . . .

His revengeful wrath is as melodramatic as its cause is, for us, unreal; but it is desperately sincere. And his words are more veracious than he knows. His "love" is indeed royal in mien, though not in quality, like the "crown" and "throne"; it is intensely "hearted" but self-centeredly "fond": that is the essence of his tragedy. He cannot rid himself of that love, as he here fancies: the very histrionism of his effort to "blow" it "all" into the air assures us that it is very far from "gone." But the "vengeance" rising now in his heart is indeed "black"; the "hollow hell" echoes to his invocation of it. And his new "hate," thoroughly "tyrannous," will enslave and batten upon his unabrogable love.

His sudden, new word "hate" crowns the precedent "revenge" and "hell." We, not Othello, know that those terms have hitherto been Iago's. In the first act they were nodes (I. i. 7, 155; I. iii. 102, 373, 375) of the jealous darkness which, through the agency of Iago, subordinately of Brabantio and Roderigo, pressed close upon the charming but dubious light of Othello's love. And now this light has yielded up itself, in Othello's phrase above (447), to that darkness. And the darkness, the black passion, is, like the devil, both serpentine and violent: insinuative, poisonous as "aspics' tongues" (450); but always ready to rage like a "foul and violent tempest" (II. i. 34), as in Othello now. His "blood," his "passion," having "collied" his "judgement," rules him absolutely and leads the "way" (II. iii. 205-207). The "way" for him now is the violent destruction of the two offenders. His "blood" burning with poisonous "fire" sends out a raging cry for "blood, blood, blood" (326-329, 389, 451). Othello, the opposite of Iago in human character, is unawares co-operating with him, in revengeful "hate," in the service of "hollow hell."

Indeed we are made to feel in the finale of this Temptation scene that the hero and the villain of the play are mysteriously coalescing under pressure of the powers of evil.[37] Each is the complement of the other. Iago has the wariness, Othello the furor, of jealous, proud, vengeful hate. And we realize that each from the beginning of the drama has had a latent capacity

[37] Later Shakespeare will combine hero and villain in a single person, Macbeth, with the Witches symbolizing the mystery and the pressure of the powers of evil.

for the other's distinctive vice. Iago, too small and hard of
heart to experience real furor, has a cold mental fury and a
"fire" (I. i. 76) of malicious fancy enabling him at the first to
enter into Brabantio's selfish rage, and into Othello's now. On
the other hand Othello's strong self-control, exhibited so nobly
in his first scene (I. ii), *not* nobly in the "government" (256)
of his feelings during his wife's presence above, enables him now
at the very height of his rage to attain a wary "patience" (452)
analogous to Iago's, though far more dreadful.

A deeply and grandly wicked composure is the essence of
Othello's Pontic Sea speech (453 ff.). Here are no "hills
of seas"; here after "tempest" comes a dreadful calm. The
lines have a "compulsive course" (454) in tragic contrast with
the "labouring" ideality of his previous sea speech: his present
thirst for "a capable and wide revenge" (459) is far stronger
than his former "soul's joy" (II. i. 185 ff.). But the present
speech, like the other, and more than it, is lacking in the noble
simplicity of tone that marked the initial story of his love
(I. iii. 128 ff.). His mood is no longer "free and open" (I. iii.
405); and his rhetorical proclivity, subordinate in the first act, is
now apt to be dominant. The present lines are too adjectival
to be noble. But their highly wrought grandeur conveys his
ambivalent passion, fierily avid yet frigidly circumspect. To
outward view his vengeful hate is to be as imperceptible as the
forward motion of the tideless Pontic Sea: the "icy current"
of it "keeps due on," on and on with secret constancy, to the
"wide," boundless ocean. To the inward view, however, i.e.
in the "thoughts" (457) of himself and "Iago" (444, 453)—
the companion soul to whom, as never before, he is now addressing all his speeches[38]—that icy, quiet current is "bloody" and
"violent" in its "pace." Othello has fused the fire and ice of
the traditional hell in one "compulsive" stream of passion.

And this, he declares, will never "ebb to humble Love"
(458)—the sole power that could save him from "fond love"

[38] Accordingly he does not invoke "*yond* marble heaven" (460) as he
did "*you* mortal engines" above (355): he makes an oath *by* that heaven *to*
himself and Iago—to the *one soul* that now animates them both.

(445) and proud hate. His Christianity, alluded to off and on, notably by Iago (II. iii. 349 f.), is utterly gone. Last night he urged that "Christian shame" should dispel "barbarous" and selfish "rage" (II. iii. 170-173). This sort of rage he himself exhibited extremely, above, when he cried out for "blood" (451), for tearing "her all to pieces" (431). But instead of dispelling that rage he has mastered, conserved, and deepened it. His present state is not mere barbarity: it is hell, the direct opposite of religious humility. The least touch of "Christian shame" would give him some concern, however faint, for the welfare of his wife's supposedly guilty soul. But he is concerned, absolutely and entirely, for "wronged Othello" (467). And the "sacred vow" he proceeds to take "by yond marble heaven," a logical sequel of the "hollow hell" above (447), engages "my words" (460-462) along with "my bloody thoughts" (457), engages them *religiously*, in the service of the black powers opposed to "humble Love."[39]

The Christian Moor, chief warrior of Christian Venice against "the Ottomites" (II. iii. 171), dedicates himself, on his knees[40] and with dark face upraised, to the supernatural powers of "black vengeance" (447)! His "very quality" (I. iii. 252) has for the time being become entirely "collied" (II. iii. 206), "begrimed and black" (387).

The "practices of cunning hell" (I. iii. 102) are far blacker and craftier than Brabantio could foresee, and more so than Iago could possibly believe. In the close of each of the first two acts the villain cited the powers of evil mockingly: "Hell

[39] Thus the phrase "marble heaven," common in Renaissance literature, is here used by Shakespeare with unique suggestiveness, its chief suggestion, surely, being that of pride. In the Pontic Sea speech F1 capitalizes (in addition to the proper nouns) the following: Icie Current, Love, Revenge, Marble Heaven, Sacred. The speech is omitted in Q1; Q2 capitalizes Heaven. The reader would do well to note all of Othello's previous and subsequent uses of the word "heaven" in their various contexts.

[40] F1 has no stage direction here, but the modern custom of having Othello kneel when, and not before, he speaks his "sacred vow" is justified and effective. Yet the fact that the quartos place "*he kneels*" at the close of his "black vengeance" speech above (442-450) is very suggestive. Othello's soul, if not his body, bows to the "hollow hell" as well as to the "marble heaven."

and night" (I. iii. 409), the "Divinity of hell" and the devils' "blackest sins" (II. iii. 356 f.). But now, in the close of the Temptation scene, he suddenly kneels beside Othello and shares his "sacred vow," with a grotesque yet mystic combination of cynicism and truthfulness:

> Witness you ever-burning Lights above,
> You Elements, that clip us round about . . . .

Iago, swayed by Othello's evil enthusiasm but skeptical, unlike him, in regard to "heaven" and "hell," can bow sincerely enough to the material "Elements," the "fruitful" and "free Elements" (II. iii. 347 f.), fire, air, water, earth. He believes that natural forces can abet the egoistic "will" and "reason" that are "in ourselves" (I. iii. 322 ff.). So here, for once, he can feel a half-sincere reverence for something larger than himself: the material universe, "round about" us, in which we live and move and have our selfish being. The "Elements" have apparently favored the efforts of "his wit, hands, heart" in the "service" of his revengeful hate; which is now to be fulfilled— such is the transcendent, cynical irony here—by his devotedly fulfilling whatever Othello shall "command" (465-469). The naturalistic villain and the idealistic hero kneel side by side in religious dedication of their souls to the "service" of evil: so extremely cunning is the "Divinity of hell."

Each fosters and augments the evil in the other; but Iago, while swaying Othello, is *over*swayed by him. The villain's "patience" (452, II. iii. 378) aids his master's habitual self-control; but a desire habitually alien to this villain is kindled in him by his master, namely blood lust. Far more unexpected than Othello's new term "hate" above (449) is Iago's new term "bloody business" (469). Swayed by his master's "bloody thoughts" (457) Iago's "conscience" is now for the first time readying itself for "contrived murder" (I. ii. 2 f.).[41] His hate, of course, has always been as murderously wicked as

---

[41] The passage referred to is of course hypocritical. But Iago's there expressed aversion to murder is not feigned: what he feigns is that he "had thought" (I. ii. 5) of doing the (to him) extremely silly deed of murdering Brabantio.

Othello's is now; but he has never shown the least inclination
to destroy anyone bodily. The dead cannot be tortured: he
has wanted his victims to be very much alive to their misery.
Nor did it ever occur to him that Othello, even in jealous "madness" (II. i. 320), would desire to *kill* the supposed offenders.
And in the present episode he was at first dismayed by his
master's lust for blood: he hoped his "mind" would presently
"change" enough to "be content" with the Iagoan sort of vengeance, so much more "wise" (432, 450, 452). But the Pontic Sea speech, while dashing that hope, infected Iago, as his
reply indicates and as later scenes will fully show, with the
lust for a revenge at once circumspect and "bloody," at once
Iagoan and Othelloan. Thus the villain's murderous hate,
stimulated by the hero, and by the powers of evil, turns to
actual murder.

Accordingly Othello's demand that Iago shall kill Cassio
elicits the following slow, significant response; at once, like
his preceding speech, hypocritic and sincere:

> My friend is dead:
> 'Tis done at your request.
> But let *her* live!

That last line, dramatically startling, is a notable instance of
a fact well known to us all: our conscience, slumbering easily
in the midst of habitual sins, is awakened by a new one, especially if the new sin is not entirely accordant with our interests.
Here the suppressed conscience of Iago, roused by the "bloody
business" (469) so foreign to him, utters a passing but very real
protest, while his mouth grimaces queerly. As to Cassio, Iago
would have loved to continue gloating upon that "friend" of
his "alive" (473) and in total disgrace: in that respect the villain's interests are in line with his feeble conscience. On the
other hand his conscience can shift the blame of Cassio's murder
to Othello: the deed is "done" at his "request." (Incidentally
Iago avoids promising to do the deed with his own hands;
presently he will have the bright idea of getting Roderigo to
do it.) And he can take a real though second-best satisfaction,

under Othello's influence, in the violent ending of Cassio; moreover it is just as well that this possible witness to Desdemona's innocence shall be destroyed. But that being done, it is useless and senseless—and morally reprehensible—to destroy her too. That would be an anticlimax to what the villain considers his own greatest achievement, and what we think of as hell's masterpiece, wrought far less through Iago than Othello: the turning of her "goodness" into a pitchy "net" enmeshing "all" (II. iii. 366 ff.). And so the fellow's composite conscience gives a systolic-diastolic throb: "My friend is dead . . . But let her live!" But Othello replies:

> Damn her, lewd minx.
> O damn her, damn her.

Those lines, spoken with all the intensity of his "sacred vow," but with hideously bare finality, condense into nine words his elaborate imprecations, above, of "heaven" and "hell" (445 ff., 460 f.). The "damnation" (372) with which he rightly but passingly threatened Iago is now pronounced, evilly and absolutely, upon "her." In his soul's hell she is now "the fair devil" (478): that is his final and summary term for her. And then he immediately declares to Iago, "Now art thou my Lieutenant." This line, Othello's last in the scene, echoes and re-echoes in our minds. His "fair" and innocent wife has become for him a "devil"; and a tool of the real "devils" (II. iii. 357), a homely emissary of "hollow hell" (447), is his lieutenant, his vice-regent and bosom friend, whose "love" he greeted a moment ago "with acceptance bounteous" (469 f.). That was the way he greeted the love of Desdemona at the beginning: his response to it was "free and bounteous" (I. iii. 266). But his love for her, so bounteous in emotion, was poor in friendship: the more his love unfolded, the more we were made to perceive his lack of friendly, and therefore trustful, intimacy with his wife. That sort of intimacy, given by him to Cassio and violently withdrawn, is now bestowed upon Iago. Previously Othello had declared to him, "I am bound to thee for ever" (213). Now the villain asserts with diabolic religiosity, "I am your own for ever." For us, he images the "black" spirit which Othello conjured to "arise" from "hell" (447), and which is indeed his "own," very possibly "for ever."

(h) *hardness to dissemble*   III. iv. 1—98

As Othello leaves the stage with "my Lieutenant," Iago, Desdemona comes on, determined to summon him whom she persists in calling "Lieutenant Cassio" (1, III. iii. 45). And the comic relief given us by her dialogue with the clown is darkened by our sense of her ominous persistence. The omen is intensified by her failure to recollect how she lost "the handkerchief" (23) and, above all, by her fixed certitude that she fully comprehends her husband's "mind" (I. iii. 253):

> . . . . my noble Moor
> Is true of mind, and made of no such baseness
> As jealous creatures are . . . .
> . . . I think the sun where he was born   30
> Drew all such humours from him.

We, however, "think" that while no lines could be more right for Othello at his best, none could be more wrong for his present state of "mind" (III. iii. 452 ff.). The very opposite of "all such humours" (i.e. vapors or moods) are his "icy current" and his "bloody thoughts"; and "the sun where he was born" is indeed very far from the "marble heaven" under which we have just seen him evilly *re*born.

When he re-enters now we see "black vengeance" (III. iii. 447) in his face. And she sees there, when he comes close, something that alarms her, a new darkness of mood. Instantly (32 f.) she postpones her urgent plea on behalf of "Cassio": she exclaims with great anxiety, and without her usual endearments, "How is't with you, my lord?"[42]

"Well, my good lady" (34). Turning aside he struggles

---

[42] Contrast her two greetings to him in the preceding scene: "How now, my lord?" and "How now, my dear Othello?" (III. iii. 41, 279). Her present cry is a very much intensified form of her troubled exclamation in the crisis of the preceding act: "What is the matter?" (II. iii. 251).

with himself: "Oh, hardness to dissemble!" We hope he will
not succeed. But he manages to say with artificial kindness,
"How do you, Desdemona?" She, however, does not respond
with *his* name: she echoes his four faint initial words (34) with
"Well, my good lord." And he, unable to lift his eyes to
hers, takes her hand—the hand that gave the handkerchief, he
believes, to Cassio. He knows he should confess that belief
to her now. He knows, as he intimates later (V. ii. 48 f.), that
elementary justice requires him to do so. But his pride and
passion conquer his conscience, far more effectively than at his
preceding conference with her (III. iii. 279 ff.), and become
thereby more viciously potent. He studies her hand with
hideous impersonality, with a morbid mixture of sensual at-
traction, moralistic revulsion, and Iagoan equivocation:

> This argues fruitfulness, and liberal heart:
> Hot, hot, and moist. This hand of yours requires
> A sequester from liberty: fasting, and prayer,   40
> Much castigation, exercise devout,
> For here's a young and sweating devil here
> That commonly rebels. 'Tis a good hand,
> A frank one . . . .
> A liberal hand. The hearts of old gave hands;
> But our new heraldry is hands, not hearts.

That which he has blazoned is indeed "hands," not Desdemona's hand. He has envisioned the "hands," so different
from those "of old," belonging to "these delicate creatures"
who, swayed by promiscuous "appetites," betray the "Great-
ones," blackening their "name" (III. iii. 268 ff., 386). Typical
of those hands, so he feels, is the one he "here" holds, "a young
and sweating devil here / That commonly rebels"—the hand
of a "fair devil" (III. iii. 478). His bitter series of ascetical
terms followed by the word "devil" (40-42) is in secret tune
with the hellish religiosity of his "sacred vow" of revenge (III.
iii. 447, 461). But what Desdemona feels is his dreadful aloofness. He will not meet her gaze; he treats her hand as if it
were something severed from herself; heedless of her remind-

ers that this is the hand which, with fresh and entire happiness
(37),[43] gave him all of herself (45). Certain that his strange
"humour" (31) has nothing of jealousy in it, she finds it utterly
baffling; but she sees that it is growing upon him. She must
bring him out of it. She will remind him of a pressing practical duty, as she did above (III. iii. 279 ff.); at the same time
she will reassert, now more strongly than before, her influence
over him. Withdrawing her hand from his she speaks with
curt though affectionate firmness.

DESDEMONA	I cannot speak of this:
	Come, now your promise.[44]
OTHELLO	What promise, Chuck? 50
DESDEMONA	I have sent to bid Cassio come speak with you.
OTHELLO	I have a salt and sorry rheum offends me:
	Lend me thy handkerchief.

Her second speech, above, reminds us of the indirect down-
rightness, so to term it, of her crucial reply to her father at the
first (I. iii. 180 ff.). It rebukes her husband with gentle strin-
gency for his obliviousness to a "promise" so deliberately and
fully given by him to her (III. iii. 75-83). But to him, of
course, the speech is brazen advocacy of her paramour. His
anger is great; great enough to show itself frankly, as on a
previous occasion (II. iii. 204 ff.), and to make him blurt out
to her its real grounds—if only his jealousy were a humanly
and healthily bad emotion! But it is morbid and diabolic; and
so is the tone of his ensuing fiery monologue upon the handkerchief.

For us that monologue is an indirect confession by Othello
that from the very beginning he was predisposed to mistrust
his wife and, far more fatefully, to hide that mistrust. Thrice

---

[43] Compare "The heavens forbid . . . as our days do grow" (II. i. 195-
197). The present lovely verse, "It *yet* hath felt no age, nor known no
sorrow," conveys a new sense of imminent trouble.

[44] Q1 reads: "I cannot speak of this, come, come, your promise." Q2
reads: "I cannot speak of this; come now your promise." Thus both texts
have one line instead of F1's two. Those two are quick trimeter, throwing
into relief the slower trimeter of Othello's dark reply. And the three short
lines are effectively succeeded by the longer fourth and fifth, which, I think,
are hexametrical: obviously they are parallel in syntactic form.

in the preceding scene we were told that the handkerchief was his "first" gift to her (III. iii. 291, 308, 436) and were made to feel that this object, extrinsically so slight in contrast with the usual first gift from a bridegroom, particularly a man of Othello's lofty station and large personal dignity, must have had for him some very extraordinary intrinsic value. And now that value is revealed. The handkerchief is a family heirloom with "magic in the web of it" (69) designed to insure harmony and happiness in marriage. But characteristically Othello concealed all that from Desdemona when, on giving her the gift, he "conjured her she should ever keep it" (III. iii. 294). And now he conceals from her, while betraying to us, the main fact of all. He tells her the handkerchief could keep a husband true to his wife (59-63): we perceive he had thought it might keep a wife true to her husband. He gave her the thing with the secret hope that it would hold her faithful to him, as faithful as his "amiable . . . . mother" (56, 59) was to his father until her death.[45]

Thus deep pathos twines with the dark roots of Othello's passion here. His story of the handkerchief sums up and symbolizes, for the present climax, the whole course and quality of his love. That story recalls inevitably his narrative before the senate of his life and love. This earlier tale, too, had "magic in the web of it";[46] white magic, indeed, but of a sort that *could* turn, as it has now turned, black. For there his strong and wrong conviction was that Desdemona fell in love with him, "in spite of nature," mainly because the way of his life was for her both "pitiful" in its "dangers" and fascinating for its extraordinary adventures: for her it held "charms" and

[45] It is surely obvious that Othello's dying mother in bidding him give the handkerchief to his future wife was concerned for the faithfulness, not of her son, but of that unknown woman. Incidentally, it is a psychologic and dramatic error to suppose that Othello invents, wholly or even partly, the story of the handkerchief on the spur of the moment. The story *may* have been Shakespeare's brilliant afterthought, but not Othello's. Similar is the case of Desdemona's story of Cassio's part in the wooing (III. iii. 70 ff.).

[46] A reader may wonder just how much Othello really believed in the supernatural power of the handkerchief. He certainly believed in it more *intensely* than he did in the "men whose heads / Grew beneath their shoulders" (I. iii. 144 f.).

"mighty magic" and "witchcraft" (I. iii. 91-96, 169). But would that "liberal heart" (38) of hers persist in its singular love of him? That silent question caused him, as we now see, to give her as his first present this potent handkerchief; given to his mother by "a Charmer" who "could almost read / The thoughts of people" (57 f.); made of "hallowed" silk and sewed by an ancient "Sibyl" in "prophetic fury" (70-73); saturated with the spirit of his mother's love, and of his own, his own colorful, high-wrought love given "entirely" (60) to his wife. This sacramental handkerchief should bind her to him, preventing her from hunting "after new fancies" (63). She should (66)

> Make it a darling like your precious eye:
> To lose't, or give't away, were such perdition
> As nothing else could match.

But "such perdition," such *damnable* loss and matchless ruin, has now occurred, he believes; while we see that *real* "perdition"[47] has caught his own "soul" and that "chaos" has "come" (III. iii. 90-92) completely upon him here. Completely his soul gives itself to fate: the "unknown fate" (II. i. 195) which he has come to know; the "destiny" that at his birth "fated" cuckoldry to him (III. iii. 275-277); "my Fate" that "would have me wived" (64). His sense of fate, running through the whole monologue, reaches "prophetic fury" (72) in his final words upon the handkerchief:

> And it was dyed in mummy which the skilful
> Conserved of maidens' hearts.

His wife's heart has not preserved its chastity: that is sure as fate. Thus fatefulness abets his pride in establishing impregnably his evil self-control. So that here more than ever he can suppress the sense of justice that would make him declare his accusation plainly: he can silence his own conscience while trying to awe and frighten *hers* into a confession of sin.

And he is sure he has succeeded when she cries out, as if

---

[47] Shakespeare does not use this word in between the two instances which I have cited.

in reference to his final dictum upon the handkerchief, "Then
would to God that I had never seen't!" (77). But her great
misery is of course due to his tone and mood, not to his words.
He has uttered things unknowable to her: she knows only that
there is a terrible "wonder" (101) in this handkerchief. Previously it had been for her a symbol of him to be caressed in
his absence but to be superseded always by his actual self: hence
her heedless loss of it in a moment when his actual presence
was demandingly real (III. iii. 285-296). It emblemized him
as she knew him. But now, suddenly, it represents, indeed it
seems to be a very part of, a personage she does not know.
That stranger is mystically African like his handkerchief; derived, as it was, from an "Egyptian . . . Charmer"; so he said
at the outset and, at the close, "dyed in mummy." For her,
however, it is dyed, saturated, with a far darker mystery: the
loss, at least for the time being, of his love. She loves "the
sun where he was born" (30); but now she fears and hates
this foreign, unsunned handkerchief. To her it means a black
mood, or spirit, foreign to her Othello though now possessing
him. But in his view, she sees, it is a mystically powerful thing
the loss of which—for she could not conceivably "make a gift
of it"—would cause him to "hold her loathed" (60-62). And
now he speaks "so startingly and rash" (79), staring at her
so vengefully, as to make her feel that she has indeed lost his
love along with the handkerchief. "Heaven bless us!" she
cries. "It is not lost. . . . " "I say, it is not lost" (81-85).

Thus his black equivocation has induced a white, but very
tragical, equivocation in her. It is not sheerly selfish. It is
similar to her deceit of her father at the first. Certainly she
feared Brabantio's tyrannous wrath in case he learned she loved
the Moor; but also for his own sake she wished "my father"
to master his "impatient thoughts": she tried with quiet, brave
firmness to lift the mind of her "noble father" from hot resentment to the thought of plain, present "duty" (I. iii. 180-
189, 242-244). And here she tries to do the same with her
noble but now frenzied husband. To admit not only that the

handkerchief is "gone" (80) but also that she does not know how or "where" (23) she lost it, would be to render him entirely frantic: so she believes, mistakenly, misled by his conduct. And she is sure she must try to lift him out of his terrible mood by resuming and carrying out, determinedly, her abortive effort (32 f., 50) to make him think of his present, plain, urgent duty regarding Cassio. Therefore when Othello, close to her and menacing—like her father previously (I. iii. 178 ff.)—commands in a voice thick with fury, "Fetch't, let me see't" (85), she, subduing her terror at its very height, speaks quietly and firmly.

DESDEMONA	Why so I can; but I will not now:
	This is a trick to put me from my suit,
	Pray you let Cassio be received again. 87
OTHELLO	Fetch me the Handkerchief,
	My mind misgives.
DESDEMONA	Come, come: you'll never meet a more sufficient man.
OTHELLO	The Handkerchief!
DESDEMONA	I pray talk me of Cassio— 92
OTHELLO	The Handkerchief!
DESDEMONA	A man that all his time
	Hath founded his good fortune on your love,
	Shared dangers with you—
OTHELLO	The Handkerchief!
DESDEMONA	In sooth, you are to blame.
OTHELLO	Zounds![48]—Away! *Exit*

"Pray you let Cassio be received again . . . . " "I pray talk me of Cassio"[49]—thus she alters and intensifies her plea. If he will not honor his sacred "promise" to let "Cassio come speak" with him (48-50) he may at least be induced to speak *about*

---

[48] From Q1, which spells it "Zouns." This word, I think, was Shakespeare's first. choice, later changed to the "Away" of F1. (See note 13, Act III, above, and note 21, Act III, in my *Scourge and Minister*, page 99.) I have ventured to keep both words for reasons that will presently appear in my text.

[49] This vital line (92) appears only in Q1; which, however, weakens its climactic effect by reading "I pray" also in the parallel antecedent line (87) instead of "Pray you." Note that she begs him to "talk [to] me" because he is staring through and *beyond her* while exclaiming about the handkerchief.

Cassio: to turn the drift of his words and thoughts away from the hateful, mystic handkerchief towards a real and loving friend, a "man" (90) who, whether or not "sufficient" as an officer, is a "man" (94)[50] who had ever relied upon Othello's "love," "shared" his "dangers," and—we easily imagine she intended to adduce again Cassio's part in the wooing (III. iii. 70 ff.). But Othello, sure that Cassio has "shared" *her* love, will hear no more. She is stopped in mid-course by his fourth and climactically violent demand for "the Handkerchief"; he lifts his hand (I think) as if to strike her. He is arrested, however, by her final words. Still mastering her terror, extremely effortfully, she looks straight into his eyes and says with loud but not ungentle firmness—echoing, it seems, his earlier "I am to blame" (III. iii. 282)—"In sooth, you are to blame." He is astounded. How can she, if guilty and sensually soft, say just that, her very first word of real "blame" for him, in just that tone, with just that mien? The hand he had lifted against her goes to his own forehead for a perplexed moment—a very brief moment. For instantly he is certain that she, far more than he had previously known, can act the innocent consummately. And so with a violent oath he sweeps her aside together with his faint, final intuition of her innocence, and rushes from the scene: "Zounds [by God's wounds]!— Away!"

Thus Othello shows in one packed moment the deficiency of his love and the abnormality of his jealous passion. He speaks "startingly and rash" (79) in the extreme, yet not so rashly as to expose to her by any least syllable his conviction that she has given the handkerchief to Cassio. Extreme and totally uncontrolled rage is bound to betray its cause; but his extreme rage in not uncontrolled. He manages to keep the word "Cassio" from his lips throughout the whole dialogue, even in its explosive close. His final words are therefore a strikingly climactic anticlimax. Normally his fury here (as

---

[50] In her initial plea, too, she had used the word "man" for the former "lieutenant" in her effort to appeal to Othello's humanity (III. iii. 43-45). This time she iterates "man" and omits "lieutenant."

Shakespeare knows we know) would force him to utter some such cry as "Away to your paramour," or "Fetch't [the handkerchief] from Cassio!" But the high tide of his wrath is governed by an "icy current" (III. iii. 454) of proud dissimulation. His initial "hardness to dissemble" has disappeared with practice: it is now easiness. Dissimulation has become in him, for the time being, a fixed habit, almost an Iagoan second nature.

Yet we know it would break down here if his love for Desdemona had been from the outset normally altruistic. Here, for the first time, he is certain from her own words and demeanor in his very presence not only that she is guilty but that she is very deeply disturbed. Beyond his expectation he has succeeded, he thinks, in rousing her conscience (75 ff.). And whether or not her conscience is merely a fear of consequences, her misery is obviously real, great, and growing: it appears in her every word and look. It shows itself particularly beneath her final speech, her extraordinary effort, as he deems it, to reassume her wonted air of innocence. At this point, if not previously, he would surely feel a little pity for her misery if his love of her had in it an habitual touch, however slight, of real unselfishness. And that habit would be stronger than his new habit of dissembling. Rage, touched with pity, would melt his proud control at her word "blame." He would let her see just how she herself, in his view, is to blame: his dissimulation would yield to a white hot, *candid* rebuke of her. As it is, however, the defect of his love stands smitingly revealed. Its egoism, natural in the first act and liable to be overcome by his wife's devotion together with his own generosity, is now habitual and seems impregnable: it bulwarks his dissimulation.

So "the handkerchief" becomes a vivid symbol both of the primal nature and the present state of his love. His initial account of his love had for its main theme his own "history": "the Story of my life . . . . all my Pilgrimage . . . . My Storie . . . . my Story" (I. iii. 129-165). But now that story, so naturally and even modestly self-centered, is succeeded by the proud, weird story of the handkerchief. And like this token his love, we are made to feel keenly, was always tenuous in itself while colorful and charming in its pattern. Now, however, the handkerchief, saturated at once with sense appeal and illusive mystery—"The worms were hallowed that did breed the silk" (73) —means that his love has become, what it was not at the first, intensely sensuous and at the same time morbidly dissimulative. And the rest of the play will show that even more tragic than his deception of his wife is his dissembling with himself. He tries desperately to hide from himself that passionate yearning for her which he ostensibly repudiates. He wants to believe it is "gone" (III. iii. 446), "lost . . . gone . . . out o' the way" (80), like the handkerchief. Actually it obsesses him, more and more, like the thought of the handkerchief. Therefore his reiterated demand for the handkerchief becomes, so to speak, profoundly melodramatic.[51] It expresses a blatantly overwrought, confused, deceptive passion. A noble and just man has allowed that passion to grow upon him till it nullifies all his justness. His final cry for "the handkerchief" means that his passion has become for him the *whole* truth, precluding any saving touch of *self*-blame. "In sooth" (in very truth)— her heart sees, as we do, his crying need—"*you* are to *blame*."[52]

(i) *be patient*   III. iv. 99-201

That last speech of hers was so entirely right that we hold our breath when Emilia exclaims urgently, "Is not this man jealous?" Normally Desdemona would face that question as downrightly as she has condemned Othello's rage. A loving

---

[51] It is *sheerly* melodramatic if its symbolic quality is not sensed. Notice that her "hand" (36 ff.) is a dramatic symbol preparing for the far more elaborately developed handkerchief. Both those objects dramatize Othello's *hateful yearning* for his wife. Moreover, the handkerchief symbolizes, in our view, his bad passion as the "hand," in his view, symbolizes hers.

[52] Observe that his final cry for the handkerchief forms with her *preceding* line a broken pentameter: "Shared dangers with you—The Handkerchief!"; while it forms with her *succeeding* line a full-flowing pentameter: "The Handkerchief! In sooth you are to blame."

but dull and timid woman would have bowed silently, in the end, to her husband's anger, letting it be its own excuse. But Desdemona has seen and said firmly, in spite of all her loving reluctance to do so, that Othello is "to blame"; and now, weeping, "most unhappy" (102), she is brooding upon the strange and terrible default of his love. All the more, then, would she be anxious to lighten the enigma and to find excuse for him in the thought of his being jealous—if only she would fairly consider that thought. But she refuses to do so: she will neither reject the thought absolutely nor confront it plainly.

"I ne'er saw this before."[53] Her reply (100-102) to her woman's question is evasively indirect, in very striking contrast with the assured negative with which she answered the same query in its preliminary and weaker form above (29-31). There, significantly, she herself instigated the question (25-29), but only to repudiate it entirely. Here she cannot do that. We see that the possibility of Othello's jealousy, blindly sensed by her on previous occasions (II. i. 195-197, III. iii. 74-89), has now entered her mind and is indelibly fixed there. But she will not ponder it; she wishes not to see it. Thus the process of her soul is tragically analogous to that which brought Othello's soul to its present state. He, refusing from the first to grapple mentally and morally with his feeling that she *could* be unfaithful, has allowed it to develop into an overwhelming conviction. She, really aware in her soul that he *may* be jealous, is so unwilling to believe it that her conduct becomes, as the rest of this scene will show, fatefully intemperate.

And unfortunately her evasion of the truth is abetted unwittingly by the ensuing speeches of the other persons in the scene. Emilia with the best of intentions tries to make her mistress realize that "a man" (103), *any* man, even "this man" (99) who is her husband, may be violently turned against his wife by jealousy.[54] But her vigorous words, "They eat us

---

[53] This verse is metrically parallel to Emilia's question and to Desdemona's own preceding line. Thus her present mental state, described in my text, is rhythmically emphasized by Shakespeare.

[54] This word, though implied, is not here (103-106) uttered by Emilia. Probably she would have uttered it presently if her speech had not been inter-

hungerly, and when they are full / They belch us," are so much too coarse for the case of Othello that they serve to divert her mistress's mind from the whole subject. Shocked silence is Desdemona's reaction.

Just the opposite, but far more obfuscating for her mind, is her response to the sorrowful, silken Cassio. His suit to "Madam" (110) is flowingly lovely in style, as not before (III. iii. 7-9, 13-18), and consummately effective. He presses now for a final decision, for or against him (114 ff.), on the part of Othello; while we of the audience sincerely wish to God that he would carry his importunacy straight to the commander himself. But he is more than ever obsessed by the unvirtuous idea, his own as much as Iago's, that he must employ her "virtuous means" (111); he must "importune her": "There is no other way" (107 f.). And she in her present unhappiness is more than ever susceptible to his. Above she said that Cassio had depended on Othello's love "all his time" (93); and now Cassio himself speaks eloquently of all his time: "service past . . . present sorrows . . . purposed merit in futurity" (116 f.). He beseeches her (110 ff.) that

> . . . . I may again
> Exist, and be a member of his love
> Whom I with all the office of my heart
> Entirely honour . . . .

He makes her feel keenly that the sole way of real life for him is that which leads "into his [Othello's] love again" (118). And of course all this, without his awareness, is now true of his

---

rupted by the newcomers. Her two final lines appear in F1 as follows except that I have substituted a dash for a period:

> They belch us—
> *Enter Iago, and Cassio*
> Looke you, *Cassio* and my Husband.

Generally editors have followed the quarto version, in which the two lines are one: "They belch us; looke you, *Cassio* and my husband." Incidentally, the emphatic "*Cassio*" in the last line, preceding Emilia's mention of her husband, in reversal of their order of entrance, is probably significant despite the fact that proper nouns are generally italicized in the early texts. Emilia seems here to give a warning hint to her mistress. Of course, she would not dare to make the hint explicit in Cassio's presence.

listener herself in her relation to Othello.   Therefore she is
far more deeply sympathetic than before (III. iii. 1 ff.) with
Cassio's distress and, above all, with his persistent and extreme
idealization of her lord.   This effectually counteracts in her
mind the critical attitude of Emilia: she yearns to "honour"
her husband, as Cassio does, "with all the office of my heart."
The following speech shows her trying to extenuate his cruelty
to her, and then seeking "to blame" (98) herself rather than
him, in emulation of his "thrice-gentle" friend and adorer:

> Alas, thrice-gentle Cassio,[55]
> My advocation is not now in tune;
> My lord is not my lord; nor should I know him
> Were he in favour as in humour altered.   125
> So help me every spirit sanctified,
> As I have spoken for you all my best
> And stood within the blank of his displeasure
> For my free speech. You must awhile be patient:
> What I can do, I will; and more I will   130
> Than for myself I dare. Let that suffice you.

Thus she glosses over her catastrophe.   Only the word
"dare," escaping her lips pathetically, refers to her hidden fear
of Othello's fury.   This she has now softened into "his displeasure."   She is determined to regard his outbreak as indicat-
ing no radical change in him but a passing, though exceedingly
strange, "humour" (125)—not, however, a mood of jealousy.
She must believe, as obviously the "thrice-gentle" Cassio would
believe, in contrast with the crude Emilia, that their "noble
Moor" is incapable of "all such humours" (26, 31).   Hence her
avoidance of any allusion to the hateful handkerchief.[56]   It
represents that extreme violence of Othello's which she is now
palliating; and also it is linked in her mind with that downright blame of him on her part, productive of Emilia's, which
she wishes now to retract.   For one fact is perfectly clear to

---

[55] Instead of the earlier "valiant" (II. i. 87) and "good" (III. iii. 1)
Cassio.

[56] Nor, such is Shakespeare's skill, does the spectator or even the reader
think of it here, ordinarily.   But if perchance he does and wishes that Desdemona would, he must feel, if not clearly see, the ground of her not doing so.

her, as it is to us: her "free speech" (129) on behalf of a discharged officer, which she knows irked her lord increasingly
at the outset (III. i. 46 ff., III. iii. 75), has exasperated him in
his present state of mind. She herself therefore is far from
blameless. Accordingly, after waiting "awhile" patiently until
his mood subsides—such is the implication of her last lines,
above—she will speak to him more moderately and tactfully on
behalf of Cassio; and thus will help her husband to do a "peculiar profit" to his "own person" (III. iii. 79 f.) by reani-
mating a vital part of his real self, "his love" (112, 118) for
his best friend. Tacitly she hopes that when he is thus restored
to himself his love for her will also be restored. Meanwhile
she will scarcely "dare" to plead with him "for myself" because she knows, what she is trying so hard *not* to know, that
for some cause far deeper than her "free speech" his "humour"
is in the main a terrific rage against herself.

Iago too knows that. He has attended sharply to her every
word and look, reading them in the light of his last talk with
Othello. She has said "my lord is not my lord" but has
avoided the word "angry." The villain echoes the "my lord"
and inserts the "angry": "Is my lord angry?" (132). She is
silent; and Emilia, moved by sympathy with her mistress, eu-
phemizes Othello's rage into a "strange unquietness." But
Iago discerns that his master has exhibited great anger against
his wife and, far more importantly, has concealed from her its
real cause by means of extraordinary self-control; the same that
he has shown in battle when the opposed artillery, "like the
devil" (136), has destroyed his soldiers, including "his own
brother." Iago gloats triumphantly, "like the devil": he is
now for the first time perfectly sure that Othello in his wife's
presence can fully maintain his "patience" (III. iii. 452). The
fellow's exulting excitement[57] and devilish looks would betray
him, we know, to persons less intent upon their own purposes
than his present hearers. As it is, he helps unintentionally, like

---

[57] Evinced by his striking anacoluthon. This logician leaves his chief sentence logically incomplete, breaking it after the word "brother."

Emilia and Cassio, to divert Desdemona's mind from the truth
and to activate her sense of her own culpability.

For when the villain declares with unwary vagueness that
Othello's anger must be due to "something of moment" (138),
Desdemona, catching up the phrase, interprets and particu-
larizes it in accordance with her own strong wishes: "Something,
sure,[58] of state . . . . " She proceeds to make herself believe
that some political matter has "puddled his clear spirit:
and in such cases / Men's natures wrangle with inferior
things"—such as the handkerchief, which she is resolved to
minimize and forget despite her deep conviction that in it
"there's some wonder" (101). The difficulty of her endeavor
is divulged by the style of her present speech, so packed and
spasmodic in contrast with her usual simple fluency. The closing verses are as factitious in manner as they are deep in pathos:

> . . . Nay, we must think men are not gods,
> Nor of them look for such observancy[59]
> As fits the bridal. Beshrew me much, Emilia,   150
> I was—unhandsome Warrior, as I am—
> Arraigning his unkindness with my soul:
> But now I find, I had suborned the witness,
> And he's indicted falsely.

The image of a trial, present to her mind in the last three lines,
comes forcefully to our minds too, but very differently. We
see that under trial her love, in smiting contrast with Othello's,
is deepening in humility and patience (129). *He* has spurned
the very idea of "humble love"; his "patience" is revengeful
and dissimulative (III. iii. 452, 458). Unfortunately, however, her own patience, while entirely sincere, is not entirely
authentic. Her very effort in the passage quoted above to view
Othello realistically throws into strong relief her failure to do

---

[58] This "sure" is opposed to her previous "sure" (101) regarding the
handkerchief.

[59] This word from the F1 text (the other folios have "observance," the
quartos "observances") is precisely right in sense and rhythm. It is not elsewhere used by Shakespeare. But its singularity, causing it to be rejected by
the majority of editors, is in keeping with the effortfulness of the speaker's
present mood and style.

so. Her opening sentence is pathetically but also very self-deceptively euphemistic: the subsidence of a husband's bridal "observancy" is one thing; quite another, Othello's violent outbreak. Presently she lets slip the phrase "his unkindness" (152), previously termed merely "his displeasure" (128); but she hides the truth under extreme, confused self-blame.[60] Certainly her "soul" (152) should maintain its charity for Othello; but true charity demands that she should plainly confront his sin. Instead she makes herself feel that she, his "fair Warrior" (II. i. 184), has become his "unhandsome [unjust] Warrior"—a phrase which we know applies now precisely to *him*. Her closing sentence is directly opposed to the truth. Her final words to her husband (97) "indicted" him truly, not "falsely"; she has now "suborned the witness" by means of specious reasonings in the service of intemperate love.

Thus while her love grows stronger, so does its defect, like a parasite feeding upon a wholesome plant. Our sympathy with her is deep: her situation is baleful, her distress extreme; and her fault is natural. But it is not inevitable. We know that when love is *rightly* humble and patient, and therefore prudent and just, it thoroughly seeks to understand, in order if possible to remove, the cause of wrongdoing on the part of the loved one. But Desdemona does not do so: her humble patience, though beautiful and increasing, is marred by self-will. She loves Othello well; but also she loves, too much, her own conception of Othello, a conception that excludes from him all jealous passion. Such is her tragedy, complementary to his. It comes out with vivid definitiveness in the dialogue, quoted below, that ends the present episode. The waiting woman, aware of the effect of her coarse outbreak above (103-106), speaks now temperately, yet with a loving, religious intensity.

EMILIA   Pray heaven it *be*[61]   155

---

[60] "Ofttimes nothing profits more / Than self-esteem, grounded on just and right, / Well managed . . . " (*Paradise Lost* VIII. 571 ff.). Milton here expresses an outstanding point in the Renaissance doctrine of temperance.

[61] In F1 the word is the emphatic "bee." The line, spoken swiftly, forms with Desdemona's preceding line, a complete verse with a very emphatic end.

>   State matters, as you think, and no conception
>   Nor no jealous toy concerning you.
> DESDEMONA   Alas the day, I never gave him cause.
> EMILIA   But jealous souls will not be answered so;
>   They are not ever jealous for the cause,   160
>   But jealous for they're jealous. It is a Monster
>   Begot upon itself, born on itself.
> DESDEMONA   Heaven keep the⁶² Monster from Othello's mind.
> EMILIA   Lady, Amen.
> DESDEMONA   I will go seek him. Cassio, walk here about: 165
>   If I do find him fit, I'll move your suit
>   And seek to effect it to my uttermost.

For us Emilia's "monster" is darkly, heavily reminiscent of
Othello's and Iago's words in the preceding scene (III. iii. 107,
166, 427). Hence we feel acutely—what Emilia herself senses
dimly yet intensely: her final line above is one of Shakespeare's
greatest—the fatuous obstinacy of Desdemona's determination
to believe that "the monster" is still absent "from Othello's
mind," the "mind" she thinks she thoroughly knows (27, I.
iii. 253). As for Othello's *soul*, she will not consider that.
We know that jealousy has been able to master his mind because, as Emilia intimates, it first, without real external "cause,"
gained possession of his "soul" (159, III. iii. 90). But Desdemona avoids the very word "soul" in relation to Othello
though she used it above in relation to herself. She accused
herself of "arraigning his unkindness with my soul" (152);
but she makes herself believe that he cannot be guilty of unkindness to her in his very soul, much less of jealousy. Subconsciously she is aware of the presence of "the monster"; but
the stronger that awareness becomes the stronger becomes her

Emilia's speech is quick, tactful, and pointed. Ignoring her mistress's special
pleading, just above, she casts back to her most plausible notion (140-143)
and throws doubt upon that. In the quartos her speech reads:
> Pray heaven it be State matters, as you think,
> And no conception nor no jealous toy
> Concerning you.
⁶² Instead of the "the" of the folios the quartos have "that," thus making
the "Monster" weightier than Desdemona desires. The "on" in the preceding line is Elizabethan for "of."

will to ignore it. Such is the meaning of her last two speeches above, taken together. In praying that "heaven keep" jealousy "from Othello's mind" she banishes the thought of it from her own, rejecting thus the warning that the same "heaven" (155) has given her through her waiting woman. "I will go seek him" (165). Her previous "I will" (130) was measured in tone and circumspect in context: now she speaks with curt, over-wrought intensity. Her love, self-willed still though patient and mainly humble, will "seek" to work in the one way apt to exasperate her husband's jealousy to the "uttermost."

Exasperating to us, more than ever, is the sleek Cassio.[63] After his long, appealing speech (110 ff.) he fell silent. Listening to the others, this fine gentleman has been impervious to all the intimations, so clear to us, that his suit to Desdemona is the reverse of gentlemanly and very disquieting, to say the least, to the general and his wife. Cassio has not the least concern for her, except in rhetorical sentiment. She is taking a tragically wrong course despite the warnings of "heaven" (163, 155, II. i. 195); he, with obstinate blindness, is helping to prevent "the grace of heaven" (II. i. 85) from helping her. As she departs he merely says, with a deep bow and for us with deep irony, "I humbly thank your ladyship"—then alters his tone with comic speed when Bianca suddenly confronts him. The first of the following lines is startled and angry; the second, in response not to her words of greeting (169) but to her loving gestures, effortfully cordial; the third, sweetly but untruthfully conciliatory:

> What make you from home?
> How is't with you, my most fair Bianca?
> Indeed, sweet love, I was coming to your house.

This closing episode of the third act, some thirty lines in length, like the opening one (III. i. 1-32) but far more deeply amusing, gives us relief from the culminating tragedy even while covertly advancing it. Shakespeare's immediate purpose,

---

[63] Compare Claudio in *Much Ado* and Bertram in *All's Well*. Shakespeare's treatment of this type of young gentleman is fundamentally sympathetic and also severe.

however, is to bring upon Cassio a comic nemesis which his conduct demands and which the audience now craves. Bianca is a delicious, prepared surprise. Hitherto ignorant of her existence we quickly perceive that she belongs inevitably in his destiny. He is just the sort of young gentleman who would have for this "fair" and "sweet" (170 f., 179) creature a tepid passion and arouse in her an embarrassingly demanding love. If not "framed to make women false" (I. iii. 404) in general, Cassio was certainly framed to make this courtesan unfaithful to her professional promiscuity! And if not "almost damned in a fair wife" (I. i. 21) he is comically damned here (later, tragically) in his infatuated mistress.

The episode is packed with complex irony. Cassio, "pressed" with "leaden thoughts" (177), as he puts it—wrapped we would say in his heavy, blinding self-concern—produces a handkerchief "spotted with strawberries" (III. iii. 435), spreads it, surveys the pattern with melancholy admiration, and sweetly enjoins Bianca to make a copy of it: this labor of love will help her endure his "absence" (179 f.). The result on her part, of course, is a violent outbreak of jealousy, parodying Othello's above, but utterly frank: this poor simple woman lacks his proud, dissimulative self-control. The handkerchief, she declares, is a "token from a newer friend" who is palpably the "cause" of Cassio's "absence." Her jealousy unlike Othello's is healthily human, not in the least devilish, though the *pure* Cassio in "sudden choler" (II. i. 279) assigns it to the "devil" and terms it "vild":

> Go to, woman:
> Throw your vild guesses in the devil's teeth,
> From whence you have them . . . .

However, he explains truthfully that he found the handkerchief in his "chamber" (188, III. iii. 321); less truthfully, that he is attending "here on the general" and does not wish "to have him see me womaned";[64] the fact being he is anxious that

---

[64] We may reflect that "the general" has seen him "womaned" clandestinely with the general's wife (III. iii. 30 ff.). We could wish that Cassio himself would reflect, once at the least, upon that fact.

the general's wife, even more than the general, shall not see him thus. Carefully he refrains from making the least allusion to Desdemona. Comically anxious to get Bianca away from "here" (193, 200) he consents reluctantly to accompany her "a little" (197, 199) on her way. "But," says he, "I'll see you soon."

" 'Tis very good: I must be circumstanced." In this final line Bianca makes an honest attempt to "be patient" (129), suppressing her doubts and her jealousy. But the attempt is clearly as effortful as Desdemona's hope, in *her* final lines above, to "find" Othello "fit" (166). And the total situation, we know, is very far from being "very good." All the characters are so "circumstanced," in a larger sense of Bianca's word, that the next step taken by each is likely to be catastrophic.

(j) infectious house   IV. i

IV. i. 1—100

Catastrophic is the diseased fixity, here, of Othello's mental image of Desdemona and Cassio in the act of adultery. Iago's "Will you think so?" is an ironic echo of Othello's line in the outset of the Temptation scene, "What dost thou think?" (III. iii. 105). This time the villain instead of the hero puts the leading question—to lead the audience to see how absolutely the "monster" of jealousy, despite Desdemona's deprecation of it above, has mastered "Othello's mind" (III. iv. 163). It was *his* mind that created the vicious vision of his wife's adulterous kisses and embraces (III. iii. 341-346), a vision copied by Iago's fiction of Cassio's "monstrous . . . dream" (III. iii. 427 f.). That "dream" was really Othello's own jealous reverie. But at that time his imagination was in its first heat of shock and rage. We could hope that when this subsided so would that dream: it would, at the least, seem to him somewhat questionable. But the opening dialogue of the present scene demonstrates the contrary. Othello, coolly discoursing, shows us that this molten hellish vision has solidified to grotesque, adamantine matter of fact.

The villain's satiric suggestion that the two lovers might kiss and embrace innocently elicits from his master a solemn strain of moralizing (5 ff.) more dreadful, really, than his rages in the preceding act:

> They that mean virtuously, and yet do so,
> The Devil their virtue tempts, and they tempt Heaven.

Here Othello's native lack of humor serves conspicuously the devil's purposes.[1] His virtuous gravity, like his self-control in the preceding scene, turns into a vice. His delusion has become so fixed, by the working of the devil through Iago and through his own will, that he gravely repudiates as devilishly immoral—such is the underlying tenor of his words—the *remotest* hint that his wife and Cassio may be innocent. Whatever they may "mean" they "yet do" serve the devil. Casually Othello takes their intimacy for granted. No matter in what light his wife may regard "her honour," the inexpugnable fact, here alluded to by him with new casual coolness, is that she has given it away—like "the handkerchief" (10-15).

That token, however, he "would most gladly have forgot" (19); not because it deepens his conviction but because it re-arouses his shattering rage. This, for the time being, he has managed to put aside. But now the handkerchief "comes o'er my memory / As doth the raven o'er the infectious[2] house: / Boding to all." The image is exact. Othello's soul houses, quietly at present and therefore the more awfully, a foul disease, infecting all his "memory" and therewith, as we know, his potent imagination. The disease became all-pervasive and raging before he had any thought of the handkerchief (III. iii. 431, 434). But now this colorful object is the blackest of omens, "boding to all."[3] It means the reawakening and con-

---

[1] The reader may wish to study this phenomenon also in Shakespeare's other tragic protagonists. All of them, excepting Hamlet, are congenitally deficient in the comic sense. But the dramatist does not emphasize that defect— "wherein they are not guilty / Since nature cannot choose his origin" (*Hamlet* I. iv. 25 f.)—unless and until it becomes *wilful*, i.e. subsidiary to actual sin.

[2] The "infected" of the quartos limits and narrows the idea. Incidentally F1's colon after "house" gives heavy emphasis.

[3] Contrast Iago's "pitch" and "net /That shall enmesh them all" (II. iii. 366-368). Othello's hovering "raven" is far more blackly and conclusively portentous for "them all."

centration of Othello's passion. His imagination sees again the precious token in Cassio's hand: "he had my handkerchief" (22). That concrete detail comprises for him all others, seen or "not seen" (16). That single spectacle, more than anything else, revolts and rouses his blinding pride.

But he merely remarks, "That's not so good now," still trying, though "now" desperately, to suppress all fury. And so Iago, here as previously (III. iii. 462 ff.) tempted to further wickedness by his master's bearing, proceeds to invent the lie of Cassio's confession. The villain begins his story with clumsy hesitation, suppressing the exceptionally energetic protests of his conscience (23-29).[4] Othello, with piercing dramatic irony, helps him to suppress them. Only with the aid of his master's insistent promptings does the fellow succeed finally in completing his "lie" (34).[5] For us that word denotes Iago's faltering falsehood; for Othello, the coitus of his wife and Cassio. Instantly seizing upon the word in that sense he repeats it five times,[6] iterating thus the fact that it is far more his own than Iago's: it denotes like the fictitious "dream" his own "foregone conclusion" (III. iii. 427 f.). Instantly, therefore, the word looses his pent-up passion. And its torrent, just because of his extraordinary effort to check it hitherto, is overwhelming, sweeping away for the first time in the play *all* his self-control.

At the end of his insane monologue he *"Falls in a Trance"*; but this is merely a dramatic sign that the speech itself is the utterance of a noble person who has fallen into a black, deep trance. His whole soul shudders with *pure* abhorrence of the lust which he has been trying so factitiously to consider coolly.

[4] Those who attribute the manner of this speech entirely to Iago's hypocritic skill dehumanize him extremely and slur the dramatic contrasts designed by the dramatist in the present dialogue.
[5] The original texts give a period after this word. Rowe's edition (1714) substituted a dash—which, generally accepted by subsequent editors, injures Shakespeare's tragicomic pun. Iago would fain come to a full stop with his ambiguous "Lie." His ensuing spasmodic line, forced from him by Othello, is suggestively punctuated in F1: "With her? On her: what you will." The first two words echo Othello's; and the line as a whole points up the fact that Othello's will, not Iago's, is of paramount importance.
[6] The fourth instance is the punning phrase "belie her," spelled in F1 "belye-her."

At the same time[7] he trembles with the *impure* passion of vengeful rage at the thought of the publicizing of his own shame:
his hands itch to "hang," to strangle,[8] Cassio more because of
his "confessions" than because of his sin. That motif dominates
the whole speech. Incidentally, however, Othello's better nature hints to him, though very faintly and obscurely now, that
his wife may be innocent, that "they," the imagined gossiping
public, may "belie her"; and that it would be right and natural
to give Cassio a chance "to confess" before dispatching him. But
those subconscious promptings are utterly submerged by his
ecstatic fury and—so he makes us feel without his own awareness—by the preternatural powers of evil. "Nature," he avers,
"would not invest herself in such shadowing passion without
some Instruction." And we know that the thing now instruct-
ing, informing, and swaying him, the power "that shakes me
thus," is the "hell" he invoked when he made his vow of "black
vengeance" (III. iii. 447). Hence the tremendous effect upon
the audience of his final cry, "O devil!" (44). The effect is
intensified by the vagueness of the cry's relation to its immediate context: it may allude to Cassio, or to the "fair devil"
(III. iii. 478) that Othello imagines his wife to be, or to each
and both of the supposed lovers at once. For us, it is addressed
to the real "Devil" whom the speaker cited in his pious moralizing above (6, 8). Semiconsciously Othello, as he sinks to entire
unconsciousness, cries out from the unspeakable depths of his
misery to the black supernatural power that seems to have taken
complete possession of him here.

Seems: for we know that the devil's possession is far from
complete. Beneath Othello's *vengeful* hate of Cassio and Desdemona is his *pure* hate of lust, dishonesty, and disloyalty. It
is his pride's commingling of those two hates, so diverse in essence, that has confounded him. His present state could not
transpire in the case of a thoroughly evil man, such as the

[7] Shakespeare's imagistic art in this speech is such as to make us see that
the speaker's various emotions, successive in language, are concurrent in reality,
mad reality.

[8] Compare his use of the words "cords" and "suffocation" in a passage
(III. iii. 386-390) that prepares for the present far more furious outbreak.

devilish Iago. "O devil!"—we can allocate to Iago Othello's
final words. And indeed as he gloats heartlessly over his fallen
master he seems the very devil incarnate. Seems: but we know
he is far too small a fellow for that, here smaller than ever.

In fact the villain is undergoing shrinkage, like his soliloquies. The climactic one preceding the Temptation scene was
long and very humanly complex and fascinating (II. iii. 342-
368); the next, far less so, though culminating in verses of
rich, evil beauty (III. iii. 321-333). There he conceitedly
ascribed too much, though not exclusive, power and effect to
"my poison." But now in a brief, crude monologue (45-48)
he credits "my medicine," totally and absurdly, with his master's downfall:

> Work on—
> My Medicine works. Thus credulous fools are caught . . . .[9]

The first line is mouthed slowly: the villain makes melodramatic passes with his hands over the prostrate figure. In the
next line he turns to the audience and speaks with a smugly conclusive confidence that bodes ill for himself. He himself is
a credulous fool, more than ever "egregiously an ass" (II. i.
318). Here and from here on his pride, like Othello's, is catastrophic; but unlike Othello's it is not a malady that is conceivably curable: it is not a diseased fixture but a fixed disease.

That fact comes out strikingly in his blatant, exultant words
to his recovering "general" (60). Othello's great agony was
and is for Iago merely "a passion most unsuiting such a man"
(78). We know that precisely the opposite is the truth; to
which Iago, despite all his astuteness, is totally blinded by his
pride. He has not the slightest inkling that Othello's trance
was due, not to weakness, but to a terrific mixture of jealous
passion and manly virtue.) Hitherto the villain has constantly
recognized, however reluctantly, such virtue in his master,
notably in the preceding scene (III. iv. 134 ff.); but now, and
from now on, he will not let himself do so. He is determined

---

[9] I have substituted a dash for the comma in F1. The quartos run the lines
together, giving the whole passage as prose, and read "work" instead of
"works": "Work on, my medicine, work: thus credulous fools" etc.

to believe that Othello, unlike himself, is really unmanly. In the first act when he compared himself with the extremely soft Roderigo his arrogation of manliness had a show of reason, but here it is fantastic in the extreme. He fools himself into conceiving Othello as made of the same stuff, essentially, as Roderigo. He adjured that "silly gentleman": "Come, be a man" (I. iii. 308, 340). Now he adjures similarly a real gentleman who is beside himself at present because of emotions too deep for Roderigo to feel or for Iago to comprehend, though certainly the shrewd villain could *apprehend* them in some degree if he were not now utterly befooled by his own conceit. Blind and absurd self-pride, far more than cruel, clever malice,[10] animates his damnable iteration here of the word "man": "Would you would bear your fortune like a man" (62), "Good Sir, be a man" (66), "Or I shall say y'are . . . nothing of a man" (89). The warped little Iago is tragicomically certain that he himself is very much of a man.

At the same time he adumbrates, here as ever, something vastly larger than himself, the "Divinity of hell" (II. iii. 356). Unlike Othello he does not believe in hell any more than in heaven. So that when he refers passingly to "the spite of hell, the Fiend's Arch-mock" (71) these words, for us, leap out of their context and hover over the speaker mockingly, like "the Fiend" himself. The devil's "Arch-mock" is directed at his unwitting slave Iago, intoxicated now with a sense of supreme *human* power. But note that also the other persons who appear in the present scene (IV. i) exhibit, each in his or her own way, a toxic obsession. The scene as a whole is at once tragic and hellishly fantastic. The mocking smile of "the Fiend," partly through but always above the agency of Iago, flickers over it all.

In the present episode Othello, for the first and last time, is bereft entirely of his innate dignity. This he maintained above even when speaking of the "forked plague" (III. iii.

[10] This point, particularly, should be considered by the modern actor of the part. At certain junctures in the scene Iago slinks; at others, he puffs out his chest.

273-277). But now in rousing from his trance he puts hand to head and *feels* his supposed horns (60, 63). Here he becomes the grotesque opposite of what he was at the first. When Brabantio heaped foul public abuse upon him with the surreptitious aid of Iago (I. ii) he was impervious to it; he stood nobly upon his inward honor. This now crumbles away; he thinks only of outward honor: he is preoccupied with the notion of his public disgrace:

> OTHELLO   Dost thou mock me?
>
> IAGO   I mock you not, by Heaven . . . .

There the villain, as he occasionally and significantly does, tells the truth: Othello is mocked by Hell. Still with hand to head, and speaking more self-revealingly than he knows, he cries, "A horned man's a monster, and a beast." The "monster" jealousy (III. iv. 161-163) has made him now more "monstrous" than he fancied his wife and Cassio to be. The thought of their sin is here entirely subordinated by his egoistic imagination to the thought of his own dishonor: the torturing pictures of his disgrace which Iago proceeds to paint are an objectification of what is going on in Othello's own mind. He himself on his own motion[11] envisions "the fleers, the gibes, and notable scorns / That dwell in every region of his [Cassio's] face" (83 f.). This, we know, is not Cassio's face: it is the present look, unheeded by Othello, of Iago and "the Fiend" (71). Such a look is so obviously the reverse of what would be the actual mien of the smooth Cassio that Othello could not believe it unless he had really invented it himself. His soul is now so diseased (21) that he takes for fact not only specious but "monstrous" suppositions.

IV. i. 101-228

Monstrous too, however, though in a lighter sense, is the conduct of Cassio during the present episode. As never elsewhere he is prone to "excess of laughter" (100) owing to his

---

[11] As the mien and gestures of a good actor will show. Significantly the dramatist has Iago use the present instead of the future tense of the verb "dwell."

sharply conflicting emotions.[12] His face when he re-enters is
gloomier than ever: his despair in regard to the lieutenancy is,
as he intimates, killingly extreme (106). Therefore by way
of instinctive relief he smiles (101), then laughs (110), at
the vision of himself pursuing his luckless "suit" through Desdemona—"your ladyship" (III. iv. 168)—while her very opposite, the "poor caitiff" Bianca, fondly pursues *him* (107-109).
We share his relieving amusement. But soon we see how prodigious, while relentlessly logical, is the tragicomic nemesis that
grips him here. His lofty chivalry for "the divine Desdemona" (II. i. 73) has been more and more tainted for us by
his blindness to her growing trouble, a failing mitigated, however, by his charm and simplicity. But these better traits dis-
appear in his talk with Iago about the poor woman who dotes
upon him: he is grossly unchivalrous and double-faced.[13] In
converse with "sweet Bianca" (III. iv. 179) herself, presently
to be addressed still more fondly as "*my* sweet Bianca" (162),
he submerges his annoyance at her under sweet affectionateness. But behind her back he ridicules her, hiding his fondness for her while pluming himself like a vain boy upon her
love of *him* (112). He is really far more flattered than disconcerted by the belief, or supposed belief, of this "customer"
(122), "monkey" (131), "bauble" (139), and "fitchew" (151)
that he intends to marry her.[14] His obtuseness, so persistent
in regard to Desdemona's plight, becomes in regard to Bianca's
outrageously cruel.

The climax of the episode shows him, and at the same time
Othello, at their very worst (136-148). Cassio tells how Bianca
embraced him openly when he was "talking on the sea-bank
with certain Venetians"—who will doubtless recount the joke
on their own sea banks at home. He "falls . . . about" Iago's
neck to show how Bianca

[12] Iago does not here (94-104) mention that conflict. Shakespeare displays it, with the help of Iago, in the ensuing dialogue.
[13] The commonly cruel Elizabethan view of "the strumpet" (97), exem-
plified in Iago's words, is no excuse for Cassio—quite the reverse from Shakespeare's standpoint.
[14] Artfully the dramatist leaves open the question as to whether Bianca's
"giving out" (118, 131) is "true" (128) or merely invented by Iago. Thus
Cassio's will to believe is emphasized vividly.

So hangs, and lolls, and weeps upon me:
So shakes, and pulls me. Ha, ha, ha![15]

His laugh, at the first low and brief (110), then louder and longer (120, 125), is now fantastically forced. Shamed and flattered by his mistress, he hugs the flattery while he tries to waive the shame by grossly deriding her. And the lurking Othello[16] mitigates his own fancied shame by deriding Cassio: "Now he tells him how she [Desdemona] pluckt him to my chamber: oh, I see that nose of yours, but not the dog I shall throw it to." It is grotesque for him to imagine that Cassio, even at his worst, would talk thus to Iago concerning Desdemona. On the other hand Cassio, at his worst, is more grotesque in his bearing towards his actual mistress than Othello could imagine. The present conduct of both these gentlemen is *devilishly natural*. It exemplifies the primitive egoism latent always in even the finest gentlemen and likely to master them when, with their charity utterly in abeyance, they are subjected at their tenderest points to vivid ridicule. Here the "Fiend" (71) in Othello and Cassio, far more than in the beckoning Iago (134), inspires and derides them both.

"Let the devil and his dam haunt you" (153). Bianca's rude accost is close to the mark! And her mood is the direct opposite of that whimpering fondness which Cassio, now so dumfounded, has just described so lusciously. We of the audience are shaken by strange hysteric laughter. The tragic grotesquerie of the scene comes to a superclimax here. The poor "perfumed" (151) harlot turns out to be the sole one of the infected (21) performers whose conduct in the end is humanly healthy. Her jealousy, restrained in the close of the preceding act, overflows the more violently now and with perfectly simple directness; and her love, when she has relieved her wrath, leaves open to the offender, Cassio, the way of explication and reconciliation (166-168). This prostitute is

---

[15] The rollicking rhythm of these verses, printed as prose in the quartos, accompanies Cassio's actions very effectively.

[16] He has made a long descent since the time when he thought of using Emilia as a spy: he has now "set on" himself "to observe" (III. iii. 240).

blessed, so we must feel, in having no reputation to sustain, and very little pride—unlike the great Othello!

His conduct the dramatist throws here into flagrant contrast with hers. When she suddenly produces the supposed "minx's token" (158) hitherto concealed on her person (154 ff.) and tosses it to Cassio, Othello, avowing "By heaven that should be my handkerchief" (165), starts out somewhat from his hiding place. And for a moment we have hope that he will be as straightforward as she is, and as he ought by nature to be. Here is his chance to challenge Cassio's claim that he found the handkerchief in his "chamber" (157). But Othello's dissimulative pride is now terribly strong from persistent exercise. Above he had whispered diabolically to Iago (90-92):

> I will be found most cunning in my Patience:
> But (dost thou hear) most bloody.

His new word "cunning" burns into our minds and stays there. Iago is cunning; the devil himself "most cunning"; but no trait could be more alien to the normal character of Othello. His honesty, along with his inward dignity, is for the time being absolutely gone. His prideful "patience," "bloody" and "icy" before (III. iii. 452 ff.), is now bloodily and morbidly "cunning," a hellish malady. It paralyzes his healthily wrathful impulse to supersede Bianca as Cassio's accuser: to seize upon the "token," make perfectly certain of its identity, and then confront its possessor with "my handkerchief."[17] The upshot is that while the dishonest Cassio moves off after Bianca (169 ff.), urged by the anxious Iago, Othello dishonestly checks his own advance, his mien fearfully contorted with diseased passion.

"How shall I murther him, Iago?" The Moor's hands

---

[17] The fact that Othello cannot here *fully* see the pattern of the handkerchief serves to stress the abnormality of his present state of mind. Normally an overpowering jealous curiosity would impel him to seize upon and scrutinize the thing. But the thing itself is here for him a relatively minor matter: he is preoccupied with its lurid image in his own soul. That image, really, is now "*my* handkerchief." In this scene, as not hitherto since III. iii. 436, he applies to the token the possessive pronouns "my" (22, 164) and "mine" (184).

writhe with the lust to strangle the laughing scorn (178-188)
of his former dear friend, forgetting for the moment that he
had deputed to Iago the destruction of Cassio (224, III. iii.
470 ff.).   But quickly his thoughts return, with the villain's
aid, to the chief source of all his insufferable dishonor, his
"wife" (10 ff.), his "whore" (186 f.)—and Cassio's too, like
Bianca. Iago dares to hint at that parallel[18] because he knows
as we do (cf. III. iii. 359) that it is at work in Othello's mind,
too maddeningly for words.   Hence Othello's horrid outbreak
now: "let her rot and perish, and be damned to-night"
(191 f.).[19]

"To-night"—reinforced soon by "this night" (216, 218)
and finally by Iago's "midnight" (225).   The darkness is
closing in.   But over against his black fury Othello sees,[20] and
then more and more feels, the "fair" sweetness of the "woman,"
the wonderful "creature," lying by his side at night in her
sovereign beauty (189, 194-196).   And now, far more fully
and poetically than before (III. iii. 184-186), he expatiates upon
all her graces (198 ff.)—except her *spiritual* grace and virtue
which he has never known.   His perception has never gone
deeper than her gentility. Obviously she is a gentlewoman, and
of gentle nature.   Hence the supposed unnaturalness, so deeply
though tacitly felt by him, of her love for the Moorish soldier
(I. iii. 94-120).   Hence, too, her emotional pity for his "dangers," which he was convinced she neither would nor could
share in actuality (I. iii. 155-170, 230-240).   His first word for
her was "gentle" (I. ii. 25); and it is his fatal word for her
now (204).   To him it signalizes all her almost irresistible
charm while it accounts for and aggravates her secret "iniquity"
(208).   For him she is devoid of moral character: she is "of

[18] The villain remarks that Desdemona gave the handkerchief to Cassio,
"and he hath giv'n it *his* whore."   With the aid of the abbreviated "giv'n"
the whole movement of this speech (which, incidentally, is omitted by the
quartos) throws a nice emphasis upon the "his."
[19] In the original editions "to night," as in line 166 above, and elsewhere.
[20] When he exclaims with slightly softened tone, "a sweet woman" (189),
he begins to look off into the distance raptly.   Hence the quick adjuration
of Iago, "Nay, you must forget that."

so gentle a condition"[21]—"Ay too gentle." The last three
words, from Iago's mouth, are really from Othello's heart;
they are paralleled in rhythm and deepened in current by the
first three words of his response:[22]

> Nay, that's certain:
> But yet the pity of it, Iago; oh, Iago, the pity of it, Iago.

Baleful beauty is in that word "Iago" and in the tidal
moaning of that whole strange line. Strange; for even while
we pity Othello keenly we realize that here is his first "pity"
for his wife and that it is somewhat, though far from wholly,
Iagoan. Above he declared rightly enough that his "heart is
turned to stone" (192 f.). This is true of his charity. The
charitable will, petrified in Iago, is lifeless as stone, at present,
in Othello. A sheerly emotional pity—like that which he believed she had at the first for him—sweeps through him like a
wave; then recedes into the billow of his cumulated fury: "I
will chop her into messes—Cuckold *me?*" (211). In his initial
rage he had yearned to "tear her all to pieces" (III. iii. 431).
Now, at the height of his "savageness" (200), he would hack
her into such bits ("messes") as men "throw" to dogs (147).
The beauty of his pity for her is dismembered into monstrous
ugliness.

But actually he will not dismember her: his craving to do
so subsides quickly. He cannot mangle what he passionately
loves, "her body and beauty"; yet he will not let that "unpro-
vide my mind again";[23] he must not "expostulate [converse]
with her": hence he will procure "some poison" for her (216-
218)—so poisoned now is his mind. But that notion, too,
passes quickly: it revolts his whole nature even while it fails
to satisfy his revengeful fury. Along with his fury his deep
instinct for justice, now horribly distorted, demands direct,

[21] Here this word *denotes* her disposition or temperament and *connotes* her
social station.
[22] Notice the effect of the parallel feminine endings "gentle" and "certain."
[23] Wisely the dramatist leaves vague the exact and nasty implications of
those words. The outstanding point is that Othello, with a deep self-disgust
which he is too proud to confess, has continued for a number of nights to
relish the "beauty" of her whom he believes to be a whore.

downright action. And so "the Fiend" (71) can whisper to him (220 f.) effectually: "Do it not with poison, strangle her in her bed, / Even the bed she hath contaminated."[24] That deed is exactly what his writhing soul and writhing hands desire. And the black grotesquerie of the scene reaches its acme when Othello proceeds to make his first mention of "justice" regarding his wife, after uttering his first "pity" for her above. Devoid of the real pity or mercy that seasons real justice, he exclaims with diabolic unction, sequel of his "virtuous" unction above (5-8):

> Good, good—
> The *justice* of it pleases—very good!

Iago's killing of Cassio (224) will complete that "justice." Othello exclaims, "Excellent good!"—then starts violently: "What Trumpet is that same?" It *could* be that of doomsday.

IV. i. 229-293

But it "sure" denotes "something from Venice" (227). And now an air of civility invades, and for a minute dispels, the scene's heaped air of monstrous barbarism. Lodovico enters with the governor's wife, both fully attended: he is an emissary "from the Duke" to the "worthy general." Othello, quickly mastering his "heart" (229), is again the dignified and devoted commander in the service of the great city. He formally kisses, then steps aside to open and read, the missive from "the Duke and the Senators of Venice." We recall the great scene wherein their kindly justice, together with Desdemona's open love, dispelled the jealous and violent atmosphere created by Brabantio. Then Othello stood free of all suspicion that he could be guilty of any procedure even faintly resembling "practices of cunning hell" (I. iii. 102). But hellish pride and jealousy have taught him to be cunning, indeed "most cunning"

---

[24] The words are Iago's; the ideas, as usual, Othello's. He has just been envisaging "her" in her contaminated bed. And the strangling project is not new; it began to take form when his prophetic soul yearned for "cords" and "suffocating streams" (III. iii. 388 f.). Those instruments, however, would not be so "swift" (III. iii. 477), nor so satisfying, as his own two hands; which in the present scene have more and more itched to *feel* "murther" (178).

(91). Having spied upon Cassio and Bianca, he now stealthily listens to her whom he views as Bianca's successful, subtle rival, his own wife. And the air of the "infectious house" closes in again.

And now, we feel, that atmosphere taints even Desdemona. Her frankness and determination, so wholesome in the Senate scene, are here unhealthy when she pursues her dubious "suit" to the "uttermost" (III. iv. 166 f.). At first she has no intention of doing so, just now, as her opening line shows;[25] a true instinct warns her to await the revealing of the "news" from Venice, obviously important, regarding Othello. But when Lodovico, instigated by Iago,[26] questions the ancient about "Lieutenant Cassio," she can no longer restrain herself. With utmost indecorum she informs the Venetian emissary of "an unkind breach" between her lord and Cassio, and invokes his intervention "to make all well," the indecorum being far more heightened than meliorated by the fact that the emissary happens to be her cousin. With lifted brows Lodovico, shocked, embarrassed, and considerably skeptical, delays his reply, then remarks composedly, "Is there division 'twixt my lord,[27] and Cassio?" The polite suggestion is that the general's devoted but too emotional lady has exaggerated a disagreement between him and his lieutenant; and that, though she may know something of her husband's side of the case, she is surely not in position to speak for my lord's associate, not hers, Cassio. Desdemona's unfortunate response to those two intimations is intense and rapt. She feels she must make her cousin feel that

[25] This line (232), together with the ensuing ones, tells us also that she has refrained off stage from mentioning Cassio to Lodovico.

[26] While Othello is occupied with the letter Lodovico naturally expects to be entertained by the second in command; and Iago, by officiously greeting him, provokes his query regarding Cassio (233-236). Iago's curt "Lives, sir" causes Lodovico to look inquiringly at *him*, not at Desdemona. Her sudden warm outbreak forestalls a cool dialogue between those two officials upon an official matter.

[27] The comma, omitted by Q1 and Q2, indicates a slight but significant pause. The abbreviated "'twixt" ("between" in Q1) provides rhythmic room for that pause. Incidentally Lodovico's "*my* Lord" ("thy Lord" in Q1, but Q2 restores the "my") is intended to remind Desdemona that her husband is a public figure. And obviously the vague "division," instead of "*a* division," softens and objectifies the event she has termed so strongly "an unkind breach."

she fully shares her husband's affection for Cassio and that the
division between *"them"* is really deep-going:

> A *most* unhappy one: I would do *much*[28]
> T'attone *them* for the love I bear to *Cassio*.

"Fire, and brimstone!" (245) exclaims the tortured Othello
to himself and to all the devils of burning hell. We are
wrenched by a sobbing laugh: the situation is amusing, hellishly
and crazily amusing. We join in his cry to his wife, "Are you
wise?" Certainly her wilful belief that he cannot be jealous,
especially not of Cassio, has here reached the peak of its un-
wisdom. But now she has to see and say what she has studiously avoided saying hitherto (III. iv. 128 ff.): he is, most apparently, "angry" (246) at her. The diplomatic Lodovico,
when the general resumes his reading of the letter with seeming absorption, is moved by sympathy for her to be somewhat
indiscreet himself. He informs her confidentially that "the
letter" may have "moved" Othello, "For as I think"—he
knows it, really, but knows he has no right to say it before the
general does[29]—"they do command him home, / Deputing
Cassio in his Government." Desdemona, deeply relieved, and
ignoring her companion's reserved manner, exclaims loudly,
"Trust me, I am glad on't." The problem of the lieutenancy
has suddenly been solved: now her husband will be able to
recall calmly all that his "love" for Cassio has meant in the
past (III. iv. 92-95). And she, with the aid of her "good
cousin" (232), will "make all well" (238), will "attone" the
noble Othello and his devoted friend.

[28] "I *could* do much," she had declared to Othello himself; he checked her
with "Prithee no more" (III. iii. 74 f.). Observe the rhythmic heapings in
the first of the two lines quoted above. In the second line, the folio text I am
using (see Note on the Text) has a comma before and after "them," which,
if not sheer misprinting, looks like a clumsy attempt to stress that significant
word. In any case my italicizing of it is justified by the rhythm of the passage
as a whole.

[29] Below, Othello assumes that Lodovico knows the contents of "the man-
date" (270 f.). It is natural that with peace assured in Cyprus the senate
should recall the wartime governor, their leading general, to "employ" (I. iii.
48) him in martial service elsewhere. Lodovico, surprised at the general's
emotion, opines that it *"may* be" due to regret at leaving Cyprus.

But the "sweet Othello" (250), suddenly lowering his letter, steps close to her with such rage in his eyes as she has never
yet seen. Echoing her word "glad" he cries, "I am glad to
see you mad." There is method in his own madness: he is
madly glad, furiously pleased, with the "justice" (222) of what
has happened. Despite her smooth hypocrisy, her yearning lust
has made her confess, to his very eyes and ears, far more plainly
than Cassio did above, the secret adultery. So now, superla-
tively, she is a "Devil" (251, 44, III. iii. 478). One hand grips
his letter; the other swiftly, involuntarily, strikes her.

"My lord, this would not be believed in Venice." No
words could be better calculated than these of Lodovico to
bring Othello to himself. Surely now his very pride, so we
hope, will force him to justify his barbarous action by blurting
out his conviction regarding his wife's paramour; then, urged
by her and Lodovico, he must at long last fulfil his "promise"
(III. iv. 48) to give a hearing to Cassio. But his pride, once
so healthy, notably in his "services" (I. ii. 18) to the Venetian
state, is terribly diseased. The great soldier and commander
would rather be disgraced in the mind of Lodovico and Venice
for a gross lapse of self-command than confess a disgrace, subject to gross mockery on the part of gross persons (61 ff.), but
for which his own will is not to blame, namely cuckoldry. To
be sure, his dread of ridicule is human enough, but not his
present great hypocrisy.

For throughout his fiery denunciation of his wife (255-271)
he cunningly avoids dropping any word that might give the
perceptive Lodovico the least clue to the real truth. So that
when he finally declares that her passionate sorrow is "well-
painted" (268) we apply that term, with a difference, to his own
passion. Indeed we perceive that his own dissembling, once
so difficult (III. iv. 34), now so complete, renders it easy
for him to attribute the same to her. He watches very closely
her motions of humble obedience (266) and, above all, her
"tears" (256, 267). Is it possible that under the stress of the
present situation she will not betray the least awareness of her

guilt? Plainly she does not do so. And he could not believe
in the almost incredible perfection of her acting unless he unconsciously read into her mien that which is governing himself,
satanic hypocrisy.[30] "Oh,[31] devil, devil" (255): she is twice
a devil now; she is doubling her sin by so consummately concealing it. And the more, as he thinks, she conceals the truth
the more his deformed pride makes him determine to do likewise. In the end he dismisses her with "Hence, avaunt!" as
though adjuring an evil spirit that has assumed a wonderfully
specious form. But the false spirit remains within his own soul.
Immediately, with a convulsive effort which he hides from
Lodovico by making it seem the aftermath of his violent command to his wife, Othello proceeds to utter his first deliberate,
outright falsehood:

> Cassio shall have my Place. And sir, tonight
> I do entreat, that we may sup together.
> You are welcome, sir, to Cyprus.

Cassio, who is to be destroyed "tonight"! And beforehand
Othello will "sup together" with the Venetian envoy to whom
he is lying. In fact, the greatly loyal commander is deceiving
and disobeying dreadfully "the Duke and the Senators of Venice" (230), his "very noble and approved good masters" (I.
iii. 77). Here the Moor of Venice sinks to the nadir of his
degradation. The "serious and great business" of the state and
of his own life is scanted (I. iii. 268) utterly. His "occupation" is indeed "gone" (III. iii. 357): his old, deep love has
been disrupted by his new love. And suddenly an overpowering sense of his "chaos" (III. iii. 92) breaks off his false words
of "welcome" to his visitor, but without causing him to disclose overtly his belief in the licentiousness of his wife and
Cassio. "Goats and Monkeys!" (274)[32] he cries wildly, as

---

[30] This is a good example of Shakespeare's tacit motivation. The alterna-
tive to perceiving it is to believe that Othello, here more than ever, is exceedingly stupid.

[31] Not "O." At this point he is thinking about her, not directly addressing
her.

[32] No doubt these words are a dramatic echo of Iago's above (III. iii. 403),
but not a conscious reminiscence on the part of Othello. His phrase is due not

though "light of brain" (280), moving off and peering into a
voiceless wilderness of leaping and grimacing sensuality, visible
to him alone. For us that galvanic cry, echoing his entranced
ejaculations at the first (35 ff.), condenses all the inhuman,
toxic grotesqueness of this amazing scene.

Now that atmosphere retreats entirely.[33] And the underlying stark tragedy stands out for us in the stately sentences
of the Venetian emissary:

> Is this the Noble Moor whom our full Senate
> Call all in all sufficient? Is this the Nature
> Whom Passion could not shake? Whose solid virtue
> The shot of Accident, nor dart of Chance,
> Could neither graze, nor pierce?

The allegoric martial images of the two last lines reflect Othello's profession but denote the whole warfare of human life;
wherein "solid virtue" is tested and established by the efforts
of "Passion" to "shake" it; and wherein Othello was adjudged
to be "all in all sufficient" by a high court of public opinion,
"our full Senate." The passage commemorates the whole
"name" (III. iii. 155, 386) and "nature" of "the Noble Moor."

And the shocked, mystified speaker, a normal gentleman
anxious to be just, wonders if Othello's reputation exceeds by
far his actual "virtue." Iago while ostensibly refusing the
question insinuates an affirmative answer: "He is much
changed"; Othello "is not" what "he might be," what his
friends "would to heaven he were" (279-283). Whether or
not it is "his use" to "strike his wife," that deed was a public
sign of something that the present crisis did not "new-create,"
a fundamental "fault" of "blood" which Iago has all along
silently "seen and known" (283 ff.). With full confidence
the villain proceeds to predict that Lodovico will see the whole
truth for himself very soon; Othello's "own courses will de-

---

to Iago's influence but, as the context shows, to his own climactic sense of chaos
together with his proud resolve to remain silent to Lodovico regarding his
cuckoldry.

[33] The opening and closing dialogues of this scene, each about eighteeen
lines in length, are both calmly questioning, and ominous, in tone.

note him so" (290); will, by showing "the worst" (285), reveal what he really is: "do but go after, / And mark how he
continues."   Just there the crude fellow betrays an overeager-
ness.   And the noble Lodovico, searching his face sharply, replies with new reserve, "I am sorry that I am deceived in
him."[34]   Thus he defers judgment as· to whether "our full
Senate" is "deceived in him," expressing merely his personal
sorrow for that which he has just been compelled to witness
in the conduct of "the Noble Moor."

And the ensuing episode seems *at first* to give the lie to
Iago.   The Moor "continues" in a manner very different from
the conceited villain's expectation.

(k) *my heart*   IV. ii. 1-94

Here the audience has a thrill of surprise and hope.   Othello
re-enters with Emilia and without Iago.   He has humbled himself sufficiently to confer with the fellow's "wife" (III. iii. 240)
and to do so calmly, mastering his "passion" (IV. i. 277).   The
opening lines tell us that off stage he has been questioning her
in regard to her mistress's conduct in general, without any
reference to the supposed paramour Cassio.   Now, however,
with a strong effort, and in striking contrast to his secretiveness
in the preceding episode, he forces himself to broach that hateful subject.   But he does this casually, as if by afterthought:
"Yes, you have seen *Cassio*, and she together" (3).[35]   And
his ensuing queries in this matter are so casual and common-
place that the blunt woman in waiting is misled.   She thinks
that her replies have exonerated Cassio and that, in any case,
this subject is quite incidental and transient in her lord's view.

[34] Note the strong contrast in tone between this line and his three preceding
speeches to Iago.   This line is spoken slowly and deliberately, and the repeated "I" is emphatically opposed to Iago's iterated "I" (281 ff.) above.
Incidentally the assertive phrase "I am," not hitherto used by Lodovico, was
uttered with crucial effect by each of the other three speakers (233, 249, 250,
269).
[35] The quartos read: "Yes, and you have seen Cassio and she together."
The extra "and" along with the omission of the second comma eliminates the
intimation that the subject is new.

Hence when he drops it curtly it passes wholly from her mind. His satiric, brooding "that's strange" (11) means to her he thinks it likely that *any* attractive near-by gallant would appeal to a woman of his wife's disposition. Emilia therefore attacks that "thought" (14) with all her power. Having declared at the outset that she had never "seen" nor "heard" anything suspicious (1 f.), i.e. regarding any man, in her mistress's *conduct* she now gives testimony to her mistress's *character*: "she is honest," "honest, chaste, and true," "the purest" of "wives"; and her lord's "thought," if really his "bosom" can harbor such, is, so Emilia implies, a devilishly (16) "foul slander" (19).

That speech of hers is at once passionate and restrained, judicious and fiery. Emilia "durst" to "wager" her "soul" (12 f.) upon her mistress's faithfulness—as Othello durst at the beginning: "My life upon her faith!" (I. iii. 295). But his asseveration, unlike hers, was proud and casual. This crude woman's love of his wife, unlike his own love, has more and more produced a true and irrefragable insight into the spirit of Desdemona. Othello is silent for a moment; quick to respond above to Emilia's every utterance, he has no reply now. His mien shows him deeply, involuntarily impressed by her words and her bearing, which, sinking into his "bosom," are likely enough, we discern, to have a good effect upon him later. But such effect is nullified now by the supreme hypocrisy, as he conceives it, of his wife in the preceding scene. Emilia, he decides, is completely under the sway of her "subtile" mistress:

> Bid *her* come hither—go![36]   *Exit Emilia*
> She says enough; yet she's a simple bawd   20
> That cannot say as much.—This is a subtile whore;
> A closet lock and key of villainous secrets,
> And yet she'll kneel and pray: I have seen her do't.

Thus the immediate result of Emilia's superb speech is to

---

[36] His exclamation shows that Emilia is reluctant to depart; she has moved off lingeringly, watching his face, hoping for some reply to her speech. In Othello's lines the words between the two dashes (mine) refer to Emilia; the rest, to Desdemona. Othello's first four words, with the emphasis on "*her*" (italicized by me), echo scornfully the rhythm of Emilia's last four, "Is foul as slander."

rearouse *and deepen* his proud, blind fury against his wife: "her" (19, 23), the "subtle whore," who with the aid of her devoted "bawd" (i.e. go-between) has tightly hidden the wickedness performed in this very "closet" where "she'll kneel and pray" as if her vicious "secrets" were unknown to very "Heaven" (36). And her "simple bawd" has pretended to know her better than he himself does! So now he will peer closely into his wife's eyes and into her very spirit: there he will *see* the concealed lust which he formerly *felt* in her "hand" (III. iv. 36 ff.). "Pray you, chuck,[37] come hither": he tries to speak with dissimulative tenderness in order to disarm her artful dissimulation. But his own face contorts horribly when he scans hers: "Let me see your eyes; look in my face." And in the depths of those eyes he can see only his own "horrible fancy" (26), the opposite of the purity that the poor Emilia sees there. When this woman now gives strong signs of intervening he checks and dismisses her with words of crude, taunting, increasing anger (27-30), then tries to resume his sightless looking into his wife's eyes.

But suddenly she kneels to him—as he has so often seen her "kneel" to heaven (23) with a mien of heavenly innocence—deprecating his "fury," claiming she does not "understand" the "import" of anything he has uttered (31-33). He steps back, startled and appalled by this superclimax of her devilish (IV. i. 255) histrionicism. Staring at her distantly, as though she were indeed a demon in angelic form, he says in a low tone, "What art thou?" She cries with a deep sob, her arms upstretched to him, "Your wife, my lord: your true and loyal wife." And now he speaks with frenzied religiosity.

OTHELLO   Come, swear it: damn thyself, lest being like one of
           Heaven, the devils themselves should fear to seize thee
           Therefore be double damned: swear thou art honest.

---

[37] On the previous occasion he began with "my good lady" in response to the "my lord" (III. iv. 33 f.) with which she greeted him, then as now (24). But this time he cannot, even formally, use any of those three words to her. He begins with the sentimental "chuck" (III. iv. 49) which previously he worked up to.

DESDEMONA   Heaven doth truly know it.
OTHELLO   Heaven truly knows that thou art false as hell.
DESDEMONA   To whom, my lord?
            With whom? How am I false?

"With whom?"   We of the audience hold our breath.
Surely the two, between them, must now bring up the subject
of Cassio, the all-important witness who is to be destroyed this
night. Desdemona, however, has learned at long last not to
utter in her husband's presence that infuriating name, now the
name of the new governor of Cyprus (III. iv. 50 ff., IV. i.
244 ff.). But that name, under the circumstances, must, as
we and Othello know, be in her mind. Hence her new and
studied avoidance of it is to him a sure sign of her love for
Cassio: this kneeling angel knows only too well "with whom,"
also "to whom" and "how," she is "false," thoroughly and
absolutely false. Accordingly he is penetrated by a new sense
of his absolute loss of her: "Ah Desdemon',[38] away, away,
away." Suddenly his grief overflows: the strong man whom
formerly no "passion" could "shake" (IV. i. 277) is shaken
with stormy weeping.

She had risen and stepped towards him as she uttered her
three questions: and now, waved "away" by him, she stands
a little distance off, full of great compassion and perplexity:

> Alas the heavy day: why do you weep?
> Am I the motive of these tears, my lord?

Still he will not reply. Obviously, then, his main trouble is
affairs of state which he will not confide to her; such, all along,
has been her resolute belief. And her premonition of trouble
for him "from Venice" has just been fulfilled (III. iv. 141,
IV. i. 271), but with herself, in some mysterious way, involved.
Here an answer to all her questions flashes upon her. Probably
enough her "father," reacting from his reluctant condoning of
the "Moor" (I. iii. 192 ff.), has urged his "calling back" (44 f.),

[38] The lovely name's last syllable (the apostrophe is mine) is blended with,
not entirely elided by, the "a" of the following word, as in III. i. 56, but with
far different effect.

and her husband imagines that she has connived, thus being false to him with her father. She urges: "If haply you my father do suspect . . . / Lay not your blame on me: if you have lost him, / I have lost him too."

But that double "if" betrays her underlying awareness that there is another and *not* dubitable cause of her husband's emotion regarding his recall: "Cassio shall have my place" (IV. i. 272).[39] All allusion to that person she has again avoided with loving, blundering tact[40]—in Othello's view, with sly deceitfulness. Her guess regarding her father, painfully lame even for us, seems to him a final, blatant, desperate blind. And her trivial question as to whether he has "lost" her father accentuates the enormous fact that he has "lost" *her*. His weeping deepens. So does his determination not to name to her the paramour whom she herself refuses to mention, much less confess. Having questioned Emilia about Cassio, above, he is now absolutely sure that her "subtile" mistress will stick at no device to keep that "villainous secret" locked (21 f.), unaware that Cassio has already blabbed it before his very eyes. Shame, wrath, grief, and pride combine here to constitute Othello himself, with dreadful irony, a "closet lock and key" of that which nature and "Heaven" (39) are urging him to cry out to her, the word "Cassio" (3).

His silence on that point is very sinful. But we cannot forget that the *immediate* cause of it is her sudden assuming of entire obliviousness to the pressing subject of Cassio. Her new and fixed resolve, tacit but dramatically obvious, is to shun that subject unless her husband brings it up. And that resolve goes back to the defect in her great love: her conviction, not free from pride, that she and she alone knows all the "quality" (I. iii. 252) of the man she has chosen for husband. She too

[39] The customary insertion of *"Exit Desdemona"* just *before* that line (the original texts omit that stage direction entirely) may cause the reader to believe that she does not hear it. But in fact the line is uttered *while* she is slowly departing, and it stamps into her mind what Lodovico had already told her (IV. i. 248).

[40] Fear is not her motive, not at least her main one. That fact is certified by the bold tone of her questions (40) and by her essential fortitude throughout the episode as a whole.

much loves her own high ideal of him. To be sure she has
been forced to see that he is greatly "to blame" (III. iv. 97)
in laying upon her the "blame" (46), "not" in the least "deserved" (IV. i. 252), for his inward turmoil occasioned by political troubles which he refuses to share with her. But the simple,
brave directness with which she faces *that* unhappy situation
throws into relief the evasive and subtly proud obstinacy of her
refusal to open her eyes to the main truth. Even at the height
of his fury and grief she will not admit to herself that "*my
noble Moor*" *may* be guilty of "such baseness" (III. iv. 26 ff.)
as to "suspect" (44)—this is her first and intensely suggestive
use of that word—his wife of being "false" (39 f.) to their
marital vow, least of all with Cassio. Hence she is still certain,
mistakenly and now fatally, that she has "never" given Othello
the least "cause" (III. iv. 158) for that sort of suspicion and
jealousy. And so she will not advert to the subject of Cassio
throughout this whole scene, and throughout the remaining
scenes until the end (V. ii. 48 ff.).

Hence our sympathy for Othello is deep even here. His
obsession regarding his wife is fed by hers regarding him: her
defect in love, in love's perceptiveness, complements and serves
to develop his. Nevertheless the upshot of the present episode
is to show him at his very worst in his attitude to her. His
sense of what he has "lost" (47) plunges him into a tide of
sheer self-pity, rising more and more to a brutal rage of denunciation, immeasurably crueler than the blow he struck her
in the preceding scene—a "foul and violent tempest" (II. i.
34).

Viewed in its whole context his monologue on "patience"
(47 ff.) is a thing of great, baleful beauty. It begins in an
ominously righteous calm[41]: "Had it pleased Heaven / To try
me with Affliction . . . . " Had the supernal powers determined to make trial of his faith and virtue by saturating with
misery and giving over to failure all his life and work in the
world, his "soul" (52) could have managed to find within it-

[41] Cf. IV. i. 5 ff.

self and to distil into his conduct "a drop of patience," that is, religious patience, acceptable to "Heaven." "But alas" those heavenly powers have destroyed the very "jewel" of his "soul," his great "name" and fame (III. iii. 155, 386), making him

> The[42] fixed Figure for the time of Scorn
> To point his slow, and moving finger at—

That wonderful hyperbole is a superb image of Othello's tragic pride. Obviously the word "Scorn" alludes covertly to the "notable scorns" (IV. i. 83) which, aggravated intolerably by his wife's "well-painted" (IV. i. 268) innocence, he believes he has seen Cassio heaping upon him. But now the contempt of the two supposed lovers for him is merged into an appalling vision of the disdain of the whole world throughout the whole of "time." Previously he had thought of himself as "fated" to share the "forked plague" of many "Great-ones" (III. iii. 273-277): now he is "the" sole one; and he is not merely "fated." The Christian "Heaven" (47) itself, so he feels with arrogant religiosity, has stationed him statuesquely as *the* "figure" focusing universal "scorn." The world of "time" will go on, and on; but ever its "finger" will shift slowly, constantly, to keep pointing back at him.[43]

"Yet," with a strong effort, Othello tells himself he could "bear that too," even that cosmic scorning, "well, very well" (56)—a sudden, extraordinary uprise in his proud soul of truly religious "patience" (52 f.); but it is very transient. That momentary check to the tide of his passion serves to make it rise all the higher:

> But there where I have garnered up my heart,
> Where either I must live, or bear no life,
> The fountain from the which my current runs,

[42] The quartos have "A" here and, in the next line, "slow unmoving." Q1 has "fingers"! The quartos end this line with "— oh, oh." I have retained the dash as preferable to F1's period.

[43] Obviously I am assuming that the dramatist has in mind here the Christian (and Hebrew) *linear* view of history. The reader may amuse himself by trying to fit the imagery into the ancient Greek *revolving* view, which elsewhere Shakespeare seems at times to employ.

Or else dries up—to be discarded thence,   60
Or keep it as a cistern for foul toads
To knot and gender in![44] Turn thy complexion there:
Patience, thou young and rose-lipped Cherubin,
Ay here[45] look grim as hell.

And "here" he turns upon his "young" and angelically fair
wife a look of hellish grimness. In his view she is *the* supremely specious symbol—in our view, a real though imperfect one—
of that heavenly "patience" which he "here" discards utterly.
In his ensuing anathematizing of her his bearing is far more
evilly specious than he conceives hers to be.

For the wickeder he deems her, the wickeder we deem his
failure to find in his "heart" for her, this "lovely fair" (68)
creature wherein he has "garnered up" his "heart" (57), the
least grain of merciful pity. Dreadful is the self-righteous
"modesty" (75) which, he says, will not let him "speak thy
deeds" even at the very height of his endeavor to bring the
foulness of whoredom (72) home to her. The slightest "drop"
(53) of merciful justness here would cause him to specify her
worst "deed," her "sin" (70) with Cassio, in order to break
through the supposed wicked persistence of her hypocrisy.
But he will not do so: pitiless pride under the cloak of "modesty" keeps him from uttering a single plain hint, even, of
all he has come to know, as he thinks, of her and Cassio. And
obviously he tries to justify himself for dissembling in that important *particular* by heaping upon her *general* objurgations,
vague in tenor but excruciatingly vivid in detail: she is sensual
as "summer flies in the shambles" (66), more whorish than
the "bawdy wind that kisses all it meets" (78). He is satisfied with the "justice" (IV. i. 222) of his powerful diatribe;
but his justice, not seasoned with mercy, is as horridly unjust
as she in his view is horridly guilty.

[44] This image is a horrid development of one he used above (III. iii. 270-
273).
[45] The "there" of F2, nicely paralleling the double "there" above (57,
62), has been accepted by most editors. But the "here" of all the other early
texts is demanded by the syntax of the speaker's passion here; as Dr. Johnson
perceived, though his comment on the passage is considerably clumsy.

His own initial words of "patience" judge and condemn
him. That religious virtue, the ground of true charity,[46] has
come close to him through his "affliction" (48); his "soul" has
felt the need of embracing it (52-56). But his "heart" (57)
and his will refuse to do so. Self-pity and fury "turn" the
"complexion"[47] of heavenly "patience," transmuting it into a
patience "grim as hell" (62-64). This passage condenses, with
dreadful imagistic power, all that he and Iago have expressed
of the kind of patience opposed to the heavenly kind: Iago's
"patience" in the service of the "Divinity of hell" (II. iii. 356,
378); Othello's invocation to "hollow hell" and his ensuing
"icy" patience of revengefulness (III. iii. 447 ff.); and finally
his determination, above, to be "most cunning" as well as "most
bloody" in his "patience" (IV. i. 91 f.). Most cunning, however, is the devil himself; that is what we are made to feel
more than ever in the upshot of the present episode. Othello's
eloquence is extraordinarily diabolic: his utterances affront the
"Heaven" he repeatedly cites (36, 39, 47, 77). When finally
he terms his wife a *"cunning* Whore," in words of controlled
fury cynically mocking her appeal to heaven's "mercy," he
signalizes for us the fact that he has yielded himself entirely
to the sway of that which is the "opposite to" supernal charity,
the *"cunning"* patience of "hell" (64, 88-92).

Moreover we realize that Othello has now reached an evil
goal towards which he has been moving, though at first guilt-
lessly, from the very beginning, because of the inadequacy of his
love. His full final title here for his wife is "that cunning
Whore of Venice / That married with Othello." The innocent
cunning with which she encouraged him to marry her (I. iii.
158-170) is now for him, in retrospect, the cunning of a "subtile whore" (21), the subtlest as well as the loveliest one "of
Venice." For us, that summary title is the ultimate emblem
of the shallowness of Othello the lover, in contrast with Othello the devoted soldier "of Venice," who "married with" Des-

---

[46] As for instance in Spenser's *Faerie Queene* I. x. 23-29.
[47] Here obviously this word denotes color and mien, mainly, but its deeper
signification is implied, i.e. constitution or temper; cf. *Hamlet* I. iv. 27.

demona. She is now for him *that* type, "that cunning Whore" etc., because she has always been for him *a* type, never a real human individual—a type ever more fascinating as he watches her: "the sense aches at thee" (69). And so he can moan for "the pity of *it*" (IV. i. 206 f.) without real pity for *her* as a person. He can say "my heart is turned to stone" (IV. i. 192 f.) . . . . "there where I have garnered up my heart" (57).[48] A stony uncharity, cold as a "marble heaven," "compulsive" as the "icy current" of the "Pontic Sea" (III. iii. 453-460), is lodged in the rich stores of his self-centered love. The present episode is a definitive exposal of his "heart" at its worst.

It is here that Othello becomes completely *at heart* the murderer of Desdemona. That fact is stamped into our minds by the cynical force of his final speech (88 ff.). In the first act he evinced an occasional touch of gently proud sarcasm (I. ii. 59, I. iii. 91-94, I. iii. 267-275), very "free and open" (I. iii. 405) in contrast with Iago's villainous bitterness. But a flair for bitter scorn rises in Othello when he begins to lead a "life" of dissembling "jealousy," and it becomes increasingly a part of the very "business of my soul"[49] (III. iii. 177, 181). The caustic sarcasm with which he watched the laughing Cassio above (IV. i. 110 ff.) was presently directed against his weeping wife (IV. i. 256 ff.). And now it culminates; and it blacks out the hope that the audience could still harbor at the close of their preceding private interview. There we could still conceive that in the end, after some reflection, he would decide merely to send her "away" (III. iv. 98), casting her off completely as he first intended (III. iii. 260-263) instead of killing her. But here his closing words to her and to Emilia indicate that *after reflection,* all the reflection of which he is now capable, his murderous decision is fixed and obdurate. This time he

---

[48] The repeated phrase "my heart" has been reserved by the poet for the present crisis. Othello's "heart" is more crucially important, more volitional and responsible, than his "soul," of which he has hitherto talked considerably (52, III. iii. 181, etc., etc.). See note 14 to Act II.

[49] This phrase seems a mocking echo of the one he used to the senate, "your serious and great business" (I. iii. 268).

does not wave his wife away nor rush away from her presence.
He pronounces upon her, to our ears, a fatal judgment which
he is now fully set to carry out "this night" (IV. i. 218). And
his sardonic, super-Iagoan tone is at once extremely furious and
extremely composed. To Emilia, whom he resummons, and
who is here in very sooth the "opposite to St. Peter," keeping
"the gate of hell" (91 f.),[50] he says with deadly nonchalance:

> We have done our course: there's money for your pains;
> I pray you turn the key, and keep our counsel.

That "key" alludes with cynical concision to her full complicity with that "lock and key of villainous secrets," his wife,
who in this scene has knelt and prayed to him in vain (22 f.).
He and she have indeed "done" their "course." He has already murdered her, along with mercy, in his strange, terrible,
yet fearfully human "heart."

We see he will not change—unless perchance he shall be
swayed, in the end, by the great change that is now beginning
in *her*. He has rejected all charity for her; but hers for him
is now changing and deepening under the stress of *her* "affliction" (48).

The dreadful close of his Patience speech forced her to
perceive, at last, that really he suspects (44) her chastity.
Shocked, recoiling from him in horror, she tries to bring him
to himself, to his "noble" (IV. i. 275)[51] self: "I hope my
Noble Lord esteems me honest!" (65). And when he ig-
nobly heaps execrations upon her, all centering in the word
"whore" (72, 86), she casts off the meekness that she has hitherto used in reproaching him (III. iv. 97, IV. i. 250-252).
With all the force of her strong character she cries out, "By
Heaven[52] you do me wrong!" (81). Religious allusion, employed by him above (47-56) with poetic elaborateness, is

---

[50] Compare the Porter of "hell-gate . . . turning the key" in *Macbeth*
II. iii. 1-3. In both cases the words are ironical while the "hell," spiritually
regarded, is very real.

[51] This adjective is the more emphatic here because *she* has not used it since
III. iv. 26.

[52] No comma here in the early texts or *before* "Heaven" below (88): she
is speaking with passionate speed.

powerfully simple on her tongue. "No, as I am a Christian
... to preserve this vessel ... From ... unlawful touch ....
No, as I shall be saved!"

But his hardening cynicism tells her, through his looks even
more than his words, that now she has utterly lost him. And
for the first time she sees, really though obscurely, that she herself is in some way and in some degree to blame. She cannot
now reproach herself, as she did earlier with large anxiety (III.
iv. 140-154), for "arraigning" him "falsely": his "unkindness"
has turned out to be very certain and very cruel. But it must
be due, however slightly, to some fault in her conduct
towards him: this much her loving instinct tells her truly.
"Alas," she asks herself while she asks him, "what ignorant
sin have I committed?" (70). And in the end she again kneels,
not to him this time but to "Heaven" (88), on behalf of him
and her. She shares his sin. His love has failed completely;
but *her* love has failed to hold his and to help it "increase"
(II. i. 196). And so, on her knees with clasped hands raised,
she prays intensely, "O[53] Heaven forgive *us.*"[54]

Thus she attains the "humble love" (III. iii. 458) that he
has vengefully disdained. In a former crisis he sincerely ad-
vocated "Christian shame" (II. iii. 172) but he did so in the
service of a true and great love, his love of soldiership and
the cause of Venice. In the service of his self-centered love,
and hate, for Desdemona he has now really renounced his
Christian "baptism"; else he would see in the kneeling figure
beside him a "symbol" of "redeemed sin" (II. iii. 349 f.): her
words would awaken in him some sense, however slight, of the
meaning of forgiveness. But he has discovered no slightest
fault in his very inadequate love for her; whilst she has discovered that her pure and mainly unselfish love for him is
crucially inadequate. *Just because* of his "alteration" (Sonnet
116) her love alters for the better. Unlike him she has never
hitherto used the word "Christian" (82): neither she nor any-

[53] "Oh" in F1, "O" in Q1 and Q2.
[54] Compare the kneeling Ophelia, *Hamlet* III. i. 89, 138. The situation
there is repeated here in far more profoundly tragic form.

one else has spoken a single word about her religion. Her love
has been, and remains, intensely connubial. But now it begins
to be also, *without her awareness*, definitely "Christian"—while
he, unawares, shuts upon himself "the gate of hell" (92).

Unlike him she has not talked eloquently about "*my* heart"
(57) in this scene; nor did she when she spoke of "my heart"
at the beginning: there, as in her present prayer, her "heart"
and "soul" (I. iii. 251, 255) were subordinate to her thought
of "him" (I. iii. 249, 260). So the present episode has developed, and conclusively exposed, the tragic contrast shown in the
first act between her "garnered up" (57) heart and his. Above
he had knelt before "Heaven" in a "sacred vow" (III. iii.
460 f.) of vengeance. Now with hopelessly hardened heart,
and for the last time, he watches *her* "kneel and pray" (23)
. . . . for "*us*" (88).[55] Here she becomes in our view an embodiment indeed of Christian "patience" (63).

[55] Compare her "our" (II. i. 196 f.) in the Storm scene.

Wedding

(a) *love*   IV. ii 95-252

BUT soon her prayer droops, beaten down by the brutal power of Othello's final words, far worse than the physical blow he struck her in the preceding scene. Then she could weep, and speak a little (IV. i. 252 ff.). Now she "cannot weep" (103), and for a moment she cannot utter a word. She gazes fixedly after him, until he disappears, as if forever; then drops her hands to the floor beside her, crouching like a dumb creature wounded mortally. "Faith, half asleep" (97), she manages to mutter to the anxious, loving Emilia; whose loud phrase "my lord" rings distantly, strangely, in the ears of her mistress (98-101). "I have none," the girl whispers; then rouses herself a little. "Prithee, tonight"— "tonight," "this night" (IV. i. 272,218), so fearful in our knowledge and in her new apprehension[56]—

Lay on my bed my wedding sheets, remember,[57]   105
And call thy husband hither.

That twofold "my" pierces us: that marriage "bed" is now hers alone. Her faithful woman has a "husband"; her faithful self, "none" (102). The rites and the consecrated companionship through which she hoped to win all of Othello's "heart" (57) have failed: she has now, in a dreadful sense, "his dear

---

[56] The effect is heightened by the fact that the word "night" has not been uttered, in any form or combination, by Othello *to Desdemona*.

[57] The comma pause before and after "remember" (in the original texts but lengthened in modern texts) makes that suggestive word an organic portion of the *whole* swift sentence. Note also that the homely, significant word "wedding" is new; and that the meaning of the line is injured by Q1's substitution of "our" for the second "my."

absence" (I. iii. 260). There has been no real "wedding":
desperately she hopes that there *may* be, still.

But now the immediate shock of disillusion and despair re-
duces her for a few minutes to a state of new, uttermost weakness (107-129).[58] The child that there is in every woman
(and in every man, though differently) complains with pathetic
petulance of her wrongs. Like a "babe" chidden and helpless
she "cannot tell" her own state of mind (111-114) nor "know"
(123, 129) any reason for Othello's. "Am I that name, Iago?"
(118). Does Othello's most intimate companion (now that
Cassio is entirely out of the picture) share his master's view
that she is that strange thing, merely a horrid "name" to a
child, a "whore"? (120). And she is childishly oblivious of
the embarrassed evasion in the villain's replies. Dumbly she
permits Emilia to term her lord worse than "a beggar in his
drink" and Iago, eventually, to "beshrew him for't" (128).
But her repressed tears (103 f.) overflow more and more; and
finally she gives way to a passionate, relieving storm of weeping (124).

The childishness passes. But the true childlikeness of the
religiously loving woman comes more than ever to the fore.
When Emilia guesses that "some eternal villain" has deceived
her lord, Desdemona exclaims, with a *devoutness* of mercy not
evinced by her in earlier scenes, "If any such there be, Heaven
pardon him" (135). This is the sequel of her cry, above,
"O Heaven forgive *us*" (88). And now she silently meditates
upon "us," her husband and herself, with growing peace in
her face, while Emilia fulminates in words of vivid vengeful-
ness against the supposed "villain" who has deceived Othello,
Iago darkly listening (136-148).

The outcome of Desdemona's meditation is her ensuing
great speech (148 ff.). It informs us tacitly[59] that she pardons

[58] Contrast the tone of " 'Tis meet I should be used so" etc. with the simple
dignity of "I have not deserved this" (IV. i. 252).

[59] If the dramatist had made her declaim her forgiveness of *Othello* in
explicit terms she would have appeared *too* angelic and probably a bit priggish.
As it is she charms us by showing that as a "Christian" (82) she can "forgive"
(88) and "pardon" (135) him without employing any of those three words
in her present long speech. This speech is the direct antithesis, without her
awareness, of *his* long speech upon "Patience" above (47-64).

not only the suppositious "cozening slave" (132) but also her husband, fully. At the same time her instinctive insight—the same that enabled her at the beginning to grasp "instinctively" the truth about her "man" behind his story (I. iii. 155, 163)— tells her, what the dramatist has shown clearly to us, that no amount of deception "by some most villainous knave" (139), as Emilia terms him, could relieve her lord of his responsibility, could assuage the guilt of his great "unkindness" (159 f.). But she too, as she feels more than ever, is in some obscure manner responsible. Her love has lost his love; though "by this light of Heaven"—her eyes search the light of her last day on earth—"I know not how I lost him" (150 f.). And now, kneeling once more, she searches with agonized intentness a thing she has hitherto not mentioned, her own "will":[60]

> If e'er my will did trespass 'gainst his love,
> Either in discourse of thought, or actual deed,
> Or that mine eyes, mine ears, or any sense
> Delighted them in any other form,   155
> Or that I do not yet, and ever did,
> And ever *will* (though he do shake me off
> To beggarly divorcement) love him dearly,
> Comfort forswear me!   Unkindness may do much,
> And his unkindness may defeat my life,   160
> But never taint my love . . . .

"Comfort," in the old and deep religious sense, can remain and increase for her because her love for him, unlike his for her, is able to "increase" and "grow" through the loss of connubial "comfort" (II. i. 194-197), in "beggarly divorcement" and in the dire shadow, now sensed by her, of death itself. As to her "will," we cannot forget her wilful blindness in her suit for Cassio. But that taint seems small now as with the aid of

---

[60] Another and very striking instance of Shakespeare's art of dictional economy. In a previous and superficial self-examination Desdemona used the phrase "my soul" (III. iv. 152). Her present phrase "my will" is in exquisite contrast with Othello's "my soul" and "my heart" above (52, 57). The will, as the poet knows—so does even Iago (I. iii. 324 ff.)—is the very center of every human being, especially from the standpoint of religion.

"Heaven" she puts her whole "will" (152, 157) and being into
the determination not to let the worst her husband can do
"taint" her "love." Here when terribly "bereft" she is able
to "consecrate" herself (I. iii. 255-258) in a new and far higher
way than at the first. We see, the more poignantly because
she herself does not assert the fact directly, that now her love
rises above all "the world's mass of vanity" (164).

While Desdemona thus rises, Iago, like Othello above, but
far more hopelessly, sinks to his lowest level. Here we are
shown the conclusive meeting, in theatric terms, of the
heroine and the villain. Occurring at the start of the play's
last phase it is the final sequel of their first interview, occurring
in the opening of the central phase (II. i. 101 ff.). There the
heroine was awaiting with great anxiety reunion, and complete
union, with the hero; here she is awaiting the complete destruction of that union and, very possibly, of herself. In both cases
dramatic providence offers the villain an alluring opportunity
for remorse. Here, however, the invitation is definitive and
almost overwhelmingly powerful. But Iago declines it, after
an unprecedented wavering. Thus he becomes for the first
time utterly unredeemable, an "eternal[61] villain" (130).

At the outset of this episode he is invited to pity a creature
that usually the worst sort of men cannot in cold blood resist,
an unhappy, helpless "child" (114). And indeed he shows
himself exceptionally nonplused. His hypocritic commisera-
tion for her has an uneasy touch of reality in it. He is much
bothered by her weeping (124). But when his wife breaks
out against him, vicariously, his absurd conceit is roused by his
sense of his great art in completely fooling her and all the
others. With flung-up hand and priggish mien he exclaims,
"Fie, there is no such man: it is impossible!" (134). No man
except himself could be so cleverly deceptive. He, the superman, has accomplished the "impossible."

But he wilts and blinks when suddenly Desdemona pardons
him, him who has so masterfully, in his opinion, brought about

[61] Obviously Emilia, unlike Shakespeare and us, means by "eternal" merely
very abhorrent.

her ruin. He was not prepared for this: he has never seen goodness go to such an amazing extreme. He watches her with fascination while she meditates, not again interrupting his wife's objurgations, in the end rebuking that "fool" (148) with sharp curtness. Then he starts back abashed when Desdemona, breaking her long silence, appeals to him piercingly: "O good Iago[62] . . . Good friend . . ." (148, 150). She believes, more simply than the others, that there is genuine goodness in him. His loquacious cynicism in their previous dialogue was due, she was sure, to "heavy ignorance" (II. i. 145) along with posturing wit. Later she remarked with the casualness of simple conviction, "Oh that's an honest fellow" (III. iii. 5). And now "Heaven" (135, 141, 150) through her, subsidiarily through his own wife, is issuing a tremendous summons to his inerted conscience. It has been thoroughly lashed by the "whip" (142) of his wife's tongue. For the first time his villainy, idealized by himself (II. iii. 342 ff.), has been thrust before his eyes in plainest terms, and by one who has been generally complacent enough towards immorality. And for the first time whatever speck of good he may have in him has been directly appealed to, and by one whom he has been forced to regard as embodied goodness.

He feels like slinking off: he makes a motion to do so (I believe) when Desdemona's word "go" (150) gives him the excuse. But his conscience, not yet perfectly lifeless, makes him stay. And now comes the superclimax. With dismay he sees her kneel and dedicate herself to love through death: for a minute the evil fellow stands "stupidly good, of enmity disarmed" (*Paradise Lost* IX. 465). In this "gentle lady" (II. i. 119), this "fair lady" (118), doomed to destruction, love and goodness are indestructible: they cannot be caught by "the net" he has made "out of her own goodness" to "enmesh them all" (II. iii. 366-368). For a moment he himself is enmeshed. Formerly he had wished to "let her live" (III. iii. 475); and now a touch of real remorse appears in his mute face and ges-

[62] The quarto reading. The folios have "Alas Iago." One is tempted to make the line: "O good Iago, alas Iago. . . ."

tures. But presently his demonic pride rouses. His proud little "soul" (I. i. 54) shakes off the forming filaments of his salvation. "I pray you be content . . . " (165). He is desperately anxious, now, to get away from her and her words. He quiets her with a cruel lie that revives for a moment her wishful self-delusion regarding her husband's "business of the State" (166, III. iv. 140). Then with cocked ear, immensely relieved, he hears "how these Instruments summon to supper." Earlier a single "trumpet" announced crucial events (II. i. 180, IV. i. 226). Now a trumpet chorus signalizes the imminence of this fatal night—and may seem to us to "summon" Iago to pull shut upon himself "the gate of hell" (92).

He does so—firmly and gently. After all, the murder of Desdemona is her husband's "business" (166), not his: all he has to do is "strangle" (IV. i. 220) his rising pity for her, and eat his "supper" in peace. More than ever he hates and fears her overawing goodness; but he cannot hate and scorn *her*, as he tried to do in the close of their previous interview (II. i. 149-161). Here he dismisses her in peace, in diabolic peace, with his hand lifted piously. He sends her to her death, employing fine biblical language and with the wry ghost of throttled pity in his leer, *to comfort himself as well as her:* "Go in, and weep not: all things shall be well" (171).[63]

But while Iago broods, alone and quietly, very much "content" (165) with his supernal cleverness, he is rudely interrupted: "How now, Roderigo?" He said that before (II. iii. 369); but his angry friend has this time two new things to talk about, justice and repentance. Roderigo's opening speech is deliberate and punctilious[64]: "I do not find / That thou dealest justly with me" (174). But with every subsequent word his excitement and conviction steadily increase. In reply to his companion's smooth counterclaim of being accused "most unjustly" he loudly avers he is speaking "nought but truth"

[63] A brilliantly intensified sequel to the pious hypocrisy of Claudius near the close of *Hamlet* (V. i. 320-322).

[64] The quartos spoil that tone by running his two lines into one. Each word, particularly "find," is pompously slow.

(187); presently he dares to denounce Iago's conduct as "scurvy," the opprobrious term used by Emilia above (140, 196); and finally, hand on sword, he is ready to "seek satisfaction of you" (203). So much for justice. But meanwhile a pious note has comically crept in. The jewels Iago has supposedly given Desdemona "would half have corrupted a Votarist" (188-190)—"half," not wholly, because Roderigo[65] has a certain respect for women religiously vowed to chastity. And now his ultimatum comes (199 ff.): "I will make myself known to Desdemona. If she will return my jewels, I will give over my suit, and repent my unlawful solicitation."

If he can save his jewels he will try to save his soul too; if his immoral suit is unsuccessful he will "repent"! He stirs in us a depth of laughing pathos. We see that all of Iago's accumulated influence has not been able to destroy the belief of this weak and foolish gentleman that love is not lust (I. iii. 336-338) and that there is something "most blessed" (II. i. 255) in Desdemona, something, as he now feels, akin to the spirit of "a Votarist" —as we of the audience felt during her great monologue above.

But Roderigo's inchoate and conditional desire for repentance is overtopped by his habitual longing to "be a man" (I. iii. 340), a real man like the strong, vital, successful Iago. And now that yearning is appealed to by the villain with a new stroke of artful hypocrisy. Roderigo's tendency to be converted *from* Iago is countered by Iago's feigned conversion *to him*, a conversion very credible to the gull just because it is so dramatically sudden and total.[66] Iago gazes at his companion with a look, entirely novel in Roderigo's experience, of richly wondering admiration. "Why, now I see there's mettle in thee; and even from this instant do build on thee a better opinion than ever before: give me thy hand, Roderigo."[67]

[65] Like Lucio in *Measure for Measure* I. iv. 30 ff.

[66] Precisely the opposite of Iago's conversion, so gradual and artfully hesitant, to his new role of Othello's intimate "friend" (III. iii. 142) in the first part of the Temptation scene.

[67] The early texts, unlike modern ones, have a longer pause after "Roderigo" than after "before."

For a moment the poor creature is motionless as a frog
under the fixed eye of a hungry snake. Then he advances his
hand just a very little, but fatally. Iago seizes it; and he holds
it in firm grasp while he speaks further, making his dupe *feel*
well-nigh his equal in "wit and judgement . . . purpose, Courage, and Valour" (215-219). The masterful Iago's previous
touches of scorn for the "silly gentleman" (I. iii. 308) are all
gone; Roderigo can no longer be classed with "base men" (II.
i. 217). Yet Iago's tone is somewhat doubtful: Roderigo's case
has in it a momentous "But . . . if" (216). Can he
"this night show," very conclusively, his manly mettle? If
so, "the next night" he shall certainly "enjoy . . . Desdemona."
Thus the villain for the first time specifies a particular and imminent hour for that rapturous event; and he stakes his "life"
(222) on his promise.

But how is Roderigo to demonstrate his manhood so conclusively tonight? Iago, keeping him in suspense, prepares
him for a new project by giving him a rapid, plausible preview
of a new situation, one which plainly demands "the removing
of Cassio" (233). How? "Why, by making him uncapable . . .
knocking out his brains." The villain's tone here is ineffably
casual, showing that a manly man's attitude towards this matter
should be just that. Roderigo has boldly threatened the "life"
of his friend, the strong Iago (203, 222): surely the "removing" of the real impediment, Cassio—obviously by "treachery"
(221) though Iago does not say so—should appear comparatively easy. However, Iago does not overtly specify the per-
former; this point he leaves to his companion's "wit and judgement" (215):

RODERIGO And that you would have me to do.   237
IAGO   Ay: if you dare do yourself a profit, and a right.[68]

[68] Instead of "a right" the quartos have "right," which seems at first blush
more suggestive but is not really. As to the suggestive word "dare," compare
Lady Macbeth's striking use of it (I. vii. 44). She has to work up its implications far more fully; but, having done so, she like Iago (239 ff.) hastens to
concentrate her companion's attention upon the feasibility of the coming deed,
which, like Iago, she will not call a murder.

No need to emphasize the delicious "profit," the enjoying of Desdemona: Iago's main ironic appeal here is to the other's manly courage and, above all, as the final word shows, to his dim sense of justice, displayed above. Roderigo readily feels that unlike Cassio, not to mention Othello, he has "a right" to Desdemona, assuming she responds to his love: the unlawfulness of his "solicitation" (202) is a comparatively minor consideration if she has been won, through the agency of the jewels and the clever Iago, to perceive that his claim to her is right and just! She can do so and still be "full of most blessed condition" (II. i. 254 f.), like a "Votarist" (190), in his romantic, immoral, confused conceit. His attitude regarding her here is a parody of hers, above, regarding Othello. Her love will be faithful to her husband through death (160). Roderigo's love-lust will be faithful to her through death—the "death" (247) of Cassio! The devil in Iago foments Roderigo's devilish implicit notion that the felling (245) of Cassio—the plain word "murder" is carefully avoided—is for him "a right."

Yet his conscience, as ever, is far from dead. He stands "amazed" (246). The gloating Iago urges, "It is now high supper time; and the night grows to waste" (248 f.)—the ultimate sequel of his earlier devilish exclamation, "By the mass, 'tis morning." Now *the night* is coming on, the final night; and more than ever "pleasure, and action, make the hours seem short" (II. iii. 384 f.): before this night wastes away he will sup full of evil. It is "high" time to begin; pulling at his motionless companion he commands sharply, "About it." But Roderigo asserts stolidly, "I will hear further reason for this." And we are not *perfectly* sure that he will be fully "satisfied" (252) by his tempter: his conscience is trying hard now to pull him the other way.

(b) *Heavenly light*   (IV. iii)

Not so with Othello; his conscience is quiet now. The last word above, "satisfied," points ominously to his mien as he enters, graciously bidding farewell to his supper company. His

careful politeness to Lodovico contrasts strongly with his parting words to him above (IV. i. 274). And his secret, strict
command to "Desdemona" (5 ff.), notably free from the brutal
sarcasm of his last speech to her (IV. ii. 88 ff.), is quite gentle
in tone. Everyone can see "he *looks* gentler than he did" (11).
And we know that a strong-willed man, normally noble, can
be (unlike Roderigo) serene in the present situation: Othello
has fully convinced himself that the murder he is going to
commit is necessary and right.

And Desdemona's will is stronger than ever. She will
give him entirely that obedience which she promised at the
beginning (I. iii. 179 ff.), which, we know, has come to seem
to him the most patent sign of her hypocritic lust (IV. i. 259
ff.), but in which she now centers her desperate hope of re-
gaining his love. In response to his injunction that she retire
at once and dismiss her attendant from her bedroom she says
with quiet firmness, "I will, my lord" (10). Yet her fore-
boding fear is now far deeper than Emilia's. But she sub-
dues it, at the same time allaying Emilia's clamorous fright,
by quiet determination and by the new religious power of her
"love" (IV. ii. 161).

EMILIA   I would you had never seen him!   18
DESDEMONA So would not I: my love doth so approve him
              That even his stubbornness, his checks, his frowns
              (Prithee, unpin me) have grace and favour.[69]

The "grace and favour" are in herself: her "love" wills to find
them in him. She knows "instinctively" (I. iii. 155) that his
dreadful harshness, which she euphemized to "chiding" (IV.
ii. 114) in her weakest moments above, and which she now
describes for the first time in realistic terms (20), has beneath
it a strong attachment to her; and she believes that her constant love may serve to revive the "grace" and goodness in him,
some way, some time.

[69] The quartos add "in them," and thus destroy the climactic stress on
"grace and favour" in order to make the line a packed pentameter with, moreover, a feminine ending.

The present time, however, is very dark. She appeals to
God against superstitious premonitions: "good Father,[70] how
foolish are our minds!" (23). And it is with studied lightness
of tone that she says, "If I do die before,[71] prithee shroud me /
In one of these same sheets," her "wedding sheets" (IV. ii.
105). But then, with head "at one side" (32) and with uplifted hand, as though hearing voices from the unseen world,
she exclaims suddenly and strangely, "My mother had a Maid
called Barbarie" (26). In the previous scene she alluded to
the hostile, selfish father whom she had "lost" (IV.ii. 44-47).
Now, pathetically, her first intimate mention of her mother
(contrast I. iii. 186) follows soon upon her first mention of
the divine "Father." But every unseen presence that she
turns to for relief is quickly related by her "mind" (23, 31) to
the unseen presence of her husband. This presence pervades
her ensuing song.

The willow song, an "old thing"[72] sung by the maid whose
lover "proved mad / And did forsake her," and who "died
singing it—That song tonight / Will not go from my mind"
(27-31). She tries hard to drive it away (33 ff.). She gives
sharp directions to her attendant. Then she turns her thoughts
to the courteous and handsome guest whom she has just made
"welcome" (4) to the island: "This Lodovico is a proper man
. . . . He speaks well." But *she* speaks listlessly; and she pays
no heed to the vivid tale begun by her woman of the Venetian
lady who "would have walked barefoot to Palestine for a
touch of his nether lip." She herself would make a hard pilgrimage for a "touch" of Othello's love. Her "soul" is "sigh-
ing" for him (41). And suddenly the repressed willow song
pours from her lips rapidly, like the "fresh streams" in "green
willow" springtime that can so beautifully murmur "moans"

---

[70] Q1 alone of the early texts reads "Good faith." This exclamation was
used by Desdemona above (IV. ii. 113) but is too weak for her present mood.
Compare Hamlet's citing, near the end of his life, the Christian belief in
"special providence" over against pagan "augury" (V. ii. 230 ff.); see the
comment in my *Scourge and Minister*, p. 188.

[71] All the early texts except F1 have "before thee," which seems to me
weaker and less suggestive. See "the rest, soon" in the F1 text of *Hamlet*
II. ii. 545 and the footnote in *Scourge and Minister*, p. 63.

[72] Compare Wordsworth's "old unhappy things" in "The Solitary Reaper."

(42, 45).[73] At the same time she hastens her disrobing: "*He'll* come anon" (50). She alters the song so as again to "approve" him (19, 52 f.). But in a sudden gust of "wind" she hears again his dreadful "scorn," along with low summoning voices, so it seems, from the spiritual realm: "Hark, who is't that knocks?" But quickly she controls herself. She sings with a rueful smile the old song's quaint ending (55-57); then says to Emilia firmly, though with warm affection and "eyes" that "itch" to weep, "So get thee gone, good night"—

But still she clings to her friend's hand. She exclaims with deep mournfulness, "Oh these Men, these men!" Thus at last she rightly *senses* in her husband, what he from the first has mistakenly and exclusively *seen* in her, a fallible human *type*. She is now deeply aware that "my noble Moor" has descended to the "baseness" of ordinary *men*, "creatures" capable of "jealous . . . ill thinking" of their wives (III. iv. 26-29). But still, and very tragically, she refuses to face that hard fact plainly and completely: her love for Othello is still not fully *just*. She persists in the delusion that she has never given him any apparent "cause" for jealousy (III. iv. 158). Instead of searching her conduct for such a cause she reiterates her entire faithfulness to him (61 ff., IV. ii. 152 ff.), as though that fact, which he has violently repudiated, must become evident to him if only she continues to obey him absolutely, thus, as we know, helping his murderous jealousy to possess him absolutely. He has no charity for her: his intense love for her is now intensely unkind and unjust. Her loving charity for him is far more kind than just and right—unlike the wise charity of the "good Father" (23) to whom she prays.

Yet we see that her love, despite its continued wilfulness, is becoming more and more religious and sacrificial. The darkness is deepening dreadfully "tonight" (30), but "grace and favour" (21) are growing in her spirit. For Iago, "the night grows . . . " (IV. ii. 249). But Desdemona finds in the last glimmers of day "this Heavenly light" (65).

[73] The "stones" (47) softened by the "salt tears" (in contrast with "fresh streams") may recall to the reader Othello's "heart . . . turned to stone" (IV. i. 192 f.).

But Emilia feels, truly, that "this Heavenly light" (66) does not condone her mistress's blind obedience to her husband tonight. So by way of counterbalance she speaks up on behalf of "the dark" (67), i.e. of the rude common sense of the "world" (69, 76, 81 f.) which her lady too much despises (IV. ii. 164). Above, Emilia proclaimed to the unbelieving Othello, with fine vigor, his wife's chaste faithfulness (IV. ii. 12 ff.). But now when her lady is carrying that faithfulness to a desperate extreme, she puts before her, with humorous vigor, the other side of the picture. Suppose a woman could by an act of adultery advance greatly her husband's welfare in the world, she might well "venture Purgatory for't" (77)—an indirect thrust at her lady's new religiosity. But that speech is merely the prologue to what follows. Emilia launches into a vivid depiction of "husbands' faults" (87 ff.) with incessant veiled criticism of Othello. Suppose our husbands turn to other women (which Othello has not done); or "break out in peevish jealousies . . . or, say, they strike us" (which Othello *has* done): "Why, we have galls; and though we have some Grace" (93)— as Desdemona has (21)—"Yet have we some Revenge."

> Then let them use us well: else let them know,
> The ills we do, their ills instruct us so.

But Desdemona, while appreciating her devoted woman's good will, rejects the good advice implicit in her speeches, rejects the good along with the bad. Rightly, of course, she rejects the doctrine of requiting "ill" with "ill." Now she repeats her "good night" (58, 105) with finality of tone—a "good night" which we feel is final in the world and, rising above "the world's mass of vanity" (IV. ii. 164), moves in a heavenly light:

> Good night, good night:
> Heaven me such uses send,[74]
> Not to pick bad, from bad; but by bad, mend.

[74] Q1 makes this line one with its predecessor and reads, "God me such usage send," which was probably enough Shakespeare's first version. F1's punctuation, reproduced by me above, indicates that the three lines are to be spoken very slowly and stressfully.

(c) *ugly* V. i

Iago's final soliloquy (11 ff.) shows his suppressed conscience making a final and extraordinary protest. He is confronted with the imminent killing of Cassio; but his desire has always been to murder souls, not bodies. Of course he has never expressed that inhuman desire in plain terms; he is not sufficiently inhuman for that; but his conduct has evinced it, especially when trying to disguise it.[1] Like other human beings he has hidden from himself the killing wickedness of hate by cherishing an aversion to actual killing; thus he has poisoned himself with that common deadly mixture, pride-and-conscience. His conscience keeps him from actual murder and so does his pride: he is above such crude procedure. Incidentally it may be dangerous; but above all it is irrelevant in the case of a person so highly gifted as he is with "will" and "reason" (I. iii. 322 ff.). He has never once wished to destroy Othello; he has yearned merely to murder (without using that word or any plain synonym) his "sweet sleep" (III. iii. 332),[2] his peace, joy, and nobility.

Iago's pride blinds him to the fact that not he but Othello himself is the main cause of Othello's ruin. On the other hand his pride-and-conscience enables him, in defiance of reason, to assign to Othello, so primitive a person in his view, the *whole* responsibility for the coming murder of Desdemona. And with still more fantastic, yet human, irrationality he has tacitly tried to hold himself excused for his own coming murder of his "friend" (III. iii. 474) Cassio because it was demanded by Othello. Iago's pride makes him claim full credit for Othello's passionate jealousy; but his conscience makes him anxious to disclaim responsibility for the most brutal results of that passion—even for that slaughter of Cassio which, when Othello

[1] Hamlet at his worst wishes to kill a "soul" (III. iii. 94) but in him the desire is a sudden rage, loudly uttered, unique, and transient. In Iago it is so constant and horrible that his conscience never dares to face it plainly.
[2] With Iago's fine euphemism in that passage contrast the inner "voice" that cried out to a deeper villain, "Macbeth does murder sleep" (II. ii. 36).

began to yearn to perform it himself, Iago had to reclaim as his own appointed task (IV. i. 146 f., 178-188, 224f.).

Yet this task is the very one that Iago most dislikes. His triumph over Cassio is peculiarly complete and satisfying. Roderigo is too easy a prey; Othello, too difficult and violent. The Moor's astoundingly powerful passion has dragged the slick Iago at its chariot wheels: only with patient, incessant effort has the villain been able to maintain, imperfectly, his feeling of being his master's master. All the more, then, has he gloated over the utter dejection and the entire subservience to his plans on the part of that very fine but weak gentleman, the former lieutenant. And Iago could have continued that cheerful gloating if only Othello's "unbookish jealousy"[3] (IV. i. 102) had not brought about the need of Cassio's bodily destruction. That crude deed is greatly deplored by the villain's pride-and-conscience.

Eagerly therefore he grasped at the opportunity of having Roderigo do "the removing of Cassio" (IV. ii. 232 f.).[4] But now that slouching gull shows even less "devotion to the deed" (8) than his master feels. Iago knows that in all probability he himself will have to end Cassio. And he knows that his own material welfare requires the death of both his dupes (12 ff.). For if Roderigo lives he will demand "restitution large . . . It must not be—[5] If Cassio do remain . . . . " And here we expect a statement, parallel to that concerning Roderigo, of the *material* danger Cassio holds for the speaker. But the villain's conscience suddenly intervenes:

> He hath a daily beauty in his life
> That makes me ugly—and besides, the Moor   20
> May unfold me to him: there stand I in much peril—
> No, he must die. But so, I hear him coming.

[3] This phrase is one of the most striking of the villain's efforts to belittle in his own mind the human strength *and art* of Othello's passion, Iago's attitude to which is really as "bookish" (I. i. 24) as, in his opinion, was Cassio's attitude to war.

[4] Obviously the situation reproduces in miniature the one in which Claudius proposes that Laertes instead of himself, though with his careful seconding, shall "requite" Hamlet (IV. vii. 140).

[5] Here, and twice in the passage quoted below, I have substituted a dash for the colon of F1.

That heavy "No," conspicuously absent from his concluding dictum upon Roderigo above, reveals the strength of Iago's impulse to let Cassio live, an impulse which he has to silence effortfully—"But so"—with the aid of the sound of Cassio's approaching footsteps.[6] That young gentleman's "daily beauty," so questionable in other respects, is outstanding in his simple, loyal, admiring devotion to "the Moor" (20). And this, despite all Iago's efforts to feel superior to such "obsequious bondage" (I. i. 46), has made him sense, increasingly, the ugliness of his own "daily" jealous and treacherous hate; and here for a moment that smoldering percept becomes a flame. But quickly he tramples it; as he did his rising pity for Desdemona above (IV. ii. 165 ff.). Tacitly he has all along recognized as his chief enemy the beautiful "goodness" (II. iii. 367) at work in the daily life of *her*. And now that same enemy at work "in" the "life" (19) of Cassio—this "pestilent complete knave" (II. i. 252)—is making an ultimate effort to unman him, to subdue his very "soul" (I. i. 54). *Incidentally* his *material* well-being is in great danger from Cassio; the profound irony for us of his phrase "and besides" (20) is entirely unintentional on the part of Iago. Here the question of his bodily safety is secondary to the question of his inward safety, the safety of his proud faith in his own egoistic self. He must destroy that "life," the life of Cassio, through the medium of which his conscience insists on telling him that his own life, the life of that masterful self of his, is "ugly." So here the villain gives his conscience a strong, ultimate "No."

Roderigo, a moment later, gives *his* conscience an ultimate yes. This foolish gentleman would fain quiet his qualms, as he has twice done before (II. iii. 153, IV. ii. 205 f.), by putting on a swaggering air. He flourishes his "sword" (10). Loudly and absurdly he addresses as "villain" (23) the man he is villainously trying to murder. But when, run through by Cas-

---

[6] Compare the effect for Macbeth of the sound of the summoning "bell" (II. i. 62). The dramatic effortfulness of Iago's final resolve is weakened in the quarto version of his last line: "No, he must die, be't so, I hear him coming."

sio's sword, he mistakenly believes he is "slain" (26) he confesses very simply his own wickedness: "Oh Villain that I am
(29) . . . . Oh wretched Villain" (41). His weak but insistent
desire to "repent" (IV. ii. 202) has been quickly matured, as
in the case of most human beings, by the approach of "death"
(45). And the true human instinct that told him at the first
that "love" is not "lust" (I. iii. 336-338) prevents him now
from trying to shift to Iago the ultimate blame for his sins:
he himself is "villain." But Roderigo feels, as we feel, that
this term is far too weak for the devilish creature who presently
assures his death by thrusting him through and through:[7]
"O damned Iago! O inhuman dog!" (62)—this subhuman
creature who at the first proclaimed his own "humanity" to
Roderigo and ridiculed damnation (I. iii. 318, 360 f.). Thus
in his last speech the stupidest person in the play can find exactly
the right terms for Iago because he has found beforehand his
own great sinfulness.

And indeed in this scene Iago (in contrast with Roderigo)
symbolizes all that is monstrous and "damned," but without
ceasing to be a human villain. Very human is his failure to
kill Cassio a moment after declaring that "he must die" (22).
Obviously Cassio's "coat,"[8] proof against Roderigo's weak
thrust, could not have saved him from an entirely ruthless Iago
resolved to end him on the spot by, if necessary, stabbing him
in the neck or cutting his throat or "knocking out his brains"
(IV. ii. 236). But Iago is not utterly ruthless. He has finally
steeled himself against any touch of repentance, but not against
subconscious touches of remorse. So now he compromises.
From behind and under the cloak of darkness he slashes Cassio's leg, cuts it well-nigh "in two" (72). Thus while re-
fraining from downright killing he can expect his hapless friend
to bleed to death; and thus, more importantly, he has the

---

[7] Q2 and Q3 have the stage direction "*Thrusts him in.*" The modern
"*Stabs Roderigo*" is much too mild for the context. The ensuing phrase
"damned Iago" may, for us, seem a sequel and synonym of Emilia's "hell gnaw
his bones" (IV. ii. 136).

[8] Cassio may or may not be wearing for the nonce a coat of mail. See the
footnote in the *Furness Variorum* edition of the play, p. 284.

malignant satisfaction of maiming "for ever" (27), though in an external fashion, the other's "daily beauty" (19). For us, the villain becomes here more monstrously "ugly" (20) than a downright killer could possibly be. And in the rest of the scene his hypocrisy, whereby he fools and comforts himself even more than he deceives others (a self-fooling far beyond the capacity of the plain fool Roderigo), becomes more and more damnable.

While Cassio cries out, "Help hoa! Murther, murther!" (27)—that term so sedulously avoided by Iago— and approaching footfalls (ironically, those of the passing Othello) seem to respond to the cry, the scared villain slinks swiftly away, a shadow darker than the night. Off stage he regains his poise sufficiently. Meanwhile Lodovico and Gratiano appear in the background. Then the villain re-enters, slowly, with perturbed mien, while Gratiano exclaims, "Here's one comes in his shirt, with Light, and Weapons" (47). The nameless "one" wears the appearance of an honest soldier roused from his bed; for us, however, he might be "one" arriving from hell to masquerade as a human rescuer. He holds high his smoking torch in the "heavy night" (42). His peering face is dark above his "shirt"; and the blade of a weapon in his hand, and the hilt of another at his side, gleam uncertainly in the meager light.

Iago for a moment is painfully uncertain. At first he hopes Cassio's cry of "murther" (48, 27)—the villain's first utterance of this gross term—was his last;[9] but presently he learns that Cassio, still alive, can repeatedly call for "help" (49-55). Iago has badly botched his evil job. As ever, his over-all strategy is weak but his tactics, in a tight place, very adroit. He delays as long as possible first aid for Cassio. He gloats over the doubly fallen "lieutenant" (56) while at the same time, as in the case of Desdemona (IV. ii. 124 ff.), indulging in pity for one he has doomed but not actually killed. Then with *good con-*

---

[9] This was Othello's assumption: he thinks Cassio "lies dead" (33). And we of the audience are uncertain until, in Iago's absence, Cassio calls out again (37, 39).

science he performs his first downright murder, that of Roderigo, a "murderous slave" (61),[10] thereupon demanding of the two aloof newcomers, with delicious hellish unctuousness, "Are you of good, or evil?" And when Lodovico, now coming closer (59), is curt and suspicious (66 ff.) the smart villain concentrates the attention of the two gentlemen upon the sufferings of Cassio, whom he dares now to address familiarly, for the first time, with mixed sentiment and triumph, as his "brother" (71); presently binding his wound assiduously with "my shirt."

He further turns suspicion from himself by casting it upon the loudly mourning Bianca, a "notable strumpet" (78), while continuing his tenderness to Cassio in curious rivalry with hers. To free his hands he had transferred his torch to the "gentlemen," requesting them to give him "light" (73); and now he loudly repeats that word (88): it echoes and gleams fitfully in the night, as it did at the very beginning (I. i. 145); while the torchlight flickers upon the villain's ghastly hypocrisy:

> Lend me a Light—know we this face, or no?
> Alas my Friend, and my dear Countryman,
> *Roderigo?*   No—Yes, sure—O heaven,[11] *Roderigo!*   90

Iago is "sure," mistakenly (V. ii. 327-329), that this friend is quite dead. And wishful thinking convinces him that his other friend, now very faint (84), will expire soon: "He that lies slain here, Cassio, / Was my dear friend (101 f.) . . . . He's almost slain, and Roderigo quite dead" (114). Iago luxuriates in his sympathy for those two: it is hypocritically sincere.

Perfectly sincere is his final pronouncement, after Cassio has been borne "carefully" (99, 104) away, upon that poor gentleman's fate: "This is the fruits of whoring" (116). Iago himself is above that vice. Strong in human "reason" he has always been able "to cool" in himself those "carnal stings" and "lusts," often called "love" (I. iii. 335 ff.), which have swayed

---

[10] Compare the unction with which the murderous Claudius condemns "murder" (*Hamlet* IV. vii. 128 f.).

[11] Q1 alone of the early texts has "O heaven"; the others read "Yes, 'tis" or "Yea, 'tis."

other men, all the way up from Roderigo to Othello. Cassio's case is outstandingly simple: he has gone in for "whoring." In contrast the rough-tongued Iago is eminently respectable. Even while he is inveighing against the "pale" Bianca (104) his wedded wife enters addressing him as "husband" (111); and presently the proper Emilia, whose secret impropriety we have overheard above (IV. iii. 66 ff.), abets his condemnation of the other woman: "Oh fie upon thee, Strumpet!" (121).

Bianca, mastering her shaking (118) sobs for Cassio—who, above, vouchsafed her not a single syllable—rejoins firmly and loudly: "I am no Strumpet, but of life as honest / As you that thus abuse me." This final speech of hers in the play rings out clearly in the ugly darkness. She is no longer a prostitute. Her love for Cassio, blind and hapless, like Desdemona's for Othello, has redeemed her past: her "life" is now "honest," as honest as her grief, in smiting contrast with Iago's, is simple and whole-hearted.

But no one believes her. Iago's different "tale" (125) is more plausible: "this trash" is a probable "party" in the mangling of Cassio (79, 85 f.). The villain's whole air in this scene is convincing to the others because he is strenuously fooling himself. He iterates the fact that Cassio "supped tonight" (117) "with a harlotry" (IV. ii. 239), a fact that enables Iago to quiet his inner qualms. This "poor Cassio" (124) is ultimately responsible for his own destruction; and obviously his "daily beauty" (19) is soiled by his "whoring" (116). The villain conceals from himself that "this is the night" (128) wherein he is making himself consummately ugly.

(d) *sword* V. ii.

V. ii. 1-96

And here the same is true, more subtly and terribly, of the hero. Othello's last speech above (V. i. 31-36), in harmony with the context, was rawly ugly. His present soliloquy is dreadfully beautiful. It weaves a veil of lovely tone and color

over the murder—he avoids that word as studiously as Iago
did before the assault on Cassio—which he is determined to
commit:

> It is the cause, it is the cause, my soul—
> Let me not name it to you, you chaste stars:
> It is the cause. Yet I'll not shed her blood,
> Nor scar that whiter skin of hers than snow,
> And smooth as monumental alabaster: 5
> Yet she must die,[12] else she'll betray more men . . . .

The vague, unique altruism of that last clause is a striking
sign of the speaker's determined effort to justify himself. He
will not face the fact that the murder of his wife is horribly
wicked no matter how wicked she may be. That fact, whispered to him by "my soul" (IV. ii. 52 ff.) in the very midst
of his furious reprobation of her, has now, when the murder
is imminent, been loudly urged by "my soul" (1). He stifles
that protest by intensely urging "the cause," not to be named
to the "chaste stars,"[13] which he invokes as sponsors of the not-
to-be-named murder. "Yet" (3) he tacitly admits what his
pride keeps him from plainly confessing, the wickedness of his
revengefulness: this evil passion he will now discard utterly.
He will execute his wife dispassionately, from motives of "Justice" (17); righteously he will end her career of secret licentiousness, to the great benefit of "more men" (6).

Accordingly he will put away that recurrent vengeful craving for "blood" (3) which culminated a little while ago in the
decision to spot her "lust-stained" bed with her lustful "blood"
(V. i. 36). He will not even "scar" her "skin" (4) by strangling her in that bed: such "justice" (IV. i. 220-222) seems now
far too harsh and primitive. Inwardly he decides to *"smother"*
her with the bed clothes (83 f.)[14] but does not utter that word

---

[12] These three words are a dramatic echo of Iago's "he must die" (V. i. 22).

[13] Contrast the "ever-burning lights" (III. iii. 463) which sponsored the
burning passion he is now about to repudiate: he wishes his mood to be cool
and serene like the "chaste stars." Incidentally Othello, coming in from the
open air beneath the "stars," carries a torch, not a taper as some have imagined;
and we recall the suggestive torches of the opening scenes of the play.

[14] F1 has the stage direction *"Smothers her"*; the quartos have *"he stifles
her."*

aloud: even the word itself sounds too ugly for his present mood. He will simply "quench" (8) her life like the torch in his hand, the "flaming minister," which he is about to extinguish: "Put out the Light, and then put out the Light." The "gentler" (IV. iii. 11) mood in which he last looked upon her quietly obedient face grows upon him now as he watches her quietly sleeping. In the low, steady shine of her nightlight she is as still as a carved figure on a tomb (5), as still as she will presently be in death. And his words, with deadly power, bring finally home to us his real ignorance of her *moving, living* self. Now more than ever she is, for him, merely a charming superficies, a "cunning'st Pattern of excelling Nature" (11), illumed with a wonderful *earthly* "light"—not at all with "Heavenly light" (IV. iii. 65).

But his "sorrow" over her, he thinks, is "heavenly" (21). Her "balmy breath," as he puts his lips to her sleeping face, could "almost persuade / Justice to break her sword" (16 f.); he "must weep" (20). And so he decides that his "cruel tears" evince the mercy that seasons heavenly justice: he feels that his "love" (19, 22) for her partakes the divine charity that is both merciful and just. Thus he becomes definitively human and tragic. That blasphemous egoism is continual in men, attesting the supreme value of the divine-human Love, just and merciful, which it perversely imitates. Desperately Othello is trying to subdue his jealous *passion* with a sincere parody of *dispassionate* charity: he tries to overcome real evil with unreal good.

He draws back into the shadows as she wakes. "Who's there? *Othello?*" (23). This anxious cry of hers startles us by condensing the import of all his lengthy "sweet" and "fatal" (20) soliloquy: not a real Othello is "there," just now, but one hovering fatally in a shadowy region between good and evil. Twice in quick succession he addresses her fondly (and for the last time in her lifetime) as "Desdemona," the beautiful name that denotes, for him, all the charms he knows and loves, "thy rose" (13)—for us, the real woman he does not lovingly know.

With specious Christianity he urges her to pray more really than she has hitherto done (25, IV. ii. 23), to "bethink your-self of any Crime / Unreconciled as yet to Heaven and Grace": the crime that his graceless pride has all along prevented him from putting clearly before her with Christian charity. All the more, therefore, is his present sort of charity anxious that she shall confess herself to Heaven: "I would not kill thy unpre-pared spirit . . . I would not kill thy soul." And so she learns she is to die. She cries out with simple fervency, "Then Heav-en have mercy on me!"[15]

But when he responds, "Amen, with all my heart," she tries hard to have "hope" (35, 45): surely he must share the mercy "all" his "heart" wants "Heaven" to bestow on her. But that very heart is filling again, swiftly, with the fury he has so re-ligiously abjured. He could abjure it when she lay sleeping as still as if "dead" (18): he could end her quiet breathing with quietness, surely, in his own soul. But her waking reawaked his evil passion. Asleep she *looked* innocent; awake she *acts* innocent: this he cannot bear. When she said with the purest wifely mien, "Will you come to bed, my lord?" (24), he could master his rage only by fervid religious words, which however have served, he thinks, to heighten her dissimulation: she too utters religious words. With "fatal" (37) though entirely hu-man irony his false religiosity finds the same in her. She can actually appeal to heaven for mercy while showing not the least touch of remorse for her sins, despite imminent death, and in the very face of all his fine Christian feelings and utter-ances. From these she merely picks a hope to live. She dis-avows all "guiltiness" and all "fear" of heaven while fearing him (37-39). He commands with loud sternness, "Think on thy *sins*."

"They are loves I bear to you." We and Othello feel, though very differently, that this declaration means more than appears. For us it means that all her errors or "sins" are ulti-

---

[15] F1 reads "mee," apparently for long tone and emphasis. This line, a single one in the early texts, has been divided in two by modern editors to make it conform with a supposed regular meter in the context.

mately due to her devotion to him, a devotion oversswaying
every desire she has: all her desires are "loves I bear to you."
For him it means that her conscience has forced her to admit,
indirectly, that her love for him is as "foul" (IV. ii. 61) as her
"lust" (V. i. 36) for others: all her "loves" are "sins"—"and
for that thou diest" (41).

His eyes "roll" (38); he gnaws his lip; his "bloody passion
shakes" his "very frame" (43 f.). He still reins in his fury;
but all his factitious quietude of soul is gone. Devoid of peace
he commands her, "Peace, and be still."

DESDEMONA   I will so—What's the matter?
OTHELLO   That Handkerchief[16]
            Which I so loved and gave thee thou gav'st to *Cassio*.
DESDEMONA   No, by my Life and Soul: send for the man,
            And ask him.

And so at last he has answered her crucial question, "To whom,
my lord? / With whom? How am I false?" (IV. ii. 40). But
he has done so in the service, not of "justice" (17), but of
proud passion. His pride has all along refused the most obvious and elementary requirement of justice: "send for the
man, / And ask him." And now, as he thinks, the "just" (V.
i. 31) Iago has killed that witness. Therefore he can manage
now, though with a convulsive effort, to mention the name of
Cassio to his wife, mastering his pride thus much—in the service of pride. His aim is not justness, as he insanely fancies,
but self-justification. Her demeanor unnerves him, far more
than Iago was unnerved above by Cassio's "daily beauty" (V.
i. 19). Her beautiful and growingly strong mien of simple
innocence appals him deeply. Surely on her very "death-bed"
she must put aside her "perjury" (51)! Iterating the fact
that she is "to die" (52, 56) he tries to make her "confess thee
freely of thy sin," not to "Heaven" (27) now but to himself.

---

[16] This word *is* "the matter." He utters it with a wrenching effort, then
goes on rushingly. The first six words of her denial are explosively quick;
the rest, progressively slow and deliberate, with heavy stress on "ask" and on
"him." The quartos give a different and metrically smoother lineation, generally followed in modern texts.

Desperately he wants her to vindicate so strongly his "strong conception" (55) of her guilt that he may kill her with a feeling of good conscience instead of sheer rage.

But she declares strongly the perfect innocence of her friendship for Cassio. Unfortunately, however, she begins with the dubious assertion, "I never did / Offend[17] you in my life" (58 f.), while we recall all the ways in which she has perturbed him. Here and in the immediate sequel we are made to realize vividly that she has "loved not wisely but too well" (344). If her love for Othello were *juster* she would now see and confess her own self-will in refusing to know his jealousy, in persistently advocating his discharged lieutenant, and in denying that his meaningful handkerchief was "lost" (III. iv. 83). No wonder her true guess that Cassio "found it" (66) seems now to Othello a desperate lie confirming his conviction that Cassio "hath confessed" (68, IV. i. 145 f.) his adultery. And her fatally tactless outcry when she learns of Cassio's supposed death, "Alas, he is betrayed, and I undone" (76), is due to the habitual tactlessness of her love.

All along she has lacked the objective sympathy that could enter *fully* into her husband's current state of mind. By giving him devoted obedience without an equal measure of loving discernment, she has blindly fed his jealousy. Rightly he has viewed her obedience as the product, not at all of weakness, but of a strong will. Wrongly, but abetted by her refusal to realize how her conduct is suspicious in his eyes, he believes she has increasingly thrown her strong will into maintaining a beautiful air of innocence. She can be a "perjured woman" (63) in the very shadow of death with wonderful art—until informed suddenly of her lover's death. Here, in his view, all her defences, just because so artificial and elaborate, suddenly collapse; this "strumpet" cannot help weeping for her lover to her husband's very "face" (77). And we, moved to our depths for him as well as for her, know that her outcry though

[17] The common denotation of this word, to annoy, vex, or affront, is prominent here in *our* minds; she, of course, means merely that she has not sinned against him sexually.

literally right—Cassio *is* "betrayed," she *is* "undone"—is spiritually wrong. Beforehand she was sure she "must not *now* displease him" (IV. iii. 17); but in the end, untaught by love's kind of justice and reason,[18] she says precisely the words that must infuriate him *now*. For us those words are a final flash revealing the defect of her spiritual sympathy, inmost fellow feeling,[19] for the extremely sinful, noble man he is.

Thus *our* sympathy *for* him is assured even while we are revolted by the ugly wickedness *in* him. This now attains its acme. We know her supposed admission of guilt should evoke in him *some* sense of his own sinfulness. At the very least her sudden helpless weeping (77) should occasion a little pause of pity before he kills her. But not so.

When she renewed, above, her appeal to the divine "mercy"[20] his repeated "amen" (57, 34) was more dreadfully hypocritic than her supposed "perjury" (51): it out-Iagoed Iago. Her simple response, "And have you mercy too," is heaven's judgment upon him. To those words he makes no reply: he silently repudiates the call of heavenly mercy in his soul. "By Heaven" (62) he presently shouts, parodying her quiet "Heaven" (60), beginning to let loose his repressed rage: what he is about to do will be indeed "a murther," not "a sacrifice" (65). His protestation to her, "thou dost stone my heart" (63), perverts his former confession, "my heart is turned to stone" (IV. i. 192 f.): he alone is responsible for the final wicked hardening of his heart. His new, fine effort to enlist himself in the service of "heavenly" (21), merciful "Justice" (17) has collapsed. The deep, long-indulged motive which he would fain abjure resumes control, "my great revenge" (74)—"my revenge," hellish "black vengeance," with its "violent pace" (III. iii. 443, 446, 457). And so when she

---

[18] Milton gives the Renaissance view of "true love" when he says that it has its "seat in Reason, and is judicious" (*Paradise Lost* VIII, 589-591).

[19] The German word *Mitgefühl* comes to mind here.

[20] Instead of the "O Heaven" (57) of the folios the quartos read, more effectively, "Then Lord," an intensified variant of her "Then Heaven" above (33). The word "Lord" is emphatically religious like the word "Father" (IV. iii. 23) in her preceding scene.

shrieks out at the last, "O banish me, my lord, but kill me not"
(78)—echoing providentially his own first and better intention
(III. iii. 260 ff.)—he will not listen, he will not pause.

She had foreseen banishment very vividly; death, very
vaguely. She saw he might "shake me off / To beggarly divorcement"; or even he might, in some obscure way, "defeat"
(ruin or destroy) "my life" (IV. ii. 157-160). Later the feeling that she was about to "die" (IV. iii. 24) grew upon her fitfully and fearfully, but with no specific image (comparable to
"beggarly divorcement") of Othello murdering her.   Hence
her *new* horror when he suddenly utters to her the word she
had not spoken to herself, the word "kill" (31-33). He, sooth-
ing his conscience, will not repeat it; but she does (35, 42), with
increasing horror.   And now at the end her death-fear, though
great, is not greater than her anguish at his crime: the husband
she loves will "kill" her (78, 80), and with "those same sheets"
(IV. iii. 24) sanctified by the "rites" of marriage (I. iii. 258).
Her final cries are an agony on his behalf as well as her own,
an agonizing craving that he should not kill her, if kill her he
must, in his present state of black, murderous rage: "Kill me
tomorrow, let me live tonight."[21] "But half an hour." "But
while I say one prayer."

That last clause appeals, in vain, to his erstwhile promise
when trying to be justly merciful: he would pause for her to
pray (25-32). And we know that her "one prayer" now (83)
would have been for both of them, imploring that "Heaven
forgive us" (IV. ii. 88) and that he be led to receive the divine
"mercy" by imitating it a little (57 f.). But he smothers her,
and her prayer, and mercy, crying out in his frenzy, "Being
done, there is no pause . . . . It is too late." The murder already "done" in his soul, done repeatedly with furious, secret,
vengeful pride, is now in his very fingers: it is being done with
every fiber of him, body and soul. The "current and compulsive course" (III. iii. 454) of that *intended* "murther"

[21] This is the last occurrence in the play of that ominous and so often
repeated word. The "night" that began in the first act culminates here, and
begins to end.

(64 f.) will have "no pause" here. It stifles and sweeps away every "drop" of religious "patience" that has tried to find lodgment in "some place" of his "soul" (1 ff., IV. ii. 52 f.). In smothering Desdemona he smothers, for one fatal, eternal minute, every motion of his own better nature and divine grace: it is indeed, but infinitely more than he knows, "too late."

Then instantly, as he withdraws his hands, dazed, shaking from head to foot, he hears at the door a clamoring summoning "noise" (85).[22] It is the voice of Emilia, the one, the sole one, who unselfishly and understandingly loves Desdemona— and the body on the bed moves a little (93).[23] "Not dead? not yet quite dead?" (85), Othello whispers hoarsely. And now a lethal air of irony palls him. Above he broke his pious promise to her regarding her prayer: here he must break his beautiful promise to himself "not" to "shed her blood" (3). To end her pain he, "yet merciful" (86)—that lovely word is cruelly ugly here—must stab her. He does so, unsteadily, with face averted, while the clamor of Emilia within rises "high" (93).[24] But the figure on the bed is quiet, "still as the grave" now, as it was when sleeping (5), though for a moment he thinks "she stirs again" (94 f.) But if Emilia is allowed to enter "she'll sure speak to my wife"—

V. ii. 97—258

Those last two words, long foreign to him, displaced by ugly stabbing epithets, rise again quietly from the depths of his soul. Long ago, so it seems, when he was trying to master his rising jealousy he recounted all the charms of "my wife" (III. iii. 184). And now when he has vented, and ended, that hellish passion his prediction, above, comes true: "Be thus when thou art dead, and I will kill thee / And love thee after" (18 f.). But he had not realized in his soul that then, i.e.

---

[22] The quartos read "voice"; and this is indeed what *we* hear (84); but the stunned Othello hears at first only an inarticulate "noise" (85, 93).

[23] Shakespeare knows that his audience knows that an essentially good man who smothers his wife is likely to bungle the job, especially when he hears an accusing "noise" at the door. Suggestively Q2 prints the following words all in one line:

OTHELLO 'Tis too late. *Emilia calls within.*

[24] Instead of "high" Q1 and Q2 have "here."

"after," she would no longer be "thou" and "thee" (87). Now he cannot ever again do what the devoted Emilia will strangely do: "speak to my wife"—

> My wife, my wife—what wife?   I have no wife.

He had not known how "insupportable" this "hour" would be, as though "sun and moon" were blotted out, and the earth a wide-gaping thing in final darkness (98-101). His soul is chaos. Emilia is "forgot." But presently her voice, now firmly beseeching, penetrates his consciousness: she wishes to "speak" (90, 96, 102) with *him*, not with that which was his wife. That, he hides by drawing the bed curtains; then gropes blindly for the door: "Where art thou?" Emilia when admitted cries, "yonder's foul murthers done," echoing unawares his own fatal "done" (82).[25]   He starts and stares, with upraised hands: the intuitions of the human mind are very strange, "mad" (111).   And he learns from Emilia that mad events have taken place. "A young Venetian" (such was that body on the bed) has been killed, a certain Roderigo; but not Cassio. Othello's chaos deepens. His own senses had told him, so he imagined, that Cassio was "dead" (V. i. 33). The "death" of Cassio and Cassio's mistress (91 f.)—that was the design of "my great revenge" (74): that, in the midst of mad chaos, was a rational though terrible thing his proud will could cling to, a great thing designed by him and done. But others are dead, not Cassio:

> Not Cassio killed?   Then Murther's out of tune,   115
> And sweet Revenge grows harsh.

Instantly is heard a voice not "harsh" but low, clear, and severe: "Oh falsely, falsely murdered."

EMILIA   Alas! what cry is that?
OTHELLO   That? . . . What?[26]

[25] Her words could of course mean: Yonder's (the bed's) foul murder is done. Compare Macbeth's "done" and Lady Macbeth's unwitting echo of it (I. vii. 1 f., II. ii. 11, 14 f.).

[26] The two question marks are in F1 and Q1. The first is commonly changed to an exclamation point in modern texts. And Emilia's line is gen-

To her it seems a "cry" from the air. To him, confounded, it is a nameless utterance from everywhere, the outward and inward sounding of a dreadful accusation. It seems to come from beyond the "curtains" (104), from that which is "still as the grave" (94). But surely the accusing words are not his former wife's: *they seem to be his own.* He told her she was *false* and that he had to *murder* her; but *she* did not, and surely would not, could not, denounce his conduct as murderous and false.[27] We, however, know what he will presently learn: her spirit, on the verge of eternity, has *in love* pronounced true judgment on his crime. Finally her love has become what it previously was not, except very inadequately, and what his own love failed utterly to be: justly merciful, mercifully just. Thus her love partakes of that complete charity which she has of late so prayerfully desired. Through her, Heaven's just, strong, burning love becomes for Othello, more and more from now on, a "flaming minister."

And the awful divine mercy, albeit in a poor, crude human guise, flames, a few minutes later, through her last words of all. Emilia, soon perceiving that the mystic "cry," above, "was my lady's voice" (119), has rushed to her bedside, clamoring for "help," throwing open the curtains, and entreating her to "speak again . . . speak!" A human whisper comes: "A guiltless death I die." But when Emilia demands in horror "who hath done this deed?" Desdemona lifts her head a little as by superhuman effort: she exclaims in a loud tone that sinks in the close and dies:

> Nobody—I myself—farewell:
> Commend me to my kind lord—oh, farewell!   125

In that sublime lie—a greater prayer, we feel, than would have been her incipient "prayer" above (83)—she "instinctive-

---

erally indented as though it and Desdemona's cry formed a single verse. But Emilia's line and Othello's are clearly parallel: his two words (the intervening dots are of course mine) echo two of hers, and require in speech about the same time as her whole line.

[27] In her song the lover was "false" (IV. iii. 55); but not till now has she applied the word directly to the conduct of Othello.

ly" (I. iii. 155) tells the truth. "Heaven" has enabled her "by bad" to "mend" (IV. iii. 105 f.). Now she is deeply aware how much "myself" has been to blame for Othello's jealousy. In reparation she takes upon herself the dire outcome, at the same time hoping fervently that he too will learn to repent. The "unkindness" (IV. ii. 160) of her "kind lord" has destroyed her earthly life and joy; but she knows that he, deep within, is kind: there she has an ultimate joy. In her final instant of earthly life her eyes turn towards him; her second "farewell" is for both the persons who love her, Emilia and him. She knows prophetically that in some unknown way he will, in the end, fare well: the good in him will rise again, dispelling his present falsity and murderousness. And he again will be hers. She is now more than ever one with him: her last speech atones; it is an intense, concrete version of her former prayer, "O Heaven forgive *us*" (IV. ii. 88). Herself needing Heaven's "mercy" (34, 57) she has it in giving it. She has utterly condemned, in her preceding speech, the evil in her husband: now she utterly forgives *him*.

But he cannot accept her forgiveness without losing his proud self. For a moment he stands stunned and silent while her words burn into him. He tries, dully, to evade their meaning: how could she say she was "murdered" and yet free him of the deed (126 f.)? But he cannot help seeing her mercy; and his pride violently hurls it away. This "whore" (132), "false as water" (134), has told a last falsehood with her last breath. To keep himself from knowing her lie as heavenly he must feel it as hellish: furiously he shouts, "She's like a Liar gone to burning hell, / 'Twas I that killed her" (129 f.).

In reality she has killed his murderous wrath; that terrible outcry was its final spasm. He cannot escape her judging, forgiving love. It has made him declare to Emilia, "I . . . killed her"; and from now on it gradually undermines his pride. First it forces him to confess himself, with a new touch of meekness, to the very woman in waiting he had so despised as a "bawd" (IV. ii. 20). Emilia echoes his own conscience when she asserts that Desdemona by reason of her dying words is "the more angel" and he "the blacker devil" (130 f.). He, instead of being wrathful, is awed by the woman's bold, righteous wrath. He tries to defend himself by reaccusing his dead wife, but now in a low tone. And he admits *tacitly* that in any case his murder of her was the act, as Emilia says, of "a devil" (133):

> Oh, I were damned beneath all depth in hell—[28]
> But that I did proceed upon just grounds
> To this extremity. Thy husband knew it all.

Iago "knew it all"! Thus at last, "too late" (83), Othello puts down his pride enough to tell Emilia what he ought to have told her and her mistress long before, notably in the Denunciation scene (IV. ii); and he knows well that he should have done so. Desperately he tries to quiet his rising sense of guilt. Had his wife been "true,"

> If Heaven would make me such another world,
> Of one entire and perfect chrysolite,   145
> I'ld not have sold her for it.

That "Heaven" recalls the plausible "heavenly" sorrow (21) and the piety towards "Heaven" (27) of his mood when the scene opened; and that world of "perfect" gold-stone (145), sequel of the "monumental alabaster" (5) above, is greatly and exquisitely factitious. Vehemently artificial is his ensuing praise of that "honest man," Emilia's husband, who "hates the slime / That sticks on filthy deeds." Othello tries frantically to suppress his growing doubt of his underling and, at the same time, to shift all responsibility to him: "My friend, thy husband; honest, honest Iago" (154).

But Emilia with a far deeper and truer vehemence avers that her husband is a "pernicious soul," and a liar through and through, "if" he said Desdemona was false; and that in any case nothing can lighten Othello's own guilt. His wife had one fault, "She was too fond of her most filthy bargain" (157).

---

[28] Here F1 has a suggestive colon (replaced by my dash); the quartos have a comma.

Filthy! That word is terrific to Othello. His love for his
wife from first to last has been, at the least, spotless: *he assumed
he was pure in heart.* That, surely, was the reason his "heart"
so hated his wife's "foul" deeds that he could not bear to
"speak" them plainly when accusing her (IV. ii. 57, 61, 76).
Never has he considered the impurity of pride, of his own
jealous and secretive pride. But now this woman boldly declares that far from his wife's "deeds" being "filthy" (149),
he himself is: his conviction of her foulness and his murderous
"deed" (160) were the outcome of a filthiness in himself.
Therefore his appeal, above, to "Heaven" (144) was impure
and impious:

> This deed of thine is no more worthy Heaven   160
> Than thou wast worthy her.

Once more, for the last time, his pride flares up furiously
in its own defense. At Emilia's word "filthy" he had cried
out "Hah?"; and now in commanding her to be silent he
actually threatens her with his "sword" (165). But his very
pride checks him. This noble gentleman, who would not let
"swords" (I. ii. 59) be used even against the scurrilous Brabantio, has for the first time in his life humiliated himself by
resorting to his sword against a railing woman. But far more
humiliating to him is the fact that even with the aid of wrath
he cannot make himself feel that this woman is merely railing.
Her courage is the courage of a great sincerity:

> Thou hast not half the power to do me harm
> As I have to be hurt. O gull, O dolt,
> As ignorant as dirt: thou hast done a deed—

The "thou" that did that unspeakable "deed" is not merely
"cruel" (21, 86) and "rash as fire" and devilish (131-134)—
he could be all that and yet feel lofty: he is now seen to be
impure, senseless, low, like the very "dirt." His own soul
is telling him this while Emilia utters it aloud with astounding
"power." This crude woman is merciless, unlike her mistress.
But she is as "heavenly true" (135) to her mistress as Desde-

mona, she asseverates, was true to him. And she is evincing
that supernal "power," far beyond his "harm," that flamed out
upon him through his dying wife's words. So he is motionless when Emilia, rushing to the door, proclaims to the world
his "deed." That deed, so *highly dreadful* in Desdemona's
cry, still ringing in his soul, "Oh falsely, falsely murdered,"
is now *dreadfully low*, drab, and brutal, ignominious "as dirt":
"The Moor hath killed my Mistress. Murther, murther!"
(167).

Thus Othello's pride begins to ebb swiftly; his agony is
commencing to be pure. Trembling he stands with sunk head
and clasped, convulsing hands, a little way from the bed, like
a soul on the verge of purgatory. He makes no reply to young
Montano's urgent queryings of the "General" (168); nor to
the question of old Gratiano (171), Desdemona's "uncle,"
scarce recognizing him (201). He is silent when Emilia designates him as "this villain" (172), urging her husband to dis-
avow all complicity. The stricken Othello gives assent by his
silence when Iago claims to have "told" him "no more / Than
what he found himself was apt and true." He hearkens like
one in a horrid dream when Emilia accuses Iago of telling an
"odious, damned . . . wicked lie" (180 ff.). But presently he
finds the eyes of the company fixed upon him with incredulous horror as committer of the "murther." Starting, and
breaking his long (161-187) silence, he says in a low tone,
"Nay stare not, Masters, / It is true indeed." And while
Emilia senses all her husband's "villainy" (190-193) Othello
senses all his own sin. Whether or not his wife was guilty his
own "act" is "monstrous" and "horrible and grim" (190, 203).
And when Emilia, commanded by her husband to go "home,"
replies that perchance she will never go "home" (197), that
meaningful word, sharpened and driven by this poor woman's
great love of his wife, pierces Othello like a sword. He falls
moaning on the bed, his marriage bed, beside the figure that
was his wife.

Louder than his moans comes a relentless voice: "thou hast

killed the sweetest innocent / That e'er did lift up eye"
(199 f.). The still figure beside him could lift up her eyes,
a little while ago, and protest her innocence with the look of
a "sweet soul" (50). But the present voice is Emilia's, giving
utterance in word to a nameless thing—"That? . . . What?"
(119)—speaking ever more loudly in his own soul. In past
days he had often heard it; it kept whispering to him that
"Desdemona's honest" (III. iii. 225), that she was his "true"
and "loyal wife" (IV. ii. 34); but his fury crushed it then.
And now with fury gone, but in great agony of spirit, he tries
once more to silence that voice.

Staggering to his feet he points behind him, face averted,
to the bed: "Oh, she was foul!" (200). And once more he
indulges the dreadful "pity" he expressed when entirely certain she was "foul" (IV. i. 206-215): he avers that her death
is "pitiful" (210), but that surely she was guilty. Yet now
he cannot heap violence and comprehensive opprobrium upon
her; no longer can he conceive her as "that cunning whore of
Venice" (IV. ii. 89). He must concentrate calmly on that one
sin of hers which, as the remnant of his pride tries hard to
make him feel, is fully demonstrable: "she with Cassio hath the
act of shame / A thousand times committed." The word
"thousand" testifies to his desperate inner effortfulness. So
does the brief, pathetic phrase, "Iago knows" (210): Othello's
soul has ceased really to "know" (III. iii. 162) that Iago knows.
More important is the supposed fact that "Cassio confessed it"
(212), confessed the thousandfold "act of shame." But here,
too, Othello's thoughts cannot pause.[29] Instantly dropping the
subject of that chimerical confession, which so horrified his wife
just before he killed her (68 ff.), his mind seizes upon one sure
and certain fact: the "Handkerchief" (216) in Cassio's possession.

He will not confess how much that fact was distorted by
his own secretive jealous passion; but the word "amorous"
(213), which he here for the first time applies to Cassio's
"works," betrays him entirely. At the first he secretly believed

---

[29] F1 and Q1 have a comma, merely, after "Cassio confest it."

that the conduct of "Cassio" towards "my wife" (III. iii. 37) was "amorous" and that she was responsive. And this belief, secretly growing, fed upon everything that could nourish it, notably the mystic handkerchief. This thing, for us the symbol of his blind fury, became for him, what he is now trying desperately to make it still seem, the "recognizance and pledge" of a perfect "love" (214): the love so pure and faithful, like that of his "Father" and "Mother" (217), which he gave to his wife and which she disdained in favor of the "amorous" Cassio. *Because* she gave Cassio her love she *must* have given him this "token." What he said with murderous fury to her (62) he now repeats weakly: "I saw it in his hand" (215).

But now he has to listen, with awful dismay, while Emilia reveals the theft of the handkerchief, "such a trifle" (228), by herself and Iago. Her valiant sincerity is apparent. And her story is rendered overwhelmingly convincing by her husband's outbreak of murderous rage against her. The clever villain loses in a crucial minute all his cleverness. He has hitherto pretty well kept his "heart" (I. i. 51, 62) attending on his self; now it overrules and ruins his self. The blind anger he mocked at in Othello (III. iv. 132 ff.) breaks forth in himself, sweeping away all his vaunted "reason" and self-control (I. iii. 330 ff.). His wife murder is a fantastic, ghastly parody of Othello's. With a blatant irrationality far exceeding his master's he shouts at Emilia, "Villainous whore! . . . Filth, thou liest!" (229, 231). But all the more do the "gentlemen" (232) believe her. And so the frenzied fellow uses "his sword upon a woman" (224) in cheap revenge: he suddenly runs his wife through—and then runs away. He makes himself, publicly, the very thing he was certain of never being: a common killer, an obvious liar, a "*notorious* villain" (239).

Thus the buffoon-scoundrel of the play is displayed in the end as what he essentially is, the veriest fool. His "gained knowledge" (I. iii. 390) of humanity is shallow and occasional; his "ignorance" is "fond" (foolish) and "heavy" (II. i. 139, 145); his pride, ridiculous in the extreme. He believed him-

self very singular when in fact he was swayed by arrogant
stupidity of a very common sort. He set himself to despise
and manipulate, to despise *in and by manipulating,* a strong
power he secretly feared and could not understand, thus ex-
posing himself to be manipulated by it. The "goodness" he
would use as a "net" (II. iii. 367) nets *him,* and ruins him. He
is a foolish fellow and small.

But here as ever he is the medium of a thing great and
terribly real, hellish hate. The heavenly goodness, as merciful as just, offered him "pardon" (IV. ii. 135) through Desdemona. But he spurned that mercy, not with passing heat
like Othello (129 ff.), but with the cold determination of diabolic pride, at the same time shutting his ears to the loud and
vivid warning given him through the lips of his own wife (IV.
ii. 130 ff.). So now he is punished through the same agency.
The goodness that worked in Desdemona flames out in the
righteousness of crude, inspired Emilia; and through Iago
comes a responsive uprush of veritable hell fire. If the fellow
had employed his usual slyness he could have thrown doubt
upon her version of the handkerchief story. But here his tactical skill is annulled by the strategy of the justice of "Heaven"
(232, 234). The fact of being unveiled by the despised person
he had deemed totally subservient to him is too much for the
villain's pride. His hidden cumulative hatred of all honest
persons, above all his awed and tacit hate of Desdemona, concentrates upon her devoted servant, his rebelling wife. That
black fire of hate, that hellishly "flaming minister," consumes
all his art, all his icy prudence. This very independent villain
is really a "damned slave" (243, 292). He mocked at the
"Divinity of hell" (II. iii. 356); but at his evil best he is the
symbol and unconscious servitor of "Hell and Night" (I. iii.
409). He is a sort of "devil" (287), a "demi-devil" (301)
at least. But pettiness of personality and greatness of evil
significance are so closely intertwined in him that no adequate
image of him can be given in few words. And we along with
Othello respect his final resolve "never" henceforth to "speak

word" (303-306). Surely here he has an inkling of the fact that he really does not understand himself or others. His *body* is to die in the torments (305, 332-335) of slow "torture" (369). But throughout the play we have watched him torturing his *soul* to death with "hellish" (368) hate of others. The devil in him succeeds in murdering no soul except his own. He dies of hate.

Othello's soul is saved as by fire.

Emilia's objurgation of him culminated in a brimstone sentence (233): "O murderous Coxcomb! what should such a Fool / Do with so good a wife?" The man once so proud listens with bowed head as to a judgment from above; then mutters:

> Are there no stones in Heaven
> But what serves for the Thunder?—[30]

Surely a *silent* fiery bolt should flash down upon him, and upon his accomplice—one more deed, certainly, he should do before his own end: execute Iago. But this obvious act of reparation and "honour" (245) is denied him. Drawing his sword he rushes upon the villain; but like a dark shadow the fellow slips away from him, wounds Emilia mortally, and disappears; while Montano, the young and flimsy former governor, wrenches the weapon from the hand of "the Moor" (240). Othello exclaims brokenly,

> I am not valiant neither,
> But every puny whipster gets my sword:
> But why should honour outlive honesty?
> Let it go, all.

His "name," once the jewel of his soul (III. iii. 155 f.), is nothing now. He impugns in himself, extremely, the "honesty"—the moral strength, the candor, the trustworthiness— he had impugned in his wife: he lacked the virtue that could find and know *her* virtue.

---

[30] Like others I have inserted a dash here. Othello pauses and lifts his head. His next words, "Precious villain!," addressed to Iago, complete this line in the quartos and modern texts; but F1 prints them, rightly, as a new and separate line.

But Emilia had it, and has it, the poor coarse Emilia, dying at his feet. He is now alone with her, and "the door" is guarded "without" (241). In an awful purgatorial solitude he listens to the accusing spirit speaking in his soul and through this woman. But she in *her* great pain is not alone. She turns her head as to an unseen presence:

> What did thy Song bode, Lady?
> Hark, canst thou hear me? . . .

that "Lady" infinitely far, as *he* now feels, from *him*. The woman's face is alight with agony and joy. She too had been dishonest to Desdemona, once and fatefully. But she confessed and repented crying, "I'll kill myself for grief" (192): she has made great reparation with the help of "heavenly Powers" (218). Grief and pain are in her, but, above them, a great joy: she will "die in music" (248). Her weak voice begins chanting a strange song of supernatural yearning, "*Willow, Willow, Willow*": she is singing it to *and with* her beloved mistress— a song *he* has never heard and cannot deserve to hear. On his knees, he bends his head close to hers, watching, listening. In agony he is learning from her, and from the "Lady" beyond, the way he had missed: the way of honest, simple, self-sacrificing love.

This is the woman he had denounced in his bitter, blinding rage as keeper of "the gate of hell," holder of "the office opposite to Saint Peter" (IV. ii. 91 f.). But her "soul," now at the gate of "bliss" (250), will not pass upon him a bitter final judgment as her lips did before the culmination of her own suffering (233 f.); now she whispers words mercifully just, words partaking the spirit of her mistress's last utterances (117-125) though far more strict and severe, words his soul needs now for its purgation:

> Moor, she was chaste—She loved thee, cruel Moor—
> So come my soul to bliss as I speak true   250

"She *loved* thee." That is what his own soul, along with Emilia's, is saying to him. She loved a "cruel Moor." Be-

cause of her love this Moor was no foreigner to her; but she
was foreign to him because he did not respond to her love
with his inmost being—until now. Emilia's word "cruel" is his
own (21, 86). His cruelty, which at its very height had seemed
to him in accord with justice and mercy, confronts him now in
all its starkness and blackness: he is the "cruel Moor." Because his love was so elaborate and self-centered it could become
barbarously cruel. The "current" of his "heart" (IV. ii. 57, 59)
was both passionate and "icy"—but now, at last, his proud
"thoughts" have ebbed to "humble love" (III. iii. 454, 457 f.).
His love is now akin to hers. And so he knows not only how
"chaste" and pure but how close to the essence of heavenly
"bliss" (250) was her love for him. With unspeakable agony
he takes the full meaning of "She *loved thee*."[31]

He sinks his head ever lower. Then with a strong effort he
gets to his feet: he lifts in his arms the body of Emilia. Tenderly and reverently he lays her, as she begged, by her "Mistress'
side" (237). He averts his face from the bed. Lifting empty,
trembling hands he gazes about the empty room. Then his
hands grope from place to place until they light upon "another
weapon," a cherished one that he has kept in "this chamber,"
a handsome, perfectly tempered "sword" (252 f.). He grasps
it, tries it lovingly, and holds it firmly. He takes the posture
of a soldier about to enter battle. He will destroy his enemy,
a great malefactor, a foe devoid of "honesty" (245), a "cruel
Moor" (249). But he must do so in the presence of a witness,
his wife's "uncle" (254) Gratiano, who, coming with the news
of her father's death, was confronted with "a strange truth":
"Poor Desdemon" herself dead, murdered by her husband, a
"desperate . . . sight" (189, 204-209). In the presence of this
good old kinsman, and of the two figures on the bed, Othello
will "speak" (257) his words, and do his deed, of repentance
and expiation.

[31] In Emilia's line the obvious stress falls on the word "loved"; but the
"thee" is strong too and becomes more so as we along with Othello reflect
upon her slow, dying speech as a whole. Her iterated "I" (250 f.) throws
back an emphasis upon "thee." She says in effect: I, unlike *thee*, loved Desdemona truly, but she *loved thee*. Incidentally, her word "music" (248) is
an antithetic sequel to her husband's earlier use of that metaphor (II. i. 203).

V. ii. 259-371

"Behold, I have a weapon . . . . " It kindles gleaming memories of his "big wars" (III. iii. 349). With "this good sword" (262) he was able singly to make his "way" through throngs of opponents. He was master of "his Fate," he thought—"But oh, vain boast! . . . 'Tis not so now." He declares that old Gratiano, who has shrunk back from the flourished weapon, could defeat the once great and proud general by wielding against him a mock sword, a mere "rush" (270), a reed. For Othello is now Othello's enemy. The one good deed left for this "good sword" to do is to pierce "Othello's breast":

> Here is my journey's end, here is my butt
> And very sea-mark of my utmost sail.[32]

His life has been warfare on land and at sea, "by flood and field" (I. iii. 135); so the "end" of it is at once the swift arrow of the field striking its "butt" and the slow vessel at sea sighting, deliberately, the sure and certain goal of a long, final voyage. But the sea image is dominant. And it recalls to us Othello's "sail" (II. i. 94) heaving at length into the harbor in the Storm scene.

His tempest of wicked passion is all gone. Now comes a beneficent storm, a passionate outbreak of repentant grief. Its prelude is fearful loneliness. "Where should Othello go?" (271). He moves towards the bed with lifted, craving hands; but these are the hands that killed her. Drawing them tight to his breast he stands a little way off from her, scrutinizing piercingly the white face. In the beginning she saw his "visage in his mind" (I. iii. 253): now, at long last, he sees her mind in her visage. "Now—how dost thou look now?" (272). He sees what he would not see while she lived, her "chastity" (276) in her very look. And there he sees something still more

[32] The last four words of the first line are rapid and abrupt; the rest of the passage, increasingly deliberate. The quick word "butt" anticipates, and swiftly yields to, the slow and significant phrase "very sea-mark." Therefore F1 is right in having no punctuation after "butt." Q2 inserts a comma, and changes the ensuing "And" to "The." (The passage is omitted in Q1.)

"Heavenly" (278), the sublime charity of her last moments: her condemnation of his sin and her forgiveness of *him*. He accepts the condemnation; but he thinks the forgiveness cannot possibly be his. Formerly he rejected it in proud fury; now he shrinks from it in humble, utter reprobation of himself. He cries out in agony: "when we shall meet at compt," at the Last Judgment,

> This look of thine will hurl my soul from Heaven,
> And Fiends will snatch at it   275

Indeed that Judgment Day is present to him *now*. The "vengeance" of "hell" (III. iii. 447) that he had invoked for her he invokes for himelf now; he consigns himself to "burning hell" (129): "O cursed, cursed slave!" (276)—

> Whip me, ye devils,
> From the possession of this Heavenly sight:
> Blow me about in winds, roast me in sulphur,
> Wash me in steep-down gulfs of liquid fire.

His soul is verily being washed in "fire." He himself is aware only of the hell he deserves in merciless justice. All the more are *we* aware of the just mercy that is giving him a purgatory, an awful fiery cleansing.[33] The heart of his torment is the full perception of the heaven he has forfeited; symbolized by the beautiful but pale and cold form—the truly "monumental" (5) form—lying on *their* bed. It at once blesses and judges him. He, the worst of sinners, the "cursed slave" of evil, of the "devils" whom he senses in all the air about him, should not have "this Heavenly sight." Yet he *does* have it: it is his "possession," the sole one he values now, his blessed, torturing possession. He tries to avert his eyes from it forever, but does not succeed. And, above, he had actually ventured to touch it, with a reverent finger tip, while he whispered brokenly, "Cold, cold, my Girl?" (275).[34]

---

[33] Compare the *purgatorial hell* of the Ghost in *Hamlet*. He is doomed to "fast in fires" till his "crimes . . . /Are burnt and purged away" (I. v. 11-13).
[34] This question is the final sequel of his two preceding ones (271 f.). But F1's question mark is absent from the quartos and has been altered to an

Those words are a sword of "ice-brook's temper" (253) drawing heart blood. At the very first he called her "the gentle Desdemona" (I. ii. 25). Presently she became, dubiously, "my soul's joy" (II. i. 186); later, a thing denounced and rejected by "my soul" (IV. ii. 52). But now that proud, magnificent "soul" is humbled and purified and simple in love—like hers. He has attained kinship with her: he is "kind" (125), and of her kind. And so she is now, what he has never before called her, nor could call her till now, simply "my Girl." His spirit weds hers now, tragically and sublimely, *without his awareness of that fact*—hence its true sublimity. He has found her in losing her. He sinks to his knees beside their marriage bed, moaning, "O Desdemon! dead Desdemon[35]—dead."

He too is "dead." Soon to be dead in body he is now dead in spirit, dead through his sin and, because of his repentance, dead *to* that sin. Lodovico, and we, now regard him in deep sympathy as "this rash and most unfortunate man" (283). But he in deep humility regards himself as "he that was Othello." And the captured Iago, staring at him with deathless hate, seems to him momentarily one of the immortal "devils" (277, 287) of the hell he has just been going through. Othello surveys him wonderingly; then tries again, but without his previous wrath (234 f.), to destroy the evil creature. But quickly his converted soul divines that the just punishment for "that demi-devil" (301) would be to have to "live: / For in my sense, 'tis happiness to die" (289 f.). Rightly enough he terms himself, in contrast with Iago, an "honourable murderer" (294). Humanly he wishes to justify himself, so far as possible, in the eyes of the assembled company, distinguishing his own case from that of the wickeder Iago, who in sheer hellish "hate" has "ensnared my soul and body." But he takes full responsibility for letting himself be thus "ensnared": he calls himself a "fool" (323), too extremely, accepting now in his

---

exclamation point by modern editors. The question hints at a hope, though cold and faint, on the part of Othello.

[35] This intimate form of her name, not used by him since IV. ii. 41, follows naturally upon "my Girl" above. The quartos, however, read "Desdemona"; so do F3 and F4.

penitence Emilia's opprobrious term (233). Alone, he had termed himself, what others have termed Iago (243, 292), a "cursed [damned] slave" (276). And he knows it is not Iago but his own guilty self—the Iago-like part of himself, in our view—that he must destroy. He is "not sorry" (289) that he has failed to kill Iago: he is too full of repentant grief to let himself live. Also he is now *just*.

In the beginning of the scene he falsely invoked "Justice" (17) to palliate his proud, murderous passion. In the end he invokes justice truly, enacting it upon himself. He does so in the name of the great "Venetian State" (337-339), which becomes here outstandingly what it has been all along, a symbol (like Hamlet's Denmark) of the whole of human society. Here Othello is really concerned, as not in the opening speech of the scene, for "more men" (6) than himself. For the commonweal, as well as for his own sake, he wishes his story (as Hamlet wished his, V. ii. 360) recounted fully and justly. He adjures *us*, as much as his listeners on the stage, to

> Speak of me as I am. Nothing extenuate,
> Nor set down aught in malice.
> Then must you speak,
> Of one that loved not wisely, but too well—[36]

That epigram is explanation, not extenuation.[37] Above he utterly condemned himself before the "Heavenly" (278) powers; so now he can sense, though distantly and silently, their charity for him. The self-righteousness with which he formerly appealed to "Heaven" (IV. ii. 47) is all gone. He dare not "bethink" himself of "Heaven and Grace" and "mercy" (26 f., 34) on his own behalf. He dare not pray, at least not vocally, as Desdemona did for him and for herself, that "Heaven forgive" (IV. ii. 88). But he can plead with his

---

[36] F1's lineation and punctuation of this passage, reproduced above except for my dash in place of a colon, are very effective. The short second and third lines (merged into one in the quartos and modern editions) prepare for the extremely significant fourth.

[37] With this veracious epigram contrast Desdemona's absolute and proud idealization of him in the third act. His ensuing word "base" (347) is a dramatically ironic echo of her phrase "no such baseness" (III. iv. 27).

fellow men to view his sin in the light of the heavenly charity,
i.e. without either softness or ill-will ("malice"), with firmness
and clear understanding. And certainly it is clear that his sin,
like the great sins of other good and great men, took its rise
from nature: his temperament and situation predisposed him
to love "not wisely but too well," with richness of emotion and
poverty of insight.

But quickly the natural became unnatural. Blameless at
the first for his lack of loving insight, he was greatly to blame
for not attaining it through his union with one who had it in
a high degree. And so superior to him does she now appear
to him to be—in extreme contrast to what she was in his initial
speech concerning her (I. ii. 17-28)—that he will not, in the
whole course of his present great speech (338-356), refer to
her *personally*. His soul may feel and hope that she is still
"my Girl" (275) and "Desdemon" (281) and "my wife"
(319), but his mind dare not conceive her as such: he even
avoids the pronouns "she" and "her" (143, 146, etc.) formerly
so frequent on his lips. Much less will he think of those defects in her conduct which he knows, as we know, served to
extenuate his own. The all-important, tragic fact is that, instead of obeying the "sweet Powers" that would have enabled
him to "increase" (II. i. 195-200) in love's wisdom, he en-
slaved himself to jealousy. Here for the first time his once
so proud lips utter, publicly, the name of his humiliating fault
(345, contrast III. iii. 176 ff.). He was "not easily jealous,
but being wrought," being worked upon by passion, he was
"perplexed in the extreme," utterly confused and blinded.
And so the noble Christian gentleman became barbarously
"cruel" (249) and "rash" (134, 283), without the barbarian's
excuse of natural ignorance. *Unlike* "the base Indian" Othello
is damnably guilty as "one whose hand, / *Like* the base Indian,[38] threw a Pearl away / Richer than all his tribe"—

Above he had compared "her," factitiously and egoistically,
to a possible "world," made by "Heaven" for "me," "of one

[38] The whole context, as interpreted above, requires the reading "Indian"
instead of "Judean," a very easily made misprint, which occurs only in F1.

entire and perfect Chrysolite" (143-146). But now the pure
and lovely person whose sacred name he will not dare again
mention is for him a real symbol of "the one pearl of great
price" (*Matthew* 13:46) worth more than that "world," worth
far more "than all his tribe," all persons of his own sort taken
together. And so he weeps bitterly. She as before is "the
motive of these tears" (IV. ii. 43); but now she is the lost
pearl, and these tears are new and different. His "subdued
eyes . . . / Drop tears as fast as the Arabian trees / Their
medicinable gumme" (348-351). In his repentance the purging "liquid fire" (280) has given place to the fast flow of drops
that can heal, medicinal tears.

But presently he lifts his head a little. Cleansed and healed
of pride of soul he can have again a measure of that right pride
submerged for the time being by his penitence: that is, true
human self-esteem.[39] Otherwise he would be false to himself
and his fellow men. In his vocation he was very far from
being a "slave" (276) and "fool" (323). On the other hand
he is now further than ever from "boasting" (I. ii. 20). For
his sin against "Heaven" (274) was also a great crime against
the state and society. Therefore "my services" (I. ii. 18),
so high in the estimation of himself and all others at the first,
are now, in view of his "unlucky [ill-omened] deeds" (341),
merely "some service" (339). Nor does he now think of that
service as consisting mainly in his "big" and "glorious" wars
(III. iii. 349, 354). His "subdued" (348) thoughts concenter
upon a certain private and elementary act of justice that he
once performed and that any humble, loyal, courageous servitor
of the Venetian state could have done just as well.

That was in Aleppo (352). His memory has swiftly ranged
from far-off India (347) to nearer but equally romantic Arabia
(350) and finally to the familiar Syrian city, Aleppo, wherein
were mingled Christian Venetians and pagan Turks, the worst
enemies of Venice and Christendom. We recall the "natural

---

[39] In accordance with the principles of Renaissance Christian humanism.
Compare the bearing of Milton's Adam and Eve after their repentance; their
"port" is not "mean" (*Paradise Lost* XI, 8 f.). See note 60 to Act III, above.

and prompt alacrity" with which he undertook "present wars" against them (I. iii. 233-235), and his stern warning to his Christian officers not to turn "Turks" and outdo "the Otto-mites" in disobeying "Heaven" through barbarous "rage" (II. iii. 170-173). But later he himself did that very thing: he has sinned worse than those barbarians against heaven and the state. Therefore he must now end "the story of my life . . . . all my pilgrimage" (I. iii. 129, 153), "my journey" (267), as he once ended the life of an obscure Turkish bully and tra-ducer—a sinner emblematic of him "that was Othello" (284). He re-enacts here and now, with tear-stained face a little raised but with a deep sense that his own crime was unspeakably greater than that of the other traducer, the deed of humble justice he did "in Aleppo once":

> Where a malignant and turbaned Turk
> Beat a Venetian, and traduced the State,
> I took by th' throat the circumcised dog,   355
> And smote him, thus.

Swiftly producing a hidden dagger,[40] Othello executes, stabs to the heart, the criminal Othello.

Dying, he turns away, as Desdemona did in the prospect of death, from "the world's mass of vanity" (IV. ii. 160, 164). She invoked God at the last (33, 57, 83): Othello in his last lines (quoted below) invokes *her*. At the outset he loved the Venetian state and his own career better than her: at the end the reverse it true; but he loves Venice more deeply and hum-bly than ever, as he has just shown, because of his regenerated love of *her*. Thus his two loves are now conjoined in his sur-passing and comprehensive devotion to the "heavenly" (278) Desdemona. In his final moment he turns from all thoughts of the state, from all memories and persons, to the one that is for him supremely real now:

> I kissed thee, ere I killed thee—No way but this,
> Killing my self, to die upon a kiss.

[40] The wrenching from him of his second sword (288) was, in dramatic economy, at once a suggestive feature of Othello's humiliation and the prepa-ration for his death in a more striking manner than the sword could have afforded.

That sudden, repeated "thee," conspicuously absent from his preceding speeches, has in its present context a gleaming dagger sharpness.[41] It invokes the supernal love that wields, above its keen justice, a piercing, forgiving, freeing mercy. *Now* her "look" does *not* "hurl" his "soul from Heaven" (274); and though in his humility he dare not aspire thither he is tacitly aware of release from his hell, his "gulfs of liquid fire" (280), and he has a rising, wordless hope. So he can touch, as not above (275), her lips with his own, accepting thus the forgiveness which he repudiated at the height of his sin (125 ff.), and despaired of in the depth of his contrition. Then his "soul" had no whither to "go" except the way of the "cursed" (271-276); now he has a way of dim but real hope— "No way but this." Then, she was "dead Desdemon—dead" (281); now, he speaks as to a living "thee" with whom his soul is in some way reuniting. "I kissed thee, ere I killed thee." That kiss, his alone, redoubled and voluptuously "sweet" (20), "cruel" (21), and selfish, is repealed now by "a kiss" pure, simple, and self-giving which is *hers as well as his*. For the love with which he has learned "to love . . . after" (19) is a new passion: he loves now, beyond her body and her charms, her devoted, pure, forgiving self. This final "kiss"—this last word of all his words, as he sinks upon their bed beside her—means the wedding of him and "thee."

Certainly he was "great of heart" (361). The human heart has shown in Othello its great capacity for good, and for evil. Love when humble is its chief good, when proud its chief evil, particularly in great persons. The small person Iago, fettered, rigid, dumb, gazes at "the tragic loading of this bed" (363), amazed by his master's "happiness to die" (290), appalled by the supernatural strength of the love he had sought to destroy.[42] He appears, over against the human-hearted

[41] The long high vowel of "thee" rings out above all the other vocables in the passage. That word is emphasized also by its alliteration with "this," and by the fact that it alone is exactly repeated, "kissed" and "killed" being altered in the second line.

[42] Iago's gaze here brings to mind the eyes of Spenser's Despair that "Lookt deadly dull and stared as astound" (*The Faerie Queene* I. ix. 35).

Moor, a subhuman creature, a "Spartan dog" (361). Yet here, conclusively, he is a figure symbolizing the evil power of proud self-love, the more greatly "tragic" the more it does its "work" (363 f.) in greatly human persons. That evil is "More fell than Anguish, Hunger, or the Sea" (362)—direr than the extremest pain, more urgent than the fiercest craving, more inhuman and cruel than the vast ocean.[43] For us (as for Shakespeare) the eventual wonder is the overcoming of that poisonous (364) and "hellish" (368) evil in Othello's heart by the ministering, purging fire of "Heaven and Grace" (27). Of these Othello spoke at the outset of this scene with formal belief but slight reality. In the end, without again naming them—his formal religiosity now entirely in abeyance—he experiences them very really, deeply, and awfully. Instead of the death in life which had obsessed him, and which Iago remains to represent, Othello has found life in death, through humble love and *new* greatness of heart. Cassio says he "was," we say he is, "great of heart."

That is what we feel when "this bed" is now "hid" (363, 365): Othello's figure is curtained off from the figure of Iago, and from all the ways of the world. But the world must go on. The material "fortunes of the Moor" (366) must be taken over by the remaining family head, old Gratiano, who has shown small understanding of spiritual fortunes.[44] And Cassio, who was once so "desperate of my fortunes" (II. iii. 337 f.), is now "Lord Governor" (367)—here so termed for the first time—of peacetime Cyprus. But as to the headship of the Venetian armed forces at large, Lodovico is very sad indeed that the "all in all sufficient" Othello (IV. i. 276), who might have been restored to that position after trial for his "fault" (336) regarding Desdemona, has brought his own life to a "bloody" end (357)!

[43] See the *Oxford English Dictionary* for all the implications of the word "fell," here occurring for the first time in this play.

[44] Gratiano's speeches in this act are worth reviewing from this standpoint, in contrast with those of Lodovico, which are very different in tenor.

> Myself will straight aboard, and to the State 370
> This heavy Act with heavy heart relate.

We know he will "relate" it as truthfully and completely as he knows how to the state and to the world. But he and the others, moving off now from the front stage, leave us with much that is "hid" (365) from them and their world—beyond the curtain.[45]

---

[45] At his best Shakespeare employs the curtain of his rear stage with proper and intense suggestiveness. Ruinous here would have been the treatment so appropriately given to the "bodies" at the close of *Hamlet* (V. ii. 388 f., 406 ff.).

Index

Spenser, Edmund (*The Faerie Queene*), xvii, xxii n., xxiv, xxvi n., 106 n., 188 n., 240 n.
Stauffer, Donald A., xxiv n.
Stoll, Elmer Edgar, xxxi n.
symbolism, 126 f., 146 f., 148, 151 f., 163 f., 171, 179, 187, 214, 228 f., 234, 236, 239, 241

temperance (intemperance), 95, 158
Tempest, The, 130 n.
Tillyard, E. M. W., viii n.
Tolstoy, xxiv

Troilus and Cressida, xxiv
Twelfth Night, xxiii n., 70 n.

Vaughan, Henry, xvii
Venice (its representativeness), xxx, xxxiv n., 55, 236, 238 f., 241 f.

Watkins, Ronald, x n., 77 n.
Watkins, W. B. C., viii n.
Wilson, Harold S., xxvii n.
Winter's Tale, The, 126 n.
Woodhouse, A. S. P., xxvi n.
Wordsworth, William, 203 n.